Reclaiming Bharatavarsha

Reclaiming Bharatavarsha

Sandeep Balakrishna

ink | OCCAM

ISBN: 978-81-968471-5-9

First published in India 2024
This edition published 2024

BluOne Ink Pvt. Ltd
A-76, 2nd Floor, Sector 136, Noida
Uttar Pradesh 201301
www.bluone.ink
publisher@bluone.ink

Printed and bound in India by Thomson Press India Ltd.

ink | OCCAM

To Sri Dharampal
for illuminating the path

Contents

Preface

This book is a collection of topical and exploratory essays organized around three broad themes. The first explores the various facets and nuances of classical Bharatavarsha, which is defined as India before the advent of alien Islamic invaders and British colonization. The second delves into the condition of an India under successive alien regimes. It opens a window to the impact that these regimes have had on our culture and society and offers a contrast with the preceding (classical) era. The third theme explores the imprint that these bouts of foreign rule have left on our contemporary national life. All three themes, taken together or separately, offer both a complementary and an informed contrast in the realms of politics, culture, society, customs, literature, and cinema.

Other important considerations, too, have instructed the selection of essays in *Reclaiming Bharatavarsha*. At the risk of sounding immodest, the topics chosen for this work have rarely appeared in mainstream discourse dating back to the previous half century or more. This, in a way, only underscores their importance. The focus is on variety and breadth rather than depth. From selected episodes drawn from the Puranas to the sacred history of the banana to 17th-century Bengali arrack, from the Mahabharata to woke cinema, from hair dyes to the 1962 war with China, this book contains an eclectic selection of atypical essays. To quote a cliché, there is something for everyone in this book. Each essay is self-contained, and while some are analytical in nature, the intent is to allow readers to draw their own conclusions.

The book's title, *Reclaiming Bharatavarsha*, also has a recent historical context. This is the unprecedented transformation of India over the last decade. A major outcome of this transformation is the huge surge of interest in recovering our national and civilizational roots. There is a visible interest in and a renewal of our sacred spaces, festivals, traditions, literature, architecture, sculpture, art, music, dance, and multidisciplinary research in all these areas. This interest and renewal are expressions of our cultural self-confidence, which had been laid low for several centuries. *Reclaiming Bharatavarsha* hopes to be a humble addition to this national endeavour.

This book is meant for both a general reader and for those who wish to dive deeper into the individual topics presented here. Essays are organized under three broad categories: classical, colonial, and post-colonial, and the rationale for the classification will become evident to the reader. The writing is imbued with a literary quality. It is event-driven and peppered with character sketches, humour, and a high degree of readability. The narrative is filled with vivid historical and contemporary details and rare anecdotes, all of which are backed by a significant amount of research.

I would like to express my gratitude to Sri Praveen Tiwari and the entire team at BlueOne Ink for their support at various stages of the publication of *Reclaiming Bharatavarsha.*

Part 1
Classical Bharatavarsha

1

An Enlivening Historical Voyage with the Banana

— 1 —

In Bharatavarsha, the plantain or banana is not merely a fruit. It is a succulent way of life and has remained so almost since the dawn of the Sanatana civilization. Among classic fruits, it arguably holds the top spot. A handy formula to identify a classic fruit is the sanctity attached to it in the Hindu cultural experience, including the annals of its sacred and earthly literature. In one sense, the banana vies with the coconut, which is known as the *kalpavṛkṣa*, whose every part is useful. Likewise, the leaf, stem, fruit, flower, and other parts of the plantain tree continue to be put to multiple uses in our society and culture.

From the spiritual heights of the Himalayas to the hill slopes of Chittagong to the fecund geography of Kerala, the banana has noiselessly established its millennial suzerainty. Throughout the same period, our ancestors inhabiting this vast expanse have extolled its glories in verse, prose, and ritual to such an extent that we don't even pause to think about the rooted significance of the mantra, *kadalīphalaṃ nivedayāmi,* uttered while offering the *Naivēdya* to our deities. The banana is clearly a fruit fit for the gods.

But when we *really* think about it, we derive a profound insight into a core element of the Sanatana culture: a deep sense of gratitude or what is known as the *Ṛṇa prajña*. Thus, the moment our ancestors discovered the inestimable value of bananas, they sanctified them. The Sanskrit synonyms for banana are endearing and expressive of its beauty, its behaviour, and the value of its products.

As *Kadaḷi,* it is the fruit that is nourished by water.
As *Rambhā*, it is the fruit that brings pleasantness to the mind.
As *Vanalakṣmi*, it is the wealth-giving goddess of the forests.
As *Bhānuphala*, it is the sun fruit.
As *Vāraṇābuṣā* and *Vāraṇavallabha*, it is the beloved of the elephants.

—2—

Another ancient Sanskrit word for banana was *Mocha,* a word infused with a profound meaning. Mocha literally means 'liberated'. In the context of the banana, it refers to the manner in which the flowering spike emerges from the parent tree like a child emerges from the mother's womb. By itself, this word is a superb tribute to the keen powers of observation of our ancestors and their innate reverence for nature.

The word Mocha also opens a beautiful chapter in the historical journey of the banana across the globe. Mocha became *Mauja* in Pali during the Buddhist and Mauryan periods. This era witnessed the briskest commercial and cultural exchanges between Bharatavarsha, pre-Islamic Arabia, and the Ionian Greeks. Thus, Mauja became *mawz* in Arabic. The Europeans took this Arabic linguistic corruption and derived the genus *Musa,* formalized in the first edition of Linnaeus' *Species Plantarum.*

The etymological origin of the words *banana* and *plantain* is equally interesting.

Some scholars argue that banana is a contraction of Vāraṇābuṣā, where *Vāraṇā* means elephant. Others claim that it is derived from *Bhānuphala.* The phonetic similarity between *Bhānu* and banana is unmistakable.

The Greek philosopher and botanist Theophrastus gave the name *Arieana* to the banana in his seminal work *Enquiry into Plants* (*Historia Plantarum*). This is how he describes it:

> There is also another tree which is very large and has wonderfully sweet and large fruit; it is used for food by the sages of India who wear no clothes . . . [its] leaf is oblong in shape, like the feathers of the ostrich; this they fasten on to their helmets, and it is about two cubits long.

According to some scholars, the word *plantain* is supposed to be derived from the word *Pala.* However, *Pala* is a corruption of *Phala*, the generic Sanskrit word for 'fruit'. The word *Pala*, denoting plantain, has undergone numerous transformations in various Indian languages. Thus, we have the following words for plantain:

Kalā = Bengali

Kēlā = Hindi, Punjabi, Gujarati

Kēḷī = Marathi

Bāḷe = Kannada

Vālapālam = Tamil and Malayalam

When we read Caius Plinius (Pliny the Elder), we get a vivid and evocative description of *P*ala in his *Historia Naturalis.* He faithfully echoes Theophrastus in *The Pala: The Fruit Called Ariena*, the twelfth chapter of this work.

> There is another tree in India . . . even more remarkable for the size and sweetness of its fruit, upon which the sages of India live. The leaf of this tree resembles, in shape, the wing of a bird, being three cubits in length, and two in breadth. It puts forth its fruit from the bark, a fruit remarkable for the sweetness of its juice, a single one containing sufficient to satisfy four persons. The name of this tree is 'pala', and of the fruit, 'ariena'. They are found in the greatest abundance in the country of the Sydraci, a territory which forms the extreme limit of the expedition of Alexander.

Pliny's description of the plantain as the food of 'the sages of India' opens up another interesting historical vista. This description generated the specific name given to the common variety of banana found across the world: *Musa sapientum*, meaning 'the *Musa* of the wise men'.

Both Theophrastus and Pliny called the banana the food of Indian sages for a practical reason. All our *Smritis* and *Dharma-Sastra* works include *Ahimsa* as part of the definition of common Dharma. The Rishis (sages) were those who lived their lives strictly adhering to these tenets of Dharma. As part of their vow of ahimsa (non-injury), some of our Rishis went to extraordinary lengths. They took a lifelong vow to not injure even plant and vegetable life. They abstained from eating seeds and grains like rice, wheat, etc. They subsisted on fallen leaves. Thus, it is unsurprising that the banana came as a huge boon for them. This is precisely what the ancient Greeks witnessed when they came to India. Hence the name *Musa sapientum.*

So, the next time you eat a banana, remember that you are eating the food of our Rishis, the spiritual sculptors of the Santana culture. In this backdrop, it is only natural that Hindus till date regard the banana with such reverence.

— 3 —

The next stop in the journey of the banana from the age of the Rishis brings us to the age of our Kavis (poets, litterateurs). Like the moon and the lotus, the banana was also a perennial favourite among Sanskrit poets. An unnamed scholar writing in 1891–92 describes this poetic fancy:

> The plantain tree is a very graceful plant, and its straight, succulent stem is a favourite object with Sanskrit poets with which to compare the lower limbs of a beautiful maiden. 'Her limbs are like the Rám-rambhá plant', is a simile which no poet of any pretension will forget to apply to his heroine.
>
> With the stem of the plantain, a beautiful comparison is made by Kálidasa in *Kumarasambhava.* Sometimes the compliment is carried a little further, when the gracefulness of the heroine comes off victorious in comparison with the poor plantain.

The love for the banana wasn't confined to poetic geniuses like Kalidasa. In fact, there is almost an inexhaustible bounty of banana-themed folklore throughout Bharatavarsha from very ancient times. This includes short stories, individual verses, and folk songs. It also expressed itself in proverbs and impromptu nuggets of wisdom as people did their routine chores like ploughing, pestling, grinding, etc. A significant portion of this folklore also talks about the ruin that will befall a person who disrespects the banana.

Here is a rather delightful and instructive verse that was wildly popular in rural Bengal even at the dawn of the 20th century.

> Dák de bale Rávan
> Kalá potoge Ashár Srávan,
> Sát háth antar savá háth bái

Kalá pute Kháo chásá-bhái.
Rávana exclaims—
Sow the plantain in the Asháda and Srávana months.
(Dig a) Two feet hole, ten feet distant,
My brother, put each plantain plant.

There is a nice rhythm in the original Bengali, which is easy to memorize. Ravana's connection is unclear in this context. Perhaps the anonymous poet who composed this found 'Rávan' as a handy rhyme for 'Srávan'. The verse is clearly meant as simple agricultural education for the proverbial unlettered farmer. But the fact that such anonymous verses have survived in our cultural and social memory without formal documentation is significant. We can find countless such verses on the same and similar themes throughout Bharatavarsha. Sadly, we've lost that cultural continuity over the last eight decades.

— 4 —

On the practical and economic planes, the banana lent itself to diverse uses throughout its history. For several centuries, Dacca was renowned for its plantain products.

We have rich historical documentation that talks about a specialized kind of cloth woven from plantain fibre. A gold-bordered handkerchief, made entirely from plantain fibre, was displayed by the Dacca weavers at the Calcutta International Exhibition of 1883–84.

The aforementioned term Mocha, a synonym for banana, eventually took on a restricted meaning in Bengali. Its flower-head was called Mocha and was lauded as an 'excellent vegetable'. It is nourishing and is said to have a salutary effect on the action of the kidneys. In former days, no feast could be complete without a hotchpotch of the plantain flower being served after the distribution of the rice. Even today, there is an endless supply of culinary videos on YouTube teaching the art of preparing *mocha'r ghonto* and *kadali bhanda patua.* The latter is predominantly a favourite in Odisha. We also notice how both Bengal and Odisha have retained intact, the original Sanskrit word kadali.

In Maharashtra, the pith of the banana tree, known as the *kelicha gavha*, was eaten cooked as a vegetable. The spicy raw banana curry and the sweet preparation, *kelyache shikharan*, are also relished in the state.

Kerala emerges as the uncrowned monarch of banana usage. Without exaggeration, the state might disappear from the face of the earth if it's deprived of the plantain. Its signature variety, the *nendran*, can be regarded as the fructuous capital of Kerala. A sub-variety of the nendran, known as the *Changalikodan*, is offered to Sri Krishna at the renowned Guruvayur Temple as a *kazhchakkula* (or naivedyam). Changalikodan is rumoured to cost anywhere between ₹1,000 and ₹2,000 per bunch. And over the last three decades, the 'Kerala banana chips' has ploughed a silent invasion across the globe, akin to how you *will* find the ubiquitous Malayali tea vendor even on the moon.

Individual states apart, the pan-Indian omnipresence of the banana is found in the banana *bajji* and its variants—plain, spiced, dressed with onions and masala, with or without chutney. It jostles for the top place in the universe of vegetable bajjis.

The most glaring and also the largest *visible* use of the kalpavṛkṣa-esque plantain is its leaf. This is the supremely delectable plate that nature has gifted us. Its ubiquity is sadly restricted to South India. Even as recently as the 1970s, the plantain leaf was the plate of choice over its metallic counterparts in the homes of the average South Indian. It continues to retain its preeminence, especially during auspicious occasions like festivals and weddings. This is a subconscious reminder of its unbroken Sanatana sanctity. Indeed, a plantain leaf meal is an experience, notwithstanding the variety or taste of the dishes served on it. It is the victual synonym for both ānanda (joy, bliss) and *rasānanda* (where rasa = taste). Here is a mouth-watering description of this plantain-leaf *ānanda,* narrated in the *Tachcholi* ballad (*Vadakkan Pattukal*), extolling the heroic feats of the 17th-century Malabar lionheart, Tachcholi Chandu. This is how Chandu has his meals on a large plantain leaf:

> Tachcholi Meppayil Kunti Odenam
> Took an oil bath, and rubbed over his body
> A mixture of perfume, sandalwood and musk,
> And sat down for dinner,
> A *Kadali* plantain leaf was spread.
> His sister Tachcholi Unchira,
> Served him the dinner of
> Fine lily-white rice,
> A large quantity of pure ghee
> And eleven kinds of vegetable curries.

That made me ravenous even as I wrote those words.

— 5 —

A twofold tragedy of the post-industrial era is rapid dehumanization and loss of memory. Both have contributed to social instability throughout the world in an unprecedented fashion. Until the 1960s, only wars and natural disasters were the prime causes of instability. Technology has taken its place today. The generation born after the advent of mobile phones has zero inkling of real human interaction and lasting relationships.

And what is true of humans is truer in the hard, complex, and unforgiving natural world.

The loss has been enormous, swift, and irreversible.

Less than a century ago, the stem of the plantain tree was used in games and amusements, both by children and adults. It was a target to shoot arrows at. Like bamboo sticks, the banana stem was used to display feats of manual dexterity requiring extraordinary skill, concentration, and coordination. It was used for sword practice as well. In the early 1920s in Kodagu, a definitive marker of a person's strength and skill was to neatly slice through a banana stem with a single blow of the deadly Kodagu knife.

The banana rind was used in some regions of India as a dye to give leather a black colour.

The banana was also a popular and inexpensive vehicle, especially in Bengal. Scores of plantain stems were joined together and made into rafts. It would easily accommodate tens of people who floated on it on the river, from town to town. R.C. Majumdar narrates his childhood experience of this mode of travel.

> In those days, there were neither buses nor trains; there were not even the roads. So learning swimming was inevitable. No need for fuel, no need to stand in the line, just jump into the water and swim to the destination! *When we went to school we used to make rafts from the banana tree stumps* or hollow palm logs to stay dry. (Emphasis added)

If plantain leaves were used as plates in South India, they were used as substitutes for paper in Bengal. Both Indian and British records describe how 'advanced students' in the traditional village schools of Bengal used plantain leaves for writing.

> At the beginning they learn to write the alphabet on the floor or on a wooden board with a piece of chalk. When they have had

> sufficient practice in this mode of writing, they next use palm-leaves. Writing on palm leaves, they learn the alphabet and make some progress in arithmetic. The next step is the plantain leaf, and lastly, paper.

The creativity of Bengalis vis-a-vis the banana was almost limitless. In villages, dry plantain leaves were burnt, and their ash was used to wash clothes—a banana detergent, if you will.

Banana leaves were also widely used in the packaging industry for centuries throughout Asia. They are making a happy resurgence even as we speak.

Medicine was another field in which banana generously gave itself. For centuries, tender, unfolded banana leaves were applied as excellent coolants to cover blisters. Its dressing procedure was described thus: 'To dress a blister, a piece of the leaf, of the required size, smeared with a bland vegetable oil, is applied to the denuded surface and kept on the place by means of a bandage. The blistered surface is generally found to heal after four or five days.' Likewise, 'in ophthalmic diseases, a piece of the banana leaf forms a good shade for the eyes'.

Like in all other areas, mother nature's free gifts were innovated to serve human vices. The banana was no exception. Bidis in western India were wrapped with dried plantain leaves and then smoked.

— 6 —

And now, we return to where we began this essay: the unbroken sanctity of the banana in Bharatavarsha. Its primacy as the food of the Devatas and the Rishis naturally evolved with the flowering of the Hindu civilization, culture, and society.

A common sight that greets our eyes throughout Bharatavarsha is the pair of banana plants with their leaves smiling widely, tied on either side of the gate or door of homes and offices celebrating an auspicious event or festival. Among other things, it signifies abundance and prosperity.

When the *upavasa* became intermixed with the daily life and lifestyle of Hindus, milk and banana were regarded as the purest foods to be consumed on those days. The practice has remained unchanged in orthodox Hindu homes.

Banana and rice balls (*piṇḍa)* are mandatory offerings made to the *pitṛs* (departed ancestors) during the annual śrāddha (honouring the departed ancestors) ceremonies.

Banana also holds special reverence in both India and Nepal for a—literally—divine reason. It is the favourite fruit of the Goddess Shashti, the Devi who protects infants and assists childbirth. Depending on the region in India, she is worshipped on the sixth, tenth, or twenty-first day after childbirth. Among the items offered to her as Naivedyam, a whole cluster of bananas is absolutely mandatory. The auspicious Chhath Puja celebrated in Bihar is in her honour, along with the puja of Surya-deva. The word *Chhath* is a corruption of Shashti.

In the grand Durga Puja celebrated in Bengal, a banana tree is tied together with a branch or stem of eight other sacred plants and worshipped. These are, respectively, pomegranate, rice, turmeric, Aruna, Bel, Asoka, Jayanti, and Bijadya (bijora in Hindi; *Citrus medica*). They each represent the Nava-Durgas.

About a century ago, on the last day of the *Pushya* month, it was a custom in Bengal and Odisha to make toy boats from the lower leafstalks of the plantain tree. The boats were tastefully decorated with marigold flowers and filled with sweets. The mother would then perform the puja of one such boat to the deities at her home. After this, she would give the boat to her young son(s) to float in the village tank or river. While this endearing custom is evidently bathed in sanctity, its origins lie in the legend of a fabulously wealthy merchant named Srimanta Saudagar (an eponymous name meaning 'wealthy merchant'). He was a maritime trader who took his fleet of ships to Southeast Asia and Sri Lanka and acquired a huge fortune. Making those banana toy boats and offering them to the Devatas were the moving prayers of those mothers who wanted the gods to bless their boys with similar wealth.

Just like gods, even ghosts were fond of bananas. The annals of our profuse folklore, all the way up to the delightful *Chandamama* comics, authoritatively declare the fondness of ghosts for milk, sweets, and plantains. Ghosts can be invoked or made to leave after being satiated with this feast. If a ghost is feeling particularly greedy, it possesses a man or woman and departs only after a gluttonous bout.

A real-life episode illustrating this ghostly propensity occurred sometime in the late 19th century in Kolhapur. One night, a woman named Sita tripped and fell. She was spotted by the ghost of a dead sepoy who was lurking around in the area. It immediately took possession of her, and Sita became a changed woman at that instant. Eventually, her family realized that she was possessed and scoured the whole land for exorcists. None of them were successful. Finally, Sita's husband brought a reputed exorcist from a faraway land. After sustained exorcism, he had the ghost in his thrall and threatened to harm it grievously. The ghost begged his forgiveness and promised to leave Sita. But before that, it confessed its story: 'O Venerable Maharaj! I am a Pardeshi Sepoy. I was a soldier in the 27th Regiment and I was killed when my Regiment mutinied against the *Firangs*. I was wandering near the pond when I saw this woman fall on the ground and I possessed her. Now I'm leaving her. But before that, feed me a good dinner comprising rice, roti, ghee and bananas.' The sepoy ghost ate the dinner and left Sita forever.

2

Public Opinion in Bharatavarsha in a Pre-News Era

In the theory and practice of Indian statecraft before the advent of the Western model of democracy, the word *Rājan* (or king) meant 'a person who could keep the people entertained and pleased'. This conception is encapsulated in a defining aphorism, *rañjanāt rājaḥ*.

Political power and authority vested in the king implicitly rested on the sanction, goodwill, and consent of the people. All treatises on *Rājyaśastra* (statecraft, governance) unequivocally recognize the ultimate right of the citizens—or collective will—as the sole arbiters of the kind of government they wanted. This recognition was given concrete and practical form in two restraints placed on the power of the king:

1. The primacy and supremacy of Dharma as the guiding force of the State.
2. The counsel of the wise people, whose gentle but firm persuasion kept the king from committing excesses.

Then there was the third restraint as well: public opinion. In our own time, public opinion has almost been exclusively associated with the media, especially after the advent of the printing press. It appears that the invention of the printing press has almost obliterated the historical memory of how public opinion was gathered and shaped in the preceding eras.

In Bharatavarsha, public opinion has always been a force to be reckoned with since the time of the Vedic kings. This essay narrates the delightful and ennobling history of public opinion from that ancient period roughly up to the fall of the Vijayanagara Empire.

Narada, the Sage of News and Public Opinion

The impulse for news is innate in human nature because it arises from curiosity. The first recorded usage of the word *news*, dates back to no earlier than the late 14th century. Its original meaning was 'new things', and for about 150 years, it was used as the plural of 'new'. Early definitions of the word include 'tidings, intelligence of something that has lately taken place'. However, the current association of news as inseparable from the mediums that carry it is not older than a century. In 1923, news was defined as a 'radio or television program presenting current events'. Roughly around the same period, news also began to be referred to as 'media', denoting the collective of newspapers, radio, and television. This term was abstracted from mass media, which was considered a technical term in advertising.

In Indian tradition, what is known as news was understood as a hunger or curiosity for learning new or unfamiliar things in the world. Narada is regarded as the first journalist. He was a newsgatherer, reporter, and newsmaker. However, calling him a mere journalist would be doing injustice to him and limiting his genius. Our tradition correctly regards Narada as a maharshi or sage. He did not merely transmit news but worked actively towards stirring action. Unlike our current understanding of journalism, Narada's journalism was not passive reportage. He drew the attention of our gods, sages, and kings (to borrow the title of Dr David Frawley's book) to evils occurring in various worlds and spurred them to destroy such evils.

This is the great lesson that Narada teaches us: the herald of the news cannot pretend to remain unattached to the consequences of his news. The legendary D.V. Gundappa puts this in perspective:

> In the present day, we require this Naradaesque duty. But then, there is no Narada today. News reporters and journalists need to fill his place. However, *if Narada was to come to our present world, there is every reason to doubt whether he would enjoy the same reverence as before. This is because in our time 'independent thinking' has replaced Narada.* (Emphasis added)

The Vedic Era

In the Vedic era, the election of the king was in the hands of the people. Dr K.P. Jayaswal's brilliant work *Hindu Polity* contains rich descriptions of this electoral process. Every village, town, and city had public halls (akin to modern town halls). The village and townsfolk regularly gathered there to discuss issues of public importance. These halls also served as the location for general social gatherings. Vigorous debates were held. Local and non-local issues were sorted out after heated discussions that sometimes lasted for weeks. These halls were also venues for verbal contests. The *Tattiriya Brahmana* has a brilliant verse that encourages young men to actively participate in public assemblies and speak their minds on social and national issues without fear.

The king studiously compiled reports of all such debates and generally followed the current of public opinion. He would consult the prominent and wise people in his kingdom before implementing a policy that he felt could go against public opinion.

These foundational principles and practices proved to be durable throughout our history, as we shall see.

Epics and Puranas

The force of public opinion became stronger as Bharatavarsha evolved politically. As monarchy became the dominant system of political organization, public opinion became institutionalized from the very top. Nowhere was the king more cautious than in appointing his successor.

The Ramayana is a classic case in this regard. An insightful section in the epic describes how Dasharatha invited the heads of all the villages in his kingdom and placed his proposal in full public view: do I have your consent for nominating Rama as my successor? After they heard it, the chiefs went away and formed a separate assembly to discuss the matter. Here, they dissected Dasharatha's proposal threadbare by discussing Rama's qualities, character, and competence, and compared notes with one another on what they had heard about Rama. Finally, they reconvened before Dasharatha and said they had no objection to Rama's succession. The gratified father and monarch said to them with folded hands, 'I accept your verdict.'

Then we have numerous instances of the fabled Mithila King, Janaka, whose respect for public opinion bordered on reverence.

The world-renowned story of Yayati is another illustrious case in point. When Yayati announced that his youngest son, Puru, would be his successor, a great uproar erupted. The *Paura* and *Janapada*—representative bodies of the State—strongly opposed the king's decision on the grounds of sastra and time-honoured usage: the eldest son must be the successor. Yayati had to go to extraordinary lengths to convince them of the wisdom of his choice by quoting other respected sastric injunctions. The Paura and Janapada leaders finally agreed after being convinced in this fashion.

The Mahabharata goes a step further. The *Shanti Parva* makes the following recommendation: the king should send secret agents and loyal spies throughout the kingdom to ascertain whether the conduct of his government on the previous day has or has not met with public approval. Further, they should ascertain whether his conduct has or has not met with the approval of people in rural areas. There should be no divergence between what has met with approval in the capital and what has met with approval in the villages.

However, there were downsides to such a system of seeking the 'perfect' public opinion, i.e., an opinion that is accepted by everyone. From one perspective, the most tragic consequence of a king trying to please everyone was Sri Ramachandra, who parted with his queen and dear wife, Sita. Although his trust in her was unshakeable, he decided to forsake her to please a loose-tongued and petty-minded citizen.

The Buddhist Period

The Buddhist period not only continued the earlier tradition of debates, discussions, and decisions in public assemblies but also made its own valuable contributions. It is noteworthy that in a philosophical treatise like the *Mahaparinibbana Sutta*, Bhagavan Buddha found it necessary to tell his disciple Ananda that 'so long as the people of the *Vajji-Gana* hold full and frequent public assemblies, so long they may be expected not to decline but to prosper'.

Indeed, Buddha repeatedly emphasized the point that such public assemblies had to compulsorily meet frequently and attendance had to be full. The success of each such public discussion was measured by decision-making and problem-solving; solutions had to be found in a timely manner. This is the direct opposite of the national malaise that has been plaguing for more than half a century: of indefinitely postponing solutions to placate every two-bit faction.

Our ancients were far wiser than we can ever fathom.

The Buddhist period, which was dominated by powerful clans (*gaṇas*), had a flourishing system of collecting public opinion . . . *publicly*. Every city and town had a common *sanghāgāra* (town hall) where citizens of all ages—as young as 14 and as old as 80—participated in vigorous public debates on various issues. The other vital point that captivates our attention is the fact that they all had full freedom to discuss the business of the State itself. A brilliant story illustrates this point like no other.

Maharaja Pasenadi of the Aikṣvāka dynasty ruling from Shravasti (Sāvatthī) proposed to marry a princess belonging to the Sākya clan. The proposal itself was quite routine. But what makes it interesting is the fact that he made it public and asked the permission of his people. Members of the Sākya clan met in their own Sanghāgāra to discuss the proposal. This episode opens two important insights:

1. Each clan or Gaṇa had its own assembly hall apart from the common sanghāgāra.
2. The importance that the general public attaches to even the private affairs of their ruler.

The importance of the second point cannot be underemphasized. Why was it necessary for the people to give their approval for the ruler's marriage? This is the answer our political philosophers and sages, right from the Vedic age, understood that running a society and thereby a country was essentially the delicate art of maintaining a fine balance. They grasped the fundamental human impulse that the moment one group gains disproportionate power, the entire structure will collapse sooner than later. Thus, the Gaṇa and the *Mahājanapada* system (generally speaking, republics) that characterized the Buddhist era would remain united as long as this balance was maintained among these clans. This, among others, is a major factor behind the rule of generally discouraging people from marrying outside their own Gaṇa. It is also the reason why Pasenadi sought public approval for his wedding. In hindsight, it appears that it was an extremely wise and highly prudent arrangement. The best example of how things can go horribly wrong for the nation is available in our own time: the marriage of an Italian lady to the son of a former prime minister of India.

This well-oiled system of the Gaṇas and Mahājanapadas was also its fatal flaw. Over time, fierce clan loyalties weakened the overall civilizational consciousness, which is the only foundation for territorial and political integrity. It was precisely this weakness that alarmed Chanakya, who understood that Hindu national unity had to be forged from a different steel. This brings us to the next epoch: how public opinion was collected in Kautilyan State.

Public Opinion in the Mauryan Era

Although the full text of the *Arthashastra* was unearthed only at the beginning of the 20th century, its imprint has remained indelible throughout Hindu political history. It is not an accident that the text itself disappeared by the 12th century CE, roughly coinciding with the rise of the Muslim sultanate in North and North-western India. Indeed, by the 17th century, the widespread opinion among Hindu litterateurs was that the *Arthashastra* was a 'wicked and cruel work'. This is a clear reflection of the weakness of a psyche that discards Chanakya.

If Kautilya established an iron-clad administrative machinery and a ruthless political apparatus, the philosopher in him had recognized the fundamental truth that the only force that could sustain all this was the goodwill of the people. And this goodwill was expressed through public opinion. When this goodwill turned to wrath, the people wouldn't hesitate to even murder the king—the *Arthashastra* mentions several kings who were killed due to public outrage.

Thus, rather than await and sense the direction of public opinion, Kautilya proactively recommends setting up what can be called the Department of News Writers. In practice, this system generally took the form of issuing royal writs (*śāsanas*) under the seal of the king. The officer in charge of these writs was called *Lekha* (literally, writer). Writs were typically classified as general purposes, royal commands, charters, gifts, donations, and remission of taxes. There were specialized writs related to commercial and merchant guilds.

The qualifications of the Lekha were exacting. The following is a partial list.

The Lekha

- had to possess neat handwriting
- be skilled in grammar, composition, and reading
- be in constant touch with day-to-day events throughout the kingdom
- keep a close watch on the events happening in other states, especially those with whom his state has an alliance

The other high office dealing with public opinion was the Espionage Bureau, which directly reported to the king. The Espionage Bureau recruited and sent spies in various disguises throughout the kingdom to collect news. No information was deemed trivial. News writers were stationed at provincial headquarters, and they, in turn, sent their reports to the Espionage Bureau at the capital. It was a three-tiered system manned by the Espionage Bureau at the top, the provincial news writers, and wandering spies. Information was encrypted using cipher writing (*gūḍhalekhya*) and transmitted through carrier pigeons. But the most remarkable feature of this system was the fact that spies and news writers were unknown to one another, and the Espionage Bureau collected information from other sources as well. News and information were collected from various sources, such as meetings at public assembly halls, parks, rest houses, festivals, fairs, and temples. Action was taken only if all versions of news related to the same event agreed with each other.

Public Opinion in Later Periods

Chanakya's system became a superb blueprint that later kings followed. For example, the rich details of the Chola and Pandyan administrative systems speak about the *Manrams* (literally, 'halls', or public assemblies), where the public met and discussed social and political questions impacting them. The practice of beating drums, blowing conches, and blowing trumpets to summon the people to these meetings was common in our villages even in the 1970s. Decisions of public importance taken in such meetings, such as sending requests for tax breaks, building tanks, making temple endowments, famine relief, etc., were binding even on the monarch.

The history of the magnificent Vijayanagara Empire is replete with examples of the manner in which the monarchs feared public opinion. A classic example is the usurpation of the throne by Saluva Narasimha, which caused a huge uproar among the public, and he, as king, had to go to extraordinary lengths to pacify the citizens. The same public opinion also welcomed the accession of Sri Krishnadevaraya with open arms. And someone as intimidating as Sri Krishnadevaraya had to abolish the marriage tax—payable both by the bride and the groom at the time of marriage—bowing to the force of public opinion.

***

When we speak of the various golden ages of Hindu rule, what we really mean is that these Hindu rulers respected and even feared public opinion. The golden age was made possible because there was this standard of genuine harmony on the part of both the ruler and the people.

In many ways, the present system of democracy makes a sham of public opinion because, for the longest time, our political class was bothered merely about perception, not public opinion. Public opinion is meaningless unless both proactive action and timely redressal occurs, and both are measured by their respective outcomes. Unlike the Hindu monarchies of the past, where direct appeal to the king was taken seriously, today's political class has insulated itself from the public using several degrees of separation. Vacillation, not decisiveness, seems to be the mantra of this brand of Indian political class.

We can close this essay with a news report I read long ago. The episode happened sometime in the early 1970s. A poor villager was embroiled in a legal case that had dragged on for years. It was time for yet another appearance in court. Accordingly, the poor man gave his testimony. After listening to him, the judge chided, 'You are lying, and you know it. Aren't you aware that it is punishable?' The villager coolly replied, 'Why shouldn't I lie? Our great ministers sitting in Parliament and Assemblies have taken oaths on all kinds of sacred books. Yet they daily lie with a clean conscience. I am merely emulating them.' The news report records how the judge expressed his regret that he had no answer to this poor villager's question.

I suppose this episode shines an illuminating light in the context of public opinion in our own time.

3

Kunti Gita as a Sagacious Guide to the Contemporary Hindu Society

— 1 —

The *Udyoga Parva* is to the Mahabharata what the *Sundara Kanda* is to Srimad Ramayana. Both are harbingers to the subsequent decisive actions taken to defend Dharma by uprooting Adharma. But there are minor differences as well.

Sri Ramachandra's job was relatively easier. He vanquished Adharma by slaying Ravana, its most representative embodiment. Ravana was not related to him in any manner. It was a straightforward fight, with clear lines separating Dharma and Adharma. Sri Rama himself frontally led the war to protect Dharma and didn't need the Bhagavad Gita to inspire his Dharma Yuddha.

But the scene dramatically changes in the Mahabharata. On the *Adhidaiva* (generally speaking, the celestial or divine) plane, the Ramayana war was fought between the deva (divine) embodied by Sri Rama and the danava (demonic) embodied by Ravana. In the Mahabharata, the Kurukshetra war was fought entirely between humans. The deva, in the form of Sri Krishna, was a guide, facilitator, and enabler of the destruction of the danava element in humans.

The Pandavas weren't exactly paragons, but they were inherently virtuous. Which is why they heeded sage counsel and actively sought out Rishis and other wise men. Which is also why Sri Krishna favoured them. But for Sri Krishna's constant guidance, confusion and vacillation were the hallmarks on the Pandava side, even when they knew that they had always abided by Dharma.

By contrast, the Kauravas were human emblems of unqualified evil. Bhagavan Veda Vyasa describes Duryodhana as an incarnation of the *Kali-Purusha* and Shakuni as the incarnation of *Dvāpara-Purusha.* In D.V. Gundappa's memorable words,

> Duryodhana, born out of Gandhari's womb is an aspect of Kali-Purusha. He has no tolerance. He is strong, valorous, and an obstinate person who listens to no one. . . . Kali-Purusha is an embodiment of jealousy. . . . The chief defect in Duryodhana is spite. Jealousy is at the root of all his thoughts and endeavours . . . it alone was enough to wipe out all of his great power and enormous wealth. That indeed, is the element of Kali. . . . Shakuni is the incarnation of Dvāpara-Purusha. Dvāpara means gambling, and deceit is the intrinsic mindset of gambling, and the implement of gambling is the dice. . . . And now, the same deity of deceit stood in support of Duryodhana, the embodiment of Kali. This is but natural.

Thus, both uncle and nephew had no ambiguity about what they were doing when they invited Yudhishtira for the gambling match. Both took pride and sadistic pleasure in inflicting wanton humiliation upon the Pandavas. Both perverted the meaning of Dharma to justify their wrongdoing. But they got away with it at a pivotal juncture because of Yudhishtira's fatal confusion regarding the real nature and essence of Dharma. Fabled as Dharmaraja, Yudhishtira was a blighted literalist of Dharma. He understood only the *Sthiti* of Dharma but not its *Gati*, i.e., he confounded the static and dynamic elements of Dharma.

Nothing else explains why he accepted the invitation to the gambling match —not once but *twice*—after he was conclusively beaten in the first round. His weakness for gambling and an exaggerated sense of his own infallibility at the dice game were the real sources of his downfall. It made him interpret Duryodhana's toxin-tipped invitation to gambling as a discharge of his Raja Dharma. It also made him forget that Raja Dharma is a mere subset of Dharma. The ill-fated gambling match was a practical demonstration of Yudhishtira abandoning Dharma itself. The price was self-inflicted slavery and the public disrobing of his own wife, who was also the queen of his kingdom and the votive mother of his citizens. The loss of his empire and the rest are secondary losses in comparison.

Duryodhana is the original progenitor of the archetypal, depraved Indian politician of today. Instead of emulating Yudhishtira's manifold virtues, he targets his weakness and drags him down to his basal level by corrupting him *just once*. And at that nadir, it naturally becomes impossible for Yudhishtira to beat his cousin, and he loses everything. The pivotal gambling episode is also the one-line verdict of seven decades of Indian democracy: corroding the country by corrupting the voter.

Thus, what Yudhishtira had lost in gambling had to be recovered by fighting a cataclysmic war. A war that was forced on him by Duryodhana.

The events leading up to this final confrontation at Kurukshetra form the contents of the *Udyoga Parva*.

— 2 —

Indeed, the whole of *Udyoga Parva* is an encyclopaedic manual of statecraft, diplomacy, ethics, ideals, values, and hard-nosed pragmatism. One of its resplendent jewels is the fabled

Vidura-niti. The *Udyoga Parva* provides the clearest exposition of Dharma Yuddha or the righteous war that must be fought and won. It is also the best rebuttal to the woolly headed and hypocritical purveyors of the perfidy that all war is bad.

Reading and contemplating the *Udyoga Parva* is an urgent imperative for contemporary Hindu society. It is a phenomenal spine-strengthening exercise. The Sri Krishna that we witness here is the Krishna that today's Hindus must really worship. It is here that Krishna sculpts the ultimate victory of the Kurukshetra war using the hammer and chisel of his shrewd diplomacy and unswerving conviction in Dharma. It is diplomacy sans weakness. It is conviction sans compromise. Confusion is the father of compromise. Conviction is the mother of Dharma.

A powerful episode illustrates these eternal truths. It occurs in Duryodhana's mansion, opulently decked up to lure and beguile Sri Krishna, now the envoy of the Pandavas. An extensive feast has been arranged. Ever smiling, Krishna politely refuses to eat. But Duryodhana, the hardened deceiver, is persistent in his forged politeness and sham hospitality. And Sri Krishna is equally persistent in his refusal. After an elaborate back and forth, Krishna finally reveals the real reason:

> I will never abandon Dharma for any reason, be it desire, greed, enmity, suspicion or wealth. O Son of Dhritarashtra, a person will eat another person's food for two reasons only. One, if he has absolutely no means of survival. Two, if he has genuine affection for that person. O King! You are not dear to me. And I am not in dire straits. Your food has been tainted by your heinousness and is therefore unpalatable to me.

This is the uncompromising spirit that Hindu society has abandoned or forgotten over the centuries for various reasons.

The spirit of unambiguously recognizing evil for what it is and telling it to its face. This is the spirit that informed fiery Hindu heroes like Maharana Pratap and Chhatrapati Shivaji.

Sri Krishna exits Duryodhana's palace of vice and sin and proceeds to Vidura's modest home to have his meals. The sublime genius of Veda Vyasa describes the value of Vidura's food using two profound adjectives: *Śuci* (hygienic, pure) and *guṇavanti* (meritorious, virtuous).

Vidura. Used by Dhritarashtra like a washcloth to assuage his permanent guilty conscience.

Vidura. Shunned by Duryodhana's evil cabal, which never fails to remind him of his low status.

Vidura. Dear to Sri Krishna.

— 3 —

Throughout his stay in Hastinavati, Sri Krishna, the envoy of the Pandavas, resolutely spurns the repeated offers of hospitality sent by the Kauravas. He knows that it is bribery disguized as generosity. Vidura's humble abode is his favoured Xanadu. His residence there is also a powerful reminder to the Kauravas: Vidura is the unfading flower of Dharma in your empire of Adharmic sludge. Vidura is the only fearless truth-teller and is therefore the genuine well-wisher of the Kaurava clan.

When we study Sri Krishna's diplomacy in the *Udyoga Parva* and contrast it with the generational record of our IFS (Indian Foreign Service) officers, we get a depressing picture. For a seat for their spawns in an elite US or European university, for business prospects, and for post-retirement sinecures, three generations of our IFS officers have sold the Indian national interest without batting an eyelid. It is unsurprising that the adult brats of such IFS officers are some of the most virulent India-haters. Among them, a majority have Hindu names.

And here was Madhava, who refused to touch Duryodhana's tainted food.

Matching this Madhavan spirit was Kunti Devi. Her extensive conversations with Sri Krishna in the *Udyoga Parva* are unalloyed gold. Here, we see Kunti commanding the summit of courage, maturity, and wisdom.

Her exposition of Kshatra Dharma is stinging, critical, and rooted in truth and experience. She asks a pointed question: 'O Destroyer of Foes, Krishna! The gambling matches and the animal-hunting expeditions that kings of the past used to perform—did these really give happiness to them?' Clearly, this is not real Kshatra Dharma but a cynical interpretation of Dharma in order to justify vices.

It is also here that Kunti reflects on her long and tragic life; of all the characters in the Mahabharata, Kunti's is the most tragic. She has never known happiness. Her indomitable inner strength is also the source of her lifelong tragedy. And there is no better person than Sri Krishna, with whom she can confide so candidly. Krishna, who is her nephew, is akin to her own son. A range of emotions hits us like a slap when we hear her say this: 'I do not blame myself or Duryodhana for my plight. I blame my father. Just like how wealth is given to scoundrels, he gave me away to Kuntibhoja.'

And yet, after her outpouring, she re-emerges as the ideal heroic Kshatriya mother. Her *Dhīrata* triumphs over her *Duḥkha*. She sends an unambiguous message to her sons through Sri Krishna:

> Madhava! I am a widow. I have lost wealth but not enemies. I am living my life depending on the largesse of others. However, it is slightly more respectable to be dependent on others than

> live the life of a beggar. Fie upon me! Tell Yudhishtira to stop his drama of peace negotiations. Else, his Dharma will become tainted!

Here, we see Kunti as the ideal mother who urges her sons to be heroic. Her voice spits fire. Her charter for them is clear: fight like real warriors and liberate me. And then she gives a steely piece of advice that has always been the ideal of Hindu mothers throughout our history:

> The time for which a Kṣātrīṇi gives birth to sons has arrived. Warlike bulls like you don't become cowards while faced with resolute foes. This is your time. If you allow it to slip away without doing anything, then, although you are respected by the whole world, you will only be inflicting harm upon it. You will be indulging in contemptible behaviour. And if contempt touches you, I will abandon you forever!

In Kunti's fiery call to heroic action, we notice how unerringly she has grasped the true character, temperament, and prowess of each of her sons. But she reserves her highest love, respect, and adoration for Draupadi. She tells Krishna: 'If my sons are truly warriors, let them first avenge Panchali. Let them slaughter the Kauravas and *then* free me from my wretched state of having to depend on others. Let Arjuna walk on the path directed by Draupadi!'

Kunti's confidence in her sons' gallantry is unwavering. She knows that, led by Arjuna, they will smash all the Kauravas and conquer the whole earth. Arjuna's fame will reach the heavens. And then she utters these immortal words, which have since become one of the definitions of Dharma: 'If there is Dharma, what I have said *will* happen. *Namō dharmāya mahatē dharmō dhārayati prajāḥ*—I bow down to Dharma. Dharma is what governs the citizens.'

She has this message for Bhima: 'Duryodhana humiliated the guileless Bhimasena in full view of the elders of the Kuru clan. He will soon eat the fruit of his sins. Vrukodara (Bhima) will not rest until his vengeance is quenched.'

Indeed, Bhima and Draupadi were the only two Pandavas who kept the flame of revenge alive in their hearts. Nothing could douse it—neither the 12 long years of arduous forest life nor the life of quasi-servitude in Virata's palace.

Likewise, to Nakula and Sahadeva, Kunti's message is clear: 'More than life itself, strive to win objects of enjoyment, procurable only by prowess.'

Kunti's message to her sons through Sri Krishna can be likened to a Kunti Gita. Its practical demonstration is most noticeable in the glorious annals of Rajput history. The centuries of ferrous resistance that they offered against Muslim oppression can be captured in three words: *Vijaya* (victory), *Vīrasvarga* (warrior's heaven), and *Vīrāgni* (jauhar). Bharatavarsha is still a Hindu majority nation, not because of Gandhian pacifism or Nehru's red-rosed cowardice disguised as diplomacy, but because of the death-daring patriotism that was inspired by generations of undaunted Hindu mothers like Kunti.

In her ripe old age, Kunti spoke of and lived by the uncompromising code of valour and heroism. Urban Hindu mothers of our time who share Kunti's vintage are busy visiting beauty parlours and spas and colouring their hair with hideous hues and grotesquely piercing their various body parts. What they have taught their sons is a question whose answer is evident and disturbing.

4

A Journey with Guilds: Business Life in Ancient India

Preface

It is instructive to delve deeper into two words that the indefatigable researcher Dharampal has mentioned repeatedly: national reconstruction. In one of his interviews, he noted with some regret that after India attained independence, the new political elite told our people:

> Your job is over. Now, go back to your daily life. We will run the country. Sadly, our political leadership did not invite the masses to join in the great task of national reconstruction. Thus, people stayed afar, they continue to stay afar.

The reason for this attitude was a deep sense of psychological colonization that this elite had imbibed under British rule. A decolonizer par excellence, Dharampal dedicated his life to a sustained study of how our society had functioned and how our traditional institutions had operated for millennia until the British systematically dismantled the native mind.

> A major evidence of colonialism is the stagnation of our country's economy and society. From time to time, our country's original

> spirt and energy renewed itself. The first war of independence in 1857 was once such epoch. *That war was far more crucial and important than the freedom struggle of our own century. Its foundational inspiration was more natural.* However, after 1857, our society's collective mind set began to steadily decline.
>
> *In order to understand how our society was structured in the past, we need utmost humility.* If we go forth with a truthful attitude of learning, people will come forward to share their knowledge. However, if we go with a know-it-all arrogance, people won't share their knowledge freely. This is but natural. (Emphases added)

And then he offers us a rather startling but, actually, a commonsense verdict about British rule.

> Rank materialism was the only yardstick that the British colonialists had used to assess India's civilization. *The system of taking bribes that we condemn today had been an accepted social system in England for several centuries.* They had prepared an elaborate system that neatly explained its fundamental ideology and justification. There was [a] marked difference between the British and us. *They had institutionalised deception, trickery and treachery in commercial transactions to the status of an art form. We continued to remain naïve.* (Emphases added)

In this light, an honest study of the comprehensive history of India's institutional, social, and commercial institutions that existed in the pre-British era is an urgent imperative for our own time.

Unfortunately, the exact opposite has occurred. Most Indian historians and scholars who studied these aspects of our past, especially our society, culture, and commerce, took the British description of our past as the starting point. These historians perhaps subconsciously believed that this description of our society was its true reflection.

The reality, however, is the exact opposite. The picture of India that the British gave was not the picture of a Bharatavarsha at her prime but at the very nadir of her downfall.

One of the chief culprits who propagated this false depiction of India was James Mill in his *The History of British India* in three volumes. Here is a sample of his description of Hindu society in a section explicitly titled, 'Of the Hindus':

> Under the glossing exterior of the Hindu, lies a general disposition to deceit and perfidy . . . the same insincerity, mendacity, and perfidy; the same indifference to the feelings of others; the same prostitution and venality . . . in truth, *the Hindoo like the eunuch, excels in the qualities of a slave . . . in physical sense, the Hindoos are disgustingly unclean* in their persons and houses. (Emphasis added)

If you start with this vile premise, it becomes effortless to justify British colonial oppression of India, which is exactly what James Mill does: 'Even the utmost abuse of European power is better, we are persuaded, than the most temperate exercise of Oriental despotism.'

Quite obviously, Mill's *History of India* is a textual reflection of his prejudiced psyche. And Mill was just one in a long line of such racist British writers, scholars, travellers, and bureaucrats who wrote about India. But he attracts our attention because his tomes became mandatory reading for every colonial British bureaucrat who wanted a stint in India.

But as terrible as this 'syllabus' was, the greater tragedy occurred after independence. It might come as a surprise, but even today, significant portions of Mill's third-rated, racist volumes have been retained in their essentials, and his diagnosis and conclusions about India are uncritically accepted as valid by our IAS class. This, among other factors, is responsible for the bureaucratic high-handedness and oppression that are rife in India till date.

However, this sorry phenomenon is very recent considering the protracted civilizational history of Bharatavarsha. That history shows us a thoroughly different and opposite picture of our society, institutions, and the people who populated them.

— 1 —

The defining and distinctive feature of life in ancient India from the Vedic era onwards was the spirit of honest cooperation and harmony. This reflected itself in all areas, including religion, society, politics, and economics.

Perhaps the best illustration of this spirit is just one word: *yajna*. Today, we associate yajna almost exclusively with a religious ceremony or what is wrongly known as ritual. But as long as India retained her original character, yajna was a profound activity of national sharing… in fact, the accurate meaning of yajna is 'sharing', and not 'sacrifice'. Yajna was an institution which provided a spiritual basis for national cooperation. It is in yajna that we notice the practical manifestations of profound conceptions such as *Rta, Rna,* Dharma, etc. It was also a great engine of economics.

The spirit of cooperation is primarily a social instinct rooted in basic human impulses. Spirit acquires meaning only through activity. And so, the aforementioned cooperative spirit derives meaning and will function in the real world only through a well-ordered social organization. This organization—its form, nature, structure, and practical operation—also depends on the circumstances that birth it and in which it operates. But while the nature of these circumstances dictates its form, functioning, etc., its evolution and development depend to a great degree on the unique genius of the society and culture in which it is incubated and fostered.

This genius is precisely what we observe in the corporate and business life of ancient India. In the real world, this life revealed itself in the following organizations, which continue to exert an enduring and invisible influence on our contemporary lives as well. Here is a partial list:

- Jati (not in the colonial sense of 'caste')
- Sangha
- Shreni
- Puga (can be likened to today's Association of Persons, a cooperative society, and so on).
- Gana

A study of business and corporate life in ancient India opens up a whole new world, to put it mildly. It reveals a stunning array of the perspectives, attitudes, and impulses of life that animated our people so far back in time. More importantly, this study of business life in ancient India shows us the innate spirit of nobility, culture, and refinement that informed and suffused all other areas of our national life.

What has been unfairly propagandized as the 'caste system' was actually two things at the same time: one, it was a social corporation much like today's Federation of Indian Chambers of Commerce and Industry (FICCI) and similar bodies; two, it was also an economic system taken as a whole.

An Exciting History

Corporate organizations in ancient India have interesting roots. The *Bṛhadāraṇyaka Upanishad*, for example, is an ancient reference to begin this historical survey. It says that just as society was divided into four *varnas*, the Devatas too had four varnas. The story that follows is rather thrilling.

Brahma, the creator of the universe, was not content with creating only the Brahmanas and Kshatriyas because these two varnas did not know how to create and acquire wealth. And so, he created the Vaishya, also known by the term *Gaṇaṣaḥ*. The word basically means that it is only through cooperation and not individual effort that wealth is acquired.

This evidently shows the fact that there was thriving corporate activity in India's economic life as early as the Vedic period. For several centuries, the business community throughout India organized itself into Gaṇas or guilds or groups. This organization of the business community into Gaṇas was also a practical necessity, as we shall see.

The following were some of the major forms of corporate bodies in ancient India:

Gaṇa: It was an overarching and highly fluid organization, which generally means an association of traders and merchants. In general, it was any corporate body in the current sense of the term.

Paṇi: Similar to Gaṇa, it is derived from the root, *Pann*, meaning 'to barter' or 'to negotiate'. Over time, it acquired other meanings, such as a miser, a path, a market, and so on.

Puga: Corporations living by the profession of arms. These were entities that supplied soldiers for hire. This genre of corporations also had a clear leadership hierarchy. We can think of them as corporations of warriors, and they were in continuous existence for several millennia.

Samavāya: In general, an assembly or congregation of people meant to discuss or carry on some kind of commercial activity.

The *Śrēṇi*

One of the most enduring and ubiquitous corporate organizations was the *śrēṇi*, and it merits some detailed examination. But before that, we can cite an interesting tidbit. The head or chief of a *śrēṇi* was the śrēṣṭhi. This is the origin of the popular surname 'Seth'.

In general, a *śrēṇi* was a guild or commercial body. We can think of it as follows: practically, all different branches of occupations, professions, and trades had a well-defined organization of some sort. Each such organization had the authority to lay down rules, laws and regulations for its members, and these were recognized as valid in the eyes of the law. The representatives of a *śrēṇi* had a right to be consulted by the government authorities, including the king himself, in any matter that concerned them.

A notable facet of *śrēṇis* is the fact that while its legal character was a guild or corporation (the terms 'guild' and 'corporation' are used interchangeably), its members belonged to the same or different varnas and jatis. But all of them followed the same trade or profession.

All branches or specializations of professions, industries, trades, etc., formed their own guilds, but their numbers varied over different periods and geographical locations throughout our history. However, the most common or standardized number of guilds starting from the Buddhist period onwards is 18. In some cases, there were as many as 32. But overall, the number of guilds or corporations in the long history of India is rather substantial, which only shows how pervasive and complex the system of our corporations was. Here is a partial list of such guilds or corporations:

- Guilds of woodworkers including carpenters, cabinet makers, wheelwrights, builders of houses, builders of ships and builders of vehicles of all sorts

- Workers in metal, including gold and silver
- Stone workers
- Leather workers
- Ivory workers
- Workers fabricating hydraulic engines (*odayantrika*)
- Bamboo workers
- Braziers or brass workers
- Jewellers
- Weavers
- Potters
- Oil millers (*tilapiśaka*)
- Basket makers
- Dyers
- Painters
- Corn-dealers
- Cultivators
- Fishermen
- Butchers
- Barbers and Shampooers
- Garland makers and flower-sellers (*mālakāra*)
- Mariners
- Herdsmen
- Traders, including caravans and merchants
- Robbers and freebooters
- Militia who guarded caravans
- Moneylenders

These professional guilds also formed part of the local political assemblies.

At a high level, there was a clear difference between trading and merchant guilds on the one hand and guilds of artisans on the other.

In that era, typically, hereditary families following certain branches of trade formed themselves into exclusive corporations with a *jyeṣṭhaka* or *jyēṣṭha* as their head.

The Brilliant World of Artisan Guilds

The artisans had a rather strict system. The son of an artisan had to compulsorily undergo an apprenticeship under his father for several years, starting from childhood. Skill, talent, and expertise in a particular craft or profession were thus honed generationally. It rarely passed out of the family.

Artisan guilds or corporations were also a powerful force to reckon with in both politics and society. An eminent proof of this fact emerges when we observe town planning methods in ancient and mediaeval India. Townships, villages, streets, and quarters were named after specific artisans. Even until recently, it was common to find streets with such names in cities and towns throughout India. In Karnataka, every city and town had a *gāṇigara keri* (quarters of oil millers), *kuṃbārara bīdi* (carpenters' street), *agasara keri* (quarters of washermen), and so on. Even here, we notice how this system of town planning and social organization indicates Hindu civilizational continuity. For example, in ancient India, the word *kammāra gāmo* meant a village of ironsmiths. The Kannada word *kammāra* even today means an ironsmith.

These artisan guilds were also highly mobile and could move or migrate over long distances at astonishing speeds. We have an example of a guild comprising one thousand families of carpenters near Varanasi who left the town during a troubled period and settled on a faraway island.

Next, we can consider some major aspects of how these artisan guilds were organized broadly around three factors:

1. Heredity of profession

2. Localization of different branches or specializations within the profession
3. The office of the jyēṣṭha, the supreme head of the guild

The jyēṣṭha was akin to an alderman in the Western parlance (who typically served on the city council county board, etc.). In ancient India, the jyēṣṭha sometimes performed the role of a governor, local magistrate, or head of a city council and generally held a powerful position in the state's administrative apparatus. Some jyēṣṭha were personal favourites of the king as well.

Thus, owing to this kind of power and prestige, quarrels and fights erupted among various jyēṣṭhas on several occasions. It is said that on several occasions, Gautama Buddha himself had to step in to settle their disputes. Over time, when the frequency of disputes increased, it led to the establishment of a special tribunal. The first recorded tribunal was the Office of the Supreme Head of Guilds in the ancient kingdom of Kashi. The *Bhāṇḍāgārika* or royal treasurer (akin to the RBI governor in contemporary parlance) himself was appointed to this post. He had full judicial powers over all the jyēṣṭhas in the kingdom.

— 2 —

Laws and Regulations

Corporations were an intrinsic part of ancient India's political, social, and cultural life. Within each corporation, rules and regulations and laws were uniformly and strictly binding on all members, from the chief to the office-bearer occupying the lowest rung. They were also entitled to arbitrate and adjudicate, even in certain personal matters concerning its members and their wives. Not infrequently, the wives were formally ordained to manage several key areas of the corporation's activities. In a highly interesting episode in the *Vinayapitaka*, we learn of how some wives of the guild's members were even permitted to become Sanyasinis.

Corporations in the Kautilyan Period

And now, we can consider some aspects of ancient India's commercial and corporate activity in the epoch-making period of Kautilya.

Here, we notice a gradual but systematic crystallization in the realms of economics, commerce, trade, and corporate activity. These areas were also arranged in a profound manner and set the tone for what followed in India's history. We can examine only some of the major features in this connection.

In the Kautilyan and, broadly speaking, the Mauryan Empire, taxes remitted by guilds and corporations were one of the most important sources of revenue. The superintendent of accounts had to enter the following information in registers and account ledgers prescribed by the government:

1. A detailed history of the customs and usages of each guild or corporation
2. Specific details of each custom
3. A list of each profession, trade, craft, industry, etc., operating in the empire
4. Details of the transactions of each guild or corporation

A well-defined process was established whereby guilds or corporations could elect three ministers who enjoyed their confidence. These ministers would be their representatives within the government machinery, who looked after their interests and presented their case. As a mark of their confidence in the ministers, guild or corporate heads voluntarily made refundable deposits to the royal treasury. A measure of the mutual trust that existed between these corporate bodies and the government was the fact that they rarely asked for a refund, except in extreme conditions such as famine, etc.

This system turned out to be phenomenally durable and was pan-Indian in scope. It was maintained almost intact even during the reign of the Nayakas in southern India after the fall of the Vijayanagara Empire.

From the Mauryan period onwards, there were entire villages comprising a single guild, and these guild-villages were given royal protection through a regulation: no guilds other than local cooperative guilds could find entrance into such villages. For a protracted period of our history, we have ample evidence showing how, in many kingdoms, some guild-villages were so wealthy that they loaned money to the king himself in times of need.

Community Service by Guilds

Guilds and corporations played a central role in executing what are today known as community projects, and they took this role seriously. They punctiliously left behind stellar track records, inscribing their demonstrated spirit of public service.

Apart from guilds, the village headman, who was also the chief of the Village Assembly, actively encouraged his people to contribute to public works. The *Arthashastra* explicitly says that 'if any one refuses to give his help in work beneficial to all, he shall be compelled to pay double the value of the aforesaid help due from him'. The village also had a common fund, to which everyone, including guilds, contributed. The fund was also augmented by fines levied on 'lazy' people or work-shirkers.

Kautilya minces no words when he says that 'the acquisition of the help of corporations is better than the acquisition of an army, a friend, or profit'. Accordingly, corporate bodies throughout Hindu history were accorded special privileges. Guilds of artisans and workmen (*sanghabhṛtraḥ*) enjoyed a grace period of seven nights over and above the project completion date. In some cases, they were even exempted from paying the mandatory security deposit to the treasury before starting a new business or project.

Some examples of guild-driven community projects included the construction of roads and bridges (*setubandha*) and community buildings of any kind (rest houses, *mandapams*, hospitals, parks, etc.). Given the cost of such large infrastructural endeavours, several guilds came together in a spirit of brotherly cooperation to fund them. The State, in turn, recognized that these initiatives were 'beneficial to the whole country' and would 'adorn the villages' and gave special concessions (*priyahitam*) and tax breaks to such guilds. But the job didn't end after the construction of such public utilities; guilds maintained their own watch-guards to patrol these roads, bridges, etc.

— 3 —

The Vibrant World of Kshatriya-*śrēṇis*

Which brings us to another marked feature in the history and evolution of our guilds and corporations. Over time, guilds and corporations had emerged as formidable, quasi-military powers—that is, they were equipped with well-trained private armies. Among others, this is indicated by the term śrēṇi-vala, which meant a class of troops that the king might call upon or enlist during war time or crises. Some powerful corporations were deliberately stationed in border towns to serve as deterrents to enemy kingdoms. In his *Arthashastra*, Kautilya mentions Kshatriya guilds that were found in abundance in the Kamboja (now eastern Afghanistan) and Saurashtra countries, and these guilds pursued war as a profession and trade and agriculture in peacetime. In the chapter titled 'The Conduct of Corporations', he clearly lauds them as being 'invincible to the enemy' and urges the king to secure their services and loyalty through gifts and conciliation.

In fact, the term *śrēṇi-vala* occurs in the Mahabharata itself, while the Ramayana gives the word *Sāyōdha-śrēṇi* or armed guilds. The other words denoting armed guilds include Āyudha-jīvi and Kshatriya-*śrēṇi*, i.e., guilds who lived by the profession of arms.

Throughout the post-Mauryan period, armed guilds played a significant and decisive role in Indian politics. Even as Hindu political power in north India was being cannibalized by alien Muslim invasions, these Hindu armed guilds maintained their dominance in South India. The Chola Era reveals an outstanding scene of the influential standard of power and prestige that these armed guilds enjoyed. The *Vēlaikkāra* community dominated the business and political life of the 10th and 11th centuries. Two of its most powerful subgroups included the *Vaḷaṅgai* (Right Hand) *Iḍaṅgai* (Left Hand). Both Rajaraja Chola I and Rajendra Chola named their army regiments after these two military guilds.

Some of the more enterprising Vaḷaṅgai and Iḍaṅgai guilds were hired by Sri Lankan rulers for participating in wars, quelling insurrections, and providing security. An incredible inscription from Polannaruwa (Sri Lanka) gives us eye-opening information about the prowess and influence of the Vēlaikkāra community of guilds. The following is a summary of the inscription.

Devasena, the chieftain of King Vijayabahu of Sri Lanka, constructed a *Dhātu-bhavana* or temple containing the relic of the tooth of the *Jina* in the city of Pulasti. After the temple was finished, Devasena enlisted an army of Vēlaikkāras from the Tamil country in India to protect it. The enlistment procedure is described as follows:

> The pious and the learned royal preceptor Vyarinimula, the *Mahāsthaviras* (literally, 'Elders of Repute') of Utturulmulai together with the king's ministers, called for a meeting of the members of the *Mahātantra* (Great Assembly). These assembled together, bringing with them their leaders, the *Vaḷḷañjiyār* and *Nagaraṭṭār* communities denominated the shrine . . . and took upon themselves the responsibility of maintaining the temple and protecting its property. As remuneration, one *Veli* (6.5 acres) of land was assigned to each member of the *Vēlaikkāras*.

The contract was ratified by the Vēlaikkāras in the following words:

> We protect the villages belonging to the temple, its servants' property and devotees, even though, in doing this, we lose ourselves [i.e., lose our lives] or otherwise suffer. We provide for all the requirements of the temple so long as our community continues to exist, repairing such parts of the temple as get dilapidated in course of time and we get this, our contract, which is attested by us, engraved on stone and copper so that it may last as long as the Moon and the Sun endure.

Outwardly, this is a commercial contract, but the wording clearly elicits awe, wonder, admiration, and deep feelings within us. It also opens a beautiful cultural casket, revealing the nuances of the guild system and the society that housed it. The inscription also gives a full list of the subgroups within the Vēlaikkāra community. Some notable groups include the Vaḷaṅgai, Iḍaṅgai, Śīrudanaṁ, *Piḷḷaigaḷ-Danaṁ, Vaḍugar, Malaiyāḷar, and Parivārakkoṇḍam.* The aforementioned *Vaḷḷañjiyār* and *Nagaraṭṭār* communities were—and remain—ubiquitous throughout South India all the way up to our own time. For example, the Kannada equivalent of Vaḷḷañjiyār is *Bañajiga*, and Nagaraṭṭār equates to *Nagartaru*; *Karaga,* the renowned annual festival of Bangalore, begins its journey from the Dharmarayaswamy Temple situated in the *Nagartarapete*, a locality named after *Nagartaru.*

The history of our corporate guilds has been preserved to this day through these surnames or family names. And so, theorists 'researching' the 'caste system' of India clearly overlook these lived realities, which, as seen so far, unambiguously show a highly harmonious society.

Legal and Judicial Aspects of Guilds and Corporations

As our guilds and corporations extended the ambit of their operations and enlarged the sphere of their influence, society, and legal system too kept pace with them. The Dharmasastra literature evolved over time to meet these changing circumstances. It contains copious rules related to guilds, corporations, caravans, and trading communities.

A key feature of this politico-legal facet was the right of corporations to have their own rules, regulations and laws, which the government not only recognized but the king was bound to consult them before taking any decision that impacted corporate bodies. In fact, as early as the 5th century BCE, this system had already been formalized. Here's a representative verse from the *Gautama Dharma-Sutra*:

> Cultivators, traders, herdsmen, money-lenders and artisans are authorised to lay down rules for their respective classes, and the king shall give the legal decision after having learned the (state of) affairs from those who have authority to speak on behalf of each class or guild.

Internally, guilds and corporations functioned according to democratic principles. The Buddhist period, for example, furnishes us with extensive evidence for this fact.

A General Assembly—akin to modern-day board meetings—was vested with supreme authority to decide on all matters. The actual procedure for conducting these meetings was described down to the last detail. All members of the guild had a right to vote unless they were incapacitated. No meeting was considered legal unless all the members entitled to vote were present. If a member was absent for some reason, he could formally declare his consent to vote, familiar in contemporary parlance as absentee voting. The formal consent of absentee members was known as *chhanda*. The *Mahavagga*, for example, contains elaborate rules formulated to constitute a quorum.

While the king did grant extraordinary autonomy to guilds and corporations, it was not a blanket licence. He was the supreme judge invested with juridical and punitive powers in both cases: one, where disputes could not be internally settled by corporate bodies, and two, in disputes between different corporate bodies. The unfairly reviled *Manusmriti* has a stately description of how the king should conduct such judicial proceedings:

> He was to enter the court preserving a dignified demeanour, together with the Brahmanas learned in the Vedas, and with experienced councillors. He was to examine the cases either seated or standing but without ostentation in his dress and

> ornaments. The decision had to be pronounced in a timely fashion. . . . The laws of various Jatis, of districts, of guilds, and of families had to be studied by the king, who was to adjudicate based on the peculiar law of every one of them.

Apart from the king, there were executive courts specifically meant for trying cases related to corporate bodies. These were helmed by three commissioners (*Pradēṣṭārāh*) or three ministers (*Amātyāh*). The following is a brief list of the corporate or quasi-corporate entities they dealt with: guilds (*Ś*rēṇi), artisans (*K*ārukāh), weavers (*Tantuvāyāha*), washermen (*Rajakāh*), goldsmiths (S*uvarṇakārāh*), sweepers and scavengers (*Jjhārakapānśudhāvākaḥ*), physicians (*Bhiṣajah*), traders (*Vanik*), musicians (*Kuśīlavā*), dancers (*C*ārāṇāvāha), mendicants (*Bhikṣukaḥ*), and cheats (*Kuhakāha*). These courts, in turn, were divided into two: *Dharmastha* and *Kaṇṭakaśōdhana*. The former dealt with cases of contract and tort, while the latter tried cases involving oppression of the people inflicted by corporate bodies. The ubiquitous corporate villain and capitalist monster is a staple of contemporary Indian cinema. Perhaps these storytellers and filmmakers might find ennobling material if they care to study the legal and judicial aspects of corporate and business life in ancient and mediaeval India.

Tradition, custom, and usage of each guild or business community played the most decisive role in two major areas:

1. Adjudication of disputes.
2. When the government allowed the starting or expansion of a new business or commercial project while levying specific classes of taxes, etc.

The primacy of guild-specific traditions, usages, and customs throughout the commercial history of India has to be grasped in order to obtain a well-rounded and error-free understanding of the subject.

We have an incredible proviso in the *Sukraniti* related to guilds of thieves, among others. This is how it reads:

> The cultivators, the artisans, the artists, the usurers, corporations, the dancers, the ascetics and thieves should decide their disputes according to the usage of their guild, etc. It is impossible to detect them through others' help. So, they are to be found out with the help of persons born in those guilds.

This injunction neatly ties in with the *Manusmriti's* dictum that the king should be well-versed in the traditions, laws, usages, and customs of each guild. The aforementioned guilds of thieves also indicate the same civilizational and social continuity; for example, the much-maligned *Kallar* tribe (literally, the tribe of thieves) that was pervasive in Tamil Nadu had existed in an unbroken manner till the end of the 19th century, when colonial British laws criminalized the tribe as a whole.

The remarkable endurance of this system can also be seen in the reign of the Hoysala monarch Vira Somesvara (1235–63 CE). His senior minister Rama Deva Nayaka issued a charter to the Acharyas of several merchant guilds of Gommatapura (Shravanabelagola). An Acharya, in this case, was the titular name given to the head of a guild. The following is the text of this rather extraordinary charter:

> In case the imposts classed as *nyaya*, *anyaya* and *mala-braya* of the palace come to be levied, the acharya . . . shall himself pay and settle the matter: it is no concern of the residents. Those who violate the terms of this charter are the destroyers of the

> *Dharma-sthala* [i.e., Shravanabelagola renowned as a sacred pilgrimage site]. If among the merchants of this holy place one or two, posing as leaders, teach the acharya deceit, and, causing confusion by taking one thing for another, encourage him to covet a *hāga* [a quarter of something including a monetary unit] and a *bēḷe* [half of something including a monetary unit] and still ask for more, they are traitors to the creed, traitors to the king, enemies of the [guild]. . . . If knowing this, merchants are indifferent, they alone are destroyers of this charity and not the acharya. If without the consent of the merchants, one or two leaders enter into the acharya's house or the palace, they are traitors to the creed. With regard to privileges, former usage [i.e., traditional customs and usages] shall be followed.

While the intent, sentiment, and legal import of the inscription are self-explanatory, the concluding sentence reaffirms a central theme of Hindu social and cultural history: the nearly paranoid care to preserve tradition. On one level, it is also rather delightful: 'former usage' can range anywhere, dating back to a few generations all the way up to the Vedic era. Every such charter, document, inscription, and epigraph found in any Hindu historical period throughout Bharatavarsha concludes with a similar injunction. Tradition is the most effective vehicle for preserving and transmitting continuity, stability, and order.

In this light, it is clear that the literate 'reformers' who tried to 'create' a 'new India' in 1947 from scratch tried to do so not only by bypassing but also by axing the very roots of tradition.

In passing, it is pertinent to mention another important feature of corporate India in ancient times. One of the mantras that has gained popularity in the contemporary world is something called ease of doing business. Accordingly, there are elaborate systems for ranking a country based on this parameter.

However, our policymakers would be greatly rewarded if they studied these aspects of business and corporate life in ancient India. Several invaluable lessons and learnings are lying in wait. In fact, the story of the gradual and organic evolution of our guilds into massive, transnational corporations is not only rewarding in the worldly sense but is a delightful study of a magnificent, kaleidoscopic universe in itself.

— 4 —

Features and Functions of Corporations in Ancient India

Next, we can examine some contours of the main features and functions of guilds and corporations in ancient India.

Guilds and corporations could own land and property in the corporation's name. They could formulate rules and regulations and draw up charters like Memorandum and Articles of Association as understood in contemporary parlance. Any member who violated it invited penal action. Corporate representatives transacted business with the court of law, where they commanded respect.

The office named *Kārya-cintaka* resembled today's board of directors. It consisted of people who were, above all, 'pure and virtuous', over and beyond their professional qualifications and competence. The *Yajnavalkya Samhita* has a beautiful line describing such men: *Kartavyaṃ vacanaṃ teṣāṃ samūhahitavādinām*. The compound word *Samūhahitavādinām* is rather poignant. What it means is that the corporate heads had to be advocates not only of their own guild but also of public welfare in the most embracive sense of the word. The Sanskrit word *Hita* has a range of meanings that can't be easily translated into English. Does this remind us of what is today known as corporate social responsibility?

Although each guild or corporation had a chief or Śrēṣṭhi, real power was vested in the board of directors or the executive council.

A mandatory clause included in the charter of each guild or corporation was a list of measures aimed at preventing corruption. At the outset, it was compulsory for any member engaged in the business of the guild who received anything of monetary value—clothes, money, gifts, etc.—to deposit it in the guild's treasury. If he did not, he had to pay 11 times that amount as a fine.

Any member who violated his agreement with the guild or corporation instantly invited various punishments, including but not limited to penalties and expulsion. An expelled member would no longer be able to conduct business with anyone, almost for life.

No member could enter into contracts with third parties using a clause that did not exist in his guild's charter.

Rules and regulations of a corporation had to be consistent with the sacred texts and the laws laid down by the king.

The World of *Nigamas*

For centuries on end, business and corporate life in India had evolved into a rather complex institution. This was the Nigama, which even today means what it originally meant in ancient India: a corporation.

Interestingly, Nigama also means the following: the Veda, city, marketplace, street, merchant, caravan, oath, an act of logical reasoning or deduction, a kind of tax, and so on. In fact, a study of the morphology of this term reveals an ocean of information about India's commercial and cultural history.

To cite just one example, a number of clay seals discovered in the ancient Buddhist city of Vaishali between 1902–15 mention the following terms:

1. Shreshti-Sarthavaha-Kulika-Nigama
2. Shreshti-Kulika-Nigama
3. Shreshti-Nigama
4. Kulika-Nigama

Pioneering scholars like D.R. Bhandarkar, R.C. Majumdar, et al. have greatly enriched this field of study. Purely going by what these seals contain, they deduce that Nigamas were cities administered either jointly or severally by *śreṣṭis, kulikās*, and *sārthavāhas*.

Generally speaking, kulikās were artisans such as sculptors, heads of specific guilds, and so on. In early mediaeval India, a kulikā was also a member of the Panchayat Board. It might be interesting to note that an inscription mentions kulikās as warriors who protected the Kullu valley in Himachal Pradesh.

Sārthavāhas were the heads of merchant caravans.

Evidence for the unbroken commercial and cultural continuity as well as the societal preeminence of these guilds is available in a Gwalior inscription dated 877 CE. In that period, the city of Gwalior was administered by a board of *śreṣṭis* and *Sārthavāhas*. The inscription explicitly mentions their names as follows: the merchant Vayyuka, the trader Ichchhuvaka, and the other members of the board of the Savviyakas were administering the city.'

In a much later period in South India, these mercantile corporations played a dominant role, as we've already seen earlier in this essay. In other words, the unbroken continuity of these institutions was retained pan-India.

Incorporation of a New Guild

Next, we can consider a few highlights regarding the incorporation of a new guild or corporation. To begin with, here's a beautiful verse from the *Brihaspati Sutra*:

> Koṣēṇa lēkhakriyayā madhyasthairvā parasparam |
> viśvāsam prathamam krtvā kuryaḥ kāryāṇi anantaram ||

We can break this verse down for the sake of convenience and to understand its practical aspects.

1. Here, the first step before incorporation was the performance of an ordeal named *Koṣa*. Accordingly, each prospective guild member had to drink three mouthfuls of water in which the *Vigraha* of his *Iṣṭa Devata* (Personal Deity) or *Kula Devata* (Deity of the Lineage) was washed. If he met with disease within a fortnight, he was considered untrustworthy and therefore denied admission into the guild. In Hindu jurisprudence, this is known as *Koṣa*-D*ivya*, part of the nine or ten Divyas or ordeals meant to prove the guilt or innocence of an accused. In this case, the term 'guilt' is synonymous with 'unfitness for membership'.
2. After passing this test of trustworthiness, a convention or agreement was drawn up detailing the rules and regulations that were binding on all members.
3. This agreement was then attested by the *Madhyastha* or guarantor. He was a man of high standing and integrity, vouching for the pure and faithful conduct of the guild itself.
4. The completion of this threefold step was what inspired mutual trust among guild members as well as in the public eye. Indeed, the phrase *viśvāsam prathamam krtvā* is actually

> quite profound and is an illustrative reflection of the defining trait and the value system of the people, society, and culture of ancient India.

The procedure was rather elaborate. It covered minute details, both in writing and in practical action. But once the guild was duly incorporated, it set to work. An elaborate Memorandum and Articles of Association were drawn up, which included the various items of the guild's business. Various annexures listed out non-business activities that the guild would carry out; these chiefly included community projects, charitable works, donations to temples, participation in festivals, etc.

A soulful verse in the *Brihaspati Sutra* says that a corporation should also perform works of public utility, such as: (1) building a house of public assembly, typically a town hall; (2) a rest house providing free accommodation and meals for travellers and pilgrims; (3) pools for supplying water to animals such as cows, bulls, buffaloes, horses and elephants; (4) constructing temples and gardens; (5) funding the poor people (*Daridrāṇām*) so that they could perform sacred *Samskaras* such as *Caula* (hair-shaving ceremony performed for young boys), *N*āmakaraṇa (naming ceremony), *Upanayana* (sacred thread ceremony), *Antyeṣṭi* (the last rites), and various Yajnas.

All these were formally written down in the corporation's charter and were legally binding. The nobler element in this is the fact that guild members were liable for judicial punishment if they transgressed or failed to perform these Dharmic duties!

And so, no matter where a guild was located in Bharatavarsha or where it travelled, it invariably carried out one or more or all of the aforementioned acts of Dharma. We literally have hundreds of inscriptions spread throughout Bharatavarsha for at least two millennia that prove this fact. Here, we can examine just three:

1. A 3rd century CE inscription at Nasik informs us that in the regime of King Isvarasena: the guilds of potters and makers of water clocks were given an endowment of 1,000 *kārṣāpaṇas* (a unit of currency) and the guild of oil millers was endowed with 500 kārṣāpaṇas. From the interest on this money, both guilds had to provide medicines for the Sangha of Buddhist monks dwelling in the caves atop the mount of Trirasmi.
2. Several inscriptions found at the Junnar caves dating back to the Indo-Greek period mention the following endowments: (i) a donation of the income of two fields with the Konachika guild for planting Karanja trees and banyan trees, (ii) an endowment of money with the guild of bamboo workers and the guild of braziers for pious activities, and (iii) the gift of a cave and a cistern to monks by the guild of corn dealers.
3. The aforementioned Gwalior inscription dated 877 CE records an endowment given by the guild of oil millers and the guild of gardeners to the Vishnu and Nava-Durga Temples. This is how it reads:

> a perpetual endowment to provide oil for the lamps, the chiefs of the guilds of oil-millers should give one *pālika* of oil per oil-mill on the ninth day of the *Shukla-Paksha* of every month. The chiefs of the guilds of gardeners should daily give for the requirements of worship, fifty garlands of the flowers available in the given season.

The government apparatus, which accorded special status to guilds and corporations, also responded in kind by enabling them to perform these Dharmic activities in a flawless manner.

The department in charge of guilds and corporations comprised the following officials:

1. A president or chief
2. Two to five executive officers

The following is a sample of their qualifications as decreed in the *Brihaspati Sutra*: deep learning in the Vedas and Dharmasastras, professional competence, impeccable honesty, firm control over the self, non-temptable, and skilled in the secret of every business operating in the kingdom.

Banking Guilds

Guilds and corporations in ancient and mediaeval India also functioned as local banks that accepted public money and paid interest in the range of 9–12 per cent. Like any bank, they also loaned money.

Larger guilds extended their banking services throughout India. There was an impressive network of such banking guilds dotting the entire geography of Bharatavarsha. Their organization was cohesive, well-linked, and above all, they operated on the basis of strict honesty, integrity, fair dealing, and a fear of incurring *paap* or sin. Measured on the parameters of professional competence, organizational efficiency, customer service, and delivery, these banking guilds can hold their own against the sophisticated banking systems of our own time. This well-oiled system existed in an era where plain, simple trust and not fraud-detection software were the norm. Like their compatriot commercial guilds, these banking guilds too performed their share of charity and piety, as we shall see.

All of these traits inspired trust among the public, which deposited large sums of money. Likewise, another significant feature of these corporations was the fact that they had a system similar to travellers' cheques. There was another side to it as well. If a traveller ran out of money in a faraway land, he could take a loan from a local guild and repay it to a guild back in his native town or village. That local guild was in turn connected with the guild from which the traveller had taken out the loan.

Village and town administrative bodies—similar to municipal councils—also provided banking services and worked closely with all denominations of commercial guilds. Banking guilds were recognized as an important constituent in the municipal government of ancient and flourishing cities such as Pataliputra, Mathura, Ujjaini, Vidisha, etc. The town corporation or municipality recognized their duties as trustees of public money. These banking guilds received not only cash deposits but also endowments of property.

Epigraphic Evidence

We can briefly examine how some of these features played out in the practical life of Hindu society throughout our history using epigraphical evidence.

A large cache of seals dating to the Gupta Era (roughly the 4th and 5th centuries CE) was discovered at Basarh, Bihar. A majority of these seals deal with corporations (nigama) of bankers. Other seals talk about guilds of mobile traders (sārthavāhas) and merchants (*kulikas*). Interestingly, one seal mentions the name of Dodda, the head of a guild of bankers and traders. Together, they had formed a body resembling the modern Chamber of Commerce. (In Kannada, the word *Dodda* still means 'elder', 'great', 'big', and 'large', indicating this linguistic continuity.)

From here, when we travel down to Lakshmeshwara in northern Karnataka two centuries later, we find an inscription dated 725 CE. It talks about the Constitution drawn up for the town of Porigere. This is how it reads: '[T]he taxes of all classes of people shall be paid to the guild of braziers in this town in the month of *kārtika*.' Clearly, this guild of braziers also doubled up as the local bank or treasury.

The Chola period supplies us with a truly spectacular portrait of the aforementioned dual role of village corporations and guilds.

A hoard of 14 inscriptions found in 1893 at a crumbling Vishnu temple in Ukkal village (Tiruvannamalai district) inspires wonder and awe. This is how R.C. Majumdar characterizes it:

> Indeed by far the most interesting examples of the village Assemblies occur in southern India. *A large number of inscriptions prove that they had a highly developed organisation and formed a very essential element in the state fabric of old.* Thus the fourteen inscriptions in the Vishnu temple at Ukkal . . . furnish a very instructive insight into their nature and constitution. (Emphasis added)

Taken as a whole, this epigraphic evidence gives us a comprehensive picture of the economic aspect of village administration in South India. Every activity that generated money was allocated a dedicated fund. Thus, there was a tank fund, a rice fund, an oil fund, a flower garden fund, a gold fund, and various donor funds. These funds were managed by their respective guilds, which had to make regular deposits with the Village Assembly at stipulated periods. It is this feature that gave a corporate character to the Village Assembly (Sabha or Mahasabha). The treasury of the Village Assembly used the interest from these deposits to fulfil the duties laid down in the village constitution, including performing works of charity.

Guilds as Trusts

Guilds and corporations were also executors of endowments and wills. Given the high degree of trust and integrity that these guilds inspired, people fearlessly made perpetual endowments and entrusted these corporate bodies to execute them. In turn, these bodies did this job flawlessly over five, six, and even ten generations. And they did this not merely as a job entrusted to them but out of a spirit of Dharma—that is, by executing the endowments, some part of that Dharma would also accrue to them. This also reveals the fact that these guilds were generational and had preserved institutional memory in a manner that can only be described as genius-level.

We need to remember that both the donor and the guild discharging the endowment regarded it as an act of piety and reverence. This is perhaps the most elevating feature of the corporate and business history of ancient India.

On the macro canvas, the intrinsic and inseparable elements of Hindu business history include spirituality, godliness, devotion, and Dharma. We have a treasure trove of records that testify to how corporations themselves made generous endowments of an astonishing variety: for lighting lamps in temples in perpetuity, for upkeep of temples, for *annadānaṃ* (charitable food distribution), for celebrating festivals, for maintaining *Go-Shalas,* for facilitating *Tirthayatras*, and other services to Sanyasins and monks.

An ennobling example will suffice to illustrate the method by which this system worked.

A Shaka prince ruling in the Sindh region in 120 CE made a perpetual endowment of 3,000 kārṣāpaṇas for the benefit of Buddhist monks engaged in penance in the caves of Nasik. He entrusted the execution of this endowment to guilds based in faraway Govardhan, Uttar Pradesh. This was 1,900 years ago.

— 5 —

Concluding Remarks

We can close this essay with where we began it: in Dharampal's passionate and sustained appeals for decolonization.

A tragic and ongoing consequence of British colonialism was the creation of the deliberate myth that only European discoveries, inventions, and innovations in science and technology had the power to unlock the mysteries of the universe. Its companion myth was that European political systems, social organizations, institutional frameworks, and intellectual traditions were the sole repositories of all the wisdom hidden in human civilization.

Quite obviously, these myths could only be sustained by the brute strength of their military dominance. It was precisely this attitude that made them confidently declare that everything in India's past was primitive and fit only to be discarded, if not annihilated. We must admit that the British succeeded phenomenally in instilling this myth among our own people.

One major, if not the central, component of this myth is directly related to the Indian corporate and business life outlined so far. It must be remembered that the British first arrived in India only to trade. In their essential position, they were supplicants before a vastly superior economic power spread across one of the largest geographies in the world. But the sort of military and political dominance that they eventually acquired made them spin exactly the opposite story. Thus, inveterate racists like James Mill deliberately invented the fiction that our guilds and corporations were closed entities working in isolation, that they were fossilized and that they resisted change, progress, and innovation.

The opposite is actually true. We can consider just a small piece of evidence that proves this historical truth. As we have seen throughout this series, our guilds and corporations enjoyed an extraordinary degree of autonomy and received royal protection as well. It was precisely this factor that made India the economic powerhouse of the world for several centuries, irrespective of the rise and fall of empires and dynasties. The fact that Indian products commanded an extraordinary premium in international markets for such a prolonged duration is one proof of our mobility, innovation, and progress.

We have the example of Sri Krishnadevaraya, who set up an entire Ministry of Perfumes, and the businessmen in his domain who prolifically imported aromatic raw materials and copious barrels of exquisite perfumes from Persia, Portugal, etc.

On a more profound plane, a study of corporate and business life in ancient India is also an invitation to a sort of penance. The names and accomplishments of some eminent businessmen have been preserved in royal edicts, epigraphs, and grant records. These are the stories we must unearth, popularize, and prescribe for both general and specialist audiences. If they reveal anything, it is this: that our business class was distinguished not just for its financial acumen; it made enormous amounts of money, but it also went far beyond this ken. In peacetime, our businessmen prolifically contributed to society and nurtured culture. In times of crisis, they stood with their chest thrust forward. When they were profoundly moved, they donated their entire wealth and renounced the world in a quest for higher callings.

The history of corporate and business life of Bharatavarsha is no less exalted than its spiritual history, which is but natural. The genius of the former is the source of the latter.

5

A Murder that Unearthed a 2nd-Century Sanskrit Manuscript on Ayurveda

— 1 —

What began as an argument between two businessmen led to the murder of one of them and launched a manhunt against the murderer and culminated in the accidental discovery of a 2nd century CE Sanskrit manuscript that rattled the world of Indology in the late 19th and early 20th centuries.

The story begins with the British explorer, tea planter, and diplomat Robert Barkley Shaw, who established the Central Asian Trading Company in 1873 to trade primarily in Indian tea.

In 1869, Shaw ventured into the badlands of Yarkand (now Yarkant County, China), scouting for business prospects. This hostile territory in the Pamir mountains was still unmapped. Shaw and his business rival, George Hayward, were the first Britons to land there.

Barkley Shaw had done his homework quite extensively. Yarkand fell under the dominion of Kashgar, the ancient and flourishing international trading post on the Silk Road. Both places were then in the grip of the tyrannical Uzbek Muslim warlord named Yaqub Beg. Shaw knew that he had to appease him to obtain permission to trade. As a first step, he sent expensive gifts to Beg. The lure worked, and Shaw found himself in Yaqub Beg's palace and then in his presence on 11 January 1869. After exchanging cordialities, Shaw made his offer: allow me to open a trading post in your territory and I can guarantee you a handsome revenue from Indian tea. There are *60 million* potential customers in the Kashgar region alone. A delighted Yaqub Beg accepted the offer, but in a bizarre twist, he placed Barkley Shaw and George Hayward under house arrest.

What both Englishmen didn't know was that they had been inadvertently drawn into the infamous Great Game fought between Russia and England for control of Central Asia. A few weeks later, Yaqub Beg met them and told a flummoxed Shaw, 'I declare you as my brother.' There was an existential reason for this. Behind the scenes, Yaqub had received confirmed intelligence that the Russians were plotting his assassination. He therefore needed support from the Queen of England and the 'Lord Sahib', the Viceroy of British India. The support was granted, but Yaqub also wanted something in return, as we shall see.

From 1873 onwards, the Central Asian Trading Company prospered on a fabulous scale, controlling trade in Indian tea and other products in the trans-Karakoram region. Ladakh and Leh were transformed into lucrative mercantile outposts.

— 2 —

Andrew Dalgleish had turned 20 in 1874. A Scot of humble origins, he had come to India at the behest and encouragement of his uncle, a bureaucrat named Thomas Russell.

That year, he found himself in a luxurious bungalow at Kashmiri Point, Murree, now in Pakistan. Murree, the birthplace of the genocide monger, General Dyer.

Andrew Dalgleish had just received a magnificent offer from Barkley Shaw: would he like to be a trader in the Central Asian Trading Company operating from Leh-Ladakh? Once more, his uncle's encouragement sealed the boy's decision. Thomas Russell was a pragmatic man. He said, '[A]ccept the offer. Men of our station in life don't often get opportunities like this.'

But the young Andrew proved even more pragmatic when he replied, 'If the Central Asian Trading Company is as successful as the East India Company, then 1874 should be a prosperous year for us.'

His maiden assignment included transporting a sizeable cargo comprising several large iron trunks and other boxes to Chinese Turkistan—specifically, Yarmand and Kashgar lying in Yaqub Beg's territory. The caravan included 30 men, 20 ponies, and 15 sheep—to be slaughtered and eaten over the course of the month-long journey.

The finest quality of Manchester cotton was a major chunk of the freight. But the contents of the iron trunks were of immense diplomatic and political value: British rifles. This was what Yaqub Beg had demanded from the British in return for permitting the Central Asian Trading Company to open their shop in his dominions.

Barkley Shaw and Lieutenant Hopkirk would lead the expedition from the front. Both were heavily armed. Shaw safeguarded the keys to the rifle-laden trunks while Hopkirk manned the ammunition just in case they encountered the 'Himalayan bandits who will murder for rifles'.

The expedition was not only successful, but it proved to be a career-altering experience for Dalgleish.

— 3 —

Andrew Dalgleish settled down in the general region of Ladakh, Leh, and the Karakoram Pass. Over time, he became somewhat of a local, mastering the Uyghur language and marrying a Yarkandi girl. He travelled incessantly and became a favourite companion of travellers, merchants, and game hunters. Dalgleish knew the whole area like the back of his hand.

Business was booming, and he was making caravan-loads of cash. One of his business associates was a volatile Pathan named Daud Mohammed Khan, well-known for operating on the trade route between Yarkand and Ladakh. Their association soon turned into a close friendship. But what Dalgleish did not know was that Daud had a torrid reputation as a smuggler and a crook.

As was his habit, Dalgleish once took off on a long expedition to Tibet. And this was when Daud revealed his real colours. He neglected his business and indulged in all sorts of vices. His ponies perished, and it wasn't long before he went bankrupt. He began borrowing indiscriminately from Hindu moneylenders, and when they finally landed on his doorstep to collect the loan, he threatened them. In turn, they complained to the British commissioner at Leh. The commissioner forbade Daud from trading on the Yarkand–Leh road until he had cleared his dues.

When Dalgleish returned and learned of Daud's fate, he took pity on him and decided to help his fallen friend. In May 1888, Dalgleish departed from Leh and travelled towards Yarkand along with some pilgrims and servants. En route, he wrote to Daud, asking him to join his caravan. A few days later, Daud met Dalgleish at some distance after the Karakoram Pass, where tents had been pitched to rest.

There are slight variations regarding the episode that follows, but the overall picture is clear.

Over tea, Dalgleish and Daud had a discussion over Daud's debts. For a long time, Daud said nothing, and then he walked out of the tent, returned with a rifle, and shot into the tent.

The bullet wounded Dalgleish's shoulder, and as he ran out to escape, Daud chased him with a lethal sword and butchered him.

Daud Mohammed Khan had now become completely unhinged. Instead of escaping, he ordered the stunned and cowering servants to prepare a meal for him. After devouring it, he slept soundly in Dalgleish's tent and left the place the next morning.

When news of this ghastly slaughter reached the British community in Yarkand, a wave of outrage erupted. Dalgleish had to be avenged at all costs, and the British Raj was only too glad to oblige. The entire government machinery launched a massive manhunt for Daud Mohammed and announced a substantial bounty for his capture. Imperial Britain's prestige was at stake. Messages, letters, and other forms of correspondence flew thick and fast.

One such communique landed on the desk of a lieutenant stationed in Kashgar. His name was Hamilton Bower.

— 4 —

The tone of the communique was grave and urgent, and it had come from the topmost bosses. It was a tersely worded, urgent order: arrest Daud Mohammed Khan at all costs and bring him to India for trial. By murdering Andrew Dalgleish, Daud has directly challenged the might of the British Empire. It ended with these words: your mission has to be kept strictly confidential.

The British government had chosen Hamilton Bower for a forthright reason. When we read between the lines, we can't help but marvel at the intricacy and effectiveness of the well-oiled British intelligence network of that era. Hamilton Bower had been stationed at Kashgar, but his bosses had more intimate knowledge about the region and the developments therein than he did.

Sometime in the recent past, Daud harassed a Hindu merchant who naturally nursed an abiding grudge against this vile Pathan. And now, Daud had become a fugitive, fleeing from place to place. His flight first led him to Kashgar. But instead of choosing caution, he began to openly gloat about his 'heroic' slaughter of Dalgleish. This news reached the Hindu merchant. Seething with vengeance, he reported the matter to the British authorities, who acted swiftly, and that was how Hamilton Bower found himself reading the aforementioned communique.

However, Daud had already outpaced him. By the time Bower took action, Daud had already decamped from Kashgar. He assembled some emissaries and intelligence agents and drew up an elaborate plan to track and arrest the murderer. Two agents went to Afghanistan and reached Balkh. There, an Amir named Abdur Rahman told them that Daud had escaped to Bokhara.

On his part, Hamilton Bower had travelled eastwards before landing in the densely populated and thriving commercial city of Kuchar (its contemporary names include Kucha, Kuche, Qiūcí, now in Aksu Prefecture, Xinjiang Uygur Autonomous Region, China). It was January or February 1890. Almost two years had passed, and the accursed Daud Mohammed was still elusive.

— 5 —

Kuchar would prove to be the unforeseen stage on which the script of a far-reaching drama was discovered. This needs to be placed in a broader political and historical context.

Ever since colonial European powers began to go on an unbridled rampage across the globe on the strength of their technological and military prowess, a parallel development had occurred in its wake. This was the upsurge of interest in rediscovering and unearthing civilizational, cultural and archaeological secrets of the ancient world. From South America to Egypt, from Arabia to India, freelance adventurers, explorers, historians, epigraphists, and archaeologists literally began to excavate the past. State-funded and private universities and academic and research institutions throughout Europe received lavish financing to pursue inquiries in these subjects.

The purpose behind these research endeavours was multi-pronged and depended on the agenda of their sponsors.

Some endeavours were based purely on a disinterested quest for knowledge. Others were motivated by unquenchable greed—epic plunderers like Cecil Rhodes fall into this category.

But topping this list was colonial-imperial arrogance, which sought to rewrite the history of the ancient world from the (White European) conqueror's perspective: the world is at our feet because our race is intrinsically superior. The clearest and most abundant proof for this racist mindset is found in the discipline miscalled Indology. In fact, the term 'Indology' itself reeks of racism. Right at the outset, adding the '-logy' suffix made it inert. 'Indology' is defined as the study of India in an all-encompassing sense. However, in practice, it has always connoted the study of an entire civilization, culture, philosophy, and people as museum artefacts. Thus, even the Indian people—mostly Hindus—have been studied and examined with the attitude and approach of a zoologist who conducts experiments on live rats and frogs in a lab.

When we return to Hamilton Bower, we observe the fact that a parallel economy was flourishing at its peak for roughly two centuries. This was the informal and underground global industry of trading in archaeological artefacts, manuscripts, scrolls, and coins.

India (in the sense of *Brihad-Bharata*) was home to the world's largest repository of these artefacts.

A complex kaleidoscope of actors populated this thriving industry. Pitched battles were fought between tribes, and bloody murders occurred to possess these artefacts. The sole goal of their possession was to sell them to the White Man at handsome rates. Almost every person in the societies conquered by the colonial Europeans intuitively knew that the artefact he had accidentally discovered would fetch him a good sum or even a fortune. Uncountable numbers of impoverished nomads, villagers, and artisans—mostly illiterate—were armed with this intuitive knowledge. And they often sold the artefact for paltry sums. What is of mere academic or colonial interest for one is often the only means of survival for another. This phenomenon is precisely what we notice in racist movies like *Indiana Jones and the Last Crusade,* a thinly veiled flaunting of the White man's burden and Christian superiority.

— 6 —

A Turkic Muslim sought Hamilton Bower's audience in Kuchar. He was a hardened professional in the aforementioned underground artefact economy. But he primarily identified himself as a treasure hunter. This is how Bower describes the meeting:

> While at Kuchar a man told me of the existence of an underground city and said that he had gone there to dig for treasure a few days previously but had only succeeded in finding what he called a book. I asked him to show it to me and he went

> away and came back bringing the manuscript as it now is. He was anxious to sell it and *I was very glad to pick up for a small sum what might prove of great value.*
>
> The same man offered to show me a subterranean town, provided I would go there in the middle of the night, as he was frightened of getting into trouble with the Chinese, if it was known that he had taken a European there. I readily agreed and we started off about midnight. The man produced me a packet of an old manuscript written on birch bark. They had been dug out of the curious old erections of which several are to be found in Kuchar District. (Emphasis added)

Clearly, both the Turkic Muslim treasure hunter and Hamilton Bower knew that they had something of great value and concluded the trade on amicable terms. The former was happy with the money, which he regarded as substantial. For Bower, the sum was trifling. He had enough knowledge and experience to understand that money was not the real value of books and manuscripts.

But before we proceed, we need to close the unfinished business of Daud Mohammed Khan.

Lieutenant Hamilton Bower was a patient man. He kept his eyes and ears open and was finally rewarded after a few months. One day, he received good news. Daud had been imprisoned in Samarkhand.

The news-bearers narrated the full story to Bower.

The characteristic recklessness of the mercurial Pathan had ultimately overwhelmed him. He was sitting on a large wooden box in the bazaar street in Samarkhand once again gloating about how he had murdered Dalgleish. Two emissaries, whom Bower had dispatched, spotted Daud. One of them quietly rushed off to General Kuropatkin, the governor of Samarkhand. Within minutes, a small unit of the Cossack army descended on the bazaar and shackled Daud Mohammed and flung him into prison.

It appeared that the imperial British had had the last laugh. The Pathan scoundrel had been caught, and now it was only a matter of formality to bring him back to India and hang him to death. However, two or three days later, Bower received another piece of news: Daud Mohammed Khan had hung himself in his cell.

Reading the full story of how the British doggedly hunted down Daud and finally captured him is a study in the temperament of a nation that takes itself seriously.

Hamilton Bower returned to India in late 1890s. He took the manuscript to Shimla and handed it over to J. Waterhouse, the then president of the Asiatic Society of Bengal. On 5 November 1890, Waterhouse placed it before the society's monthly meeting and read out Bower's note explaining the circumstances of its discovery. The board members agreed that the manuscript was of immense value, but there was a problem: at the moment, there was no scholar who could decipher it.

The manuscript was named eponymously *The Bower Manuscript*. Indeed, the nomenclature was characteristic of colonial attitudes towards India. But its real name, *Nāvanītakaṃ*, not only reveals its antiquity but is yet another proof of the scale and span of the enduring influence of the Sanatana civilization in Brihad-Bharata or Greater India.

— 7 —

The German Indologist Augustus Frederic Rudolf Hoernlé returned to India early in 1891 after finishing his annual leave. Hailing from a zealous Protestant missionary lineage, Hoernlé had learnt Sanskrit under Theodor Goldstucker's tutelage.

Over the years, he had earned acclaim as a scholar of the so-called Indo-Aryan languages and as an expert archaeologist and numismatist. He had recently stepped down as the former editor of the *Journal of the Asiatic Society* of Bengal.

And now, Hoernlé requested and got the so-called Bower Manuscript from J. Waterhouse. In the April 1891 proceedings of the Asiatic Society of Bengal, Hoernlé published the first cut of his decipherment of the manuscript.

His findings immediately overturned all the overconfident consensuses prevailing in the domain of Indology so far. Its sensational impact was comparable to or even greater than the discovery that William Jones made more than a century ago: that Sanskrit was indeed the mother of all languages.

In one stroke, the so-called *Bower Manuscript* had opened several floodgates. The most significant outcome was the birth of a whole new field of study: archaeological explorations in East Turkistan. The colonial British government splurged enormous money on this endeavour. Some scholars of that era even characterized this as a 'whole modern movement'. It appeared as though there was no limit to what they could potentially unearth in the region. But at another level, the cultural verdict was once again unambiguous: the primitive, uncivilized, and superstitious race of the Hindus had a truly glorious past, and the more the British dug and studied, the farther the frontiers of this glory extended,

The so-called *Bower Manuscript* was the first of hundreds of future conclusive proofs demonstrating the spread and impact of Sanatana and Bauddha Dharma in China and Central Asia. Bharatavarsha was clearly the selfless donor and guru of exalted philosophy, spirituality, and profound cultural values that sculpted and refined the civilizations and societies in this vast region.

When we study history from this perspective as well, we arrive at the same inescapable conclusion: the incalculable damage that Islamic ravages have caused in a substantial part of Asia. For centuries before Islam, commercial and cultural intercourse between India and the Far East was marked by continuity, amicability, and affection. The sword and fire of Islam transformed major portions of this geography into hellholes of Abrahamic barbarism and its people into semi-savages.

— 8 —

As excavations proceeded apace, Mother Earth revealed ancient historical truths anew.

Kuchar or Kucha, the site where Hamilton Bower bought the manuscript, was a flourishing city of great antiquity. In the 7th century CE, it was home to scores of temples and hundreds of Buddhist stupas. It had been ruled by Chinese kings with beautiful Sanskrit names such as Suvarna-deva and Suvarna-Pushpa, who adhered to the Hinayana sect of the Sarvāstivāda school of Bauddha Dharma. The indefatigable traveller and prolific chronicler Xuanzang, who gives us this picture of Kucha, also says that 'the doctrine and the rules of discipline of the Sarvāstivādas are like those of India, and those who read them use the same originals'.

The most eminent luminary of Kucha was a Buddhist scholar, monk, and fecund translator named Kumarajiva. Sometime in the 3rd or early 4th century CE, his father, Kumārāyana, had migrated from Kashmir to spread Bauddha Dharma. He had landed in Kucha and had married Jivaka, the sister of the king of Kucha. Showing great promise since boyhood, Kumarajiva mastered the Bauddha Agamas and Sarvāstivāda. He later journeyed to the selfsame Kashgar, which was then a great centre of Mahayana learning, and mastered Nagarjuna's Mādhyamaka philosophy.

Arguably, the whole of the Buddhist tradition in China was singlehandedly shaped by Kumarajiva. Even Communist China has gratefully preserved his memory in the form of a sculpture that greets the entrance of the Kizil Caves in Kuqa County in Xinjiang, China. But even more touchingly, in 384 CE, Kumarajiva built the artistic White Horse Pagoda to honour the memory of Tianliu, his devoted horse, which carried Buddhist scriptures from Kucha to Dunhuang.

Which brings us back to Kucha. The archaeological digs that began after the discovery of the so-called *Bower Manuscript* eventually acquired an independent life. Japanese and European explorers and archaeologists entered the scene and unearthed thousands of valuable artefacts and sites.

Of these, the Kizil and Kumtura Caves are the most significant for historical, cultural, civilizational, and artistic reasons. The Kizil Caves—also known as the Caves of the Thousand Buddhas—are the largest in number: 236. These are the indisputable physical proofs of how Sanatana and Bauddha Dharma shaped the ancient Chinese religion, culture, and society in a profound fashion. Numerous Sanskrit inscriptions in some of these caves list the names of the rulers who patronized Buddhist monks and offer invaluable historical information. Monastic cells in the caves were known by their original Sanskrit name, *Kuti*. Several wall paintings and murals in these caves exhibit distinctive influences of the Mathura, Gandhara, and Kashmir schools of art.

But the most astounding discovery was something called the Kizil Library. The scholar of history Emmanuelle Lesbre writes that this library had some of 'the oldest copies of the Indian theatre [tradition] known today' written in Sanskrit. Scripts of full-length Sanskrit plays were discovered, and they were explicitly titled *Nāṭaka.* They strictly adhered to the rules of Sanskrit drama, comprising prose, verse, music, and pantomime. They provide what is known as stage direction or scenic indications so that 'a single performer can enact a complete play by changing attitudes and voices'. Single-performer plays are typically known as *Eka-vyakti Nāṭaka.*

— 9 —

The copious wealth of literature about the Kizil Caves also reaffirms a sad fact of contemporary India: the awful squandering of Bharatavarsha's inexhaustible cultural repository and the shameful neglect of our deep, civilizational imprint across the world. That these infractions have occurred at a frenzied speed *after* 'independence' in a purposeful and sinister fashion makes this tragedy more grotesque and unforgivable.

What is our foreign policy worth if it doesn't recognize these indomitable strengths of our past? These are strengths we independently built through a complex amalgam of life-affirming philosophy, evocative spirituality, a robust and prosperous economic system, a stable and harmonious social order, and an undying spirit of Kshatra, which sustained all this. For the last 75 years, we have been unable to straighten our spine, which has been bent out of shape thanks to a defaced history that has bred four generations filled with an incurable inferiority complex.

In fact, the legendary D.V. Gundappa condemned Nehru and Indira Gandhi more than 40 years ago precisely on this point:

> Thanks to the great winner of independence and his daughter, India stands tied to the apron-strings of the mother of

> Communism even though the bulk of India's population is not communist . . . what gives poignancy to the reflection that *we are so miserably incapable of going at least to the moral support of Cambodia is the recollection of the historical fact of our ancient kinship*. Once upon a time perhaps about the time of the beginning of the Christian era—Cambodia was part of the cultural empire of Hinduism. (Emphasis added)

What applies to Cambodia also applies to China in varying degrees. If we had actually played to our strengths after independence, our foreign policy doctrine would have been perpetually reminding China of the incalculable debt it owes to the Santana civilization. The debt, among other things, is visible to the eye in the Kizil Caves and other ancient sites.

And it was the so-called *Bower Manuscript* that cut open this road of civilizational rediscovery in Brihad-Bharata.

— 10 —

Apart from precious antiquarian sites, the discovery of the so-called *Bower Manuscript* also led to the discovery of hundreds of Sanskrit and the so-called 'mixed Sanskrit'= manuscripts in East Turkistan. In general, a majority of these manuscripts were treatises or commentaries on various aspects of Bauddha Dharma. Researchers and scholars are nearly unanimous in their conclusion that the authors of these manuscripts were Buddhist monks who had typically migrated from Kashmir beginning in the early part of the 1st century CE.

The authors of the so-called *Bower Manuscript*, too, were Buddhist monks from Kashmir. Its correct name is *Nāvanītakaṃ*, literally meaning 'clarified butter'. Written on the *bhūrja-patra* or birch-bark, *Nāvanītakaṃ* is a compendium of Ayurveda compiled by four different authors belonging to the 2nd century CE. The names of the first three authors remain unknown. All four originally hailed from Udyāna or Kashmir, and migrated to Kucha and settled in the Buddhist monastery there.

Yashomitra, the fourth author, was perhaps the most eminent of the four. At Kucha, he quickly became renowned for his learning, saintliness, and piety. He was the cynosure of the monastery, and when he died, a stupa was built in his honour. Known today as the Kumtura Caves, the stupa had a Relic Chamber in which the *Nāvanītakaṃ* was deposited. Yashomitra compiled and added fresh material to the *Nāvanītakaṃ* that his predecessors had left behind.

— 11 —

The *Nāvanītakaṃ* is not an original text of Ayurveda but a collection of extracts from various Ayurvedic texts extant at the time of its composition. It quotes heavily from the *Caraka* and the *Sushruta Samhitas* and, to a lesser extent, from the *Bhela Samhita*. A fragment of the *Bhela Samhita* is available even today in the famous Saraswati Mahal Library in Thanjavur. Apart from these, the authors of the *Nāvanītakaṃ* also give original Ayurvedic formulations not found in earlier texts.

Like all ancient Indian medical treatises, the *Nāvanītakaṃ*, too, is in verse. According to scholars, the language of the treatise is a combination of Sanskrit, 'mixed Sanskrit', Prakitized Sanskrit, and what is known as 'Buddhist hybrid Sanskrit'. It primarily employs three well-known metres in Sanskrit: *Anuṣṭubh, Triṣṭubh,* and Ā*rya*. Including these, the total number of metres in the treatise is 23, spread over 1,323 verses, written on 51 birch-bark leaves.

Unfortunately, the complete manuscript is unavailable, and that which has survived is divided into seven distinct treatises. This, in turn, is divided into two major sections:

1. The 'Larger' section comprising Treatises 1, 2, 3, 4, 5, and 7.
2. The 'Smaller' section comprising Treatise 6.

The most noteworthy element in the *Nāvanītakaṃ* is the earnestness and the spirit of service of its compilers. In the opening verse of the 'Smaller' section, the author says that 'this is a compilation of extracts from the standard medical works, and the extant medical tradition of' his time. Clearly, the authors were eager to preserve the ancient medical tradition for posterity.

A glimpse into the brief contents of *Nāvanītakaṃ* is sufficient to give a delightful flavour to the work. The first three treatises deal with proper medicine, the next two deal with divination, and the last two with magical incantations (mantra). Various treatises of the work invoke Buddhist deities and Hindu deities such as Shiva, Vishnu, and Devi.

We can look at some snippets from the contents of *Nāvanītakaṃ*.

Preparation of various pastes (*lepa*) for the head and hair.

A detailed list related to the preparation of various powders (*cūrṇa*) and tablets (*guḍika* or *gulika*). Some of these are in active use in our own time.

Medicated ghee of various types. The total number is 28.

Medicated oils. The total number is 17.

Various types of elixirs, aphrodisiacs, decoctions, dyes, and ointments.

A whole treatise is devoted to the art of fortune-telling by means of throwing dice. Different types of dice are mentioned as well. This eventually became a ritualistic practice in Tibetan texts.

Another section is dedicated to magical incantations (mantra) for curing many diseases and snake bites. This ancient practice was prevalent in India until recently.

The final treatise of *Nāvanītakaṃ* extensively deals with methods for protecting a person from various types of evil.

— 12 —

The special feature of *Nāvanītakaṃ* is its elaborate disquisition on *lasuna* or garlic. In fact, *Nāvanītakaṃ* opens with a chapter titled 'Lasunakalpa', meaning 'pharmacology of garlic'. Spread over 43 verses, it is a magnificent and masterly exposition of garlic as both an item of diet and medicine. It is also a marvellous piece of storytelling that traces the origin of garlic to the Puranic episode of the *Amrita-Manthana* (Churning of the Ocean of Ambrosia).

Writing in 1923–24, Balwant Mohan, an eminent scholar and authority on *Nāvanītakaṃ* gives us this revealing piece of insight:

> The actions and uses of garlic as a remedial substance are more fully discussed in *Nāvanītakaṃ*, than in any other medical book yet published in the Western medical Literature. . . . *Its use as described in most recent western medical publications, seems to have been adopted after the publication of the first edition of the Bower Manuscript.* (Emphasis added)

This observation reflects another historical phenomenon of Westerners: stealing and appropriating scientific, medical, and other knowledge from various countries and cultures and claiming it as their own.

And so, Western medicine was another field in which *Nāvanītakaṃ* or the so-called *Bower Manuscript* left a lasting impact. As we remarked earlier in this essay, we are yet to fully explore the kind of durable influence that the ancient and classical Hindu civilization left on cultures, societies, and nations across the world.

Epilogue

The so-called *Bower Manuscript* that Rudolf Hoernlé first deciphered was finally published in 1912 in three thick volumes of gigantic size. He had spent 21 years on the work. It was doubtless an impressive feat. However, it was also a disservice because it remained inaccessible to the very audience that would benefit from it: traditional Ayurvedic Vaidyas (doctors) in India. A majority of these Vaidyas could scarcely afford the prohibitive cost of *Nāvanītakaṃ*.

The aforementioned academic and scholar, Balwant Mohan, stepped in to help them. He initiated a correspondence with the Bengal Asiatic Society, and after a sustained battle with the colonial bureaucracy, he got the full manuscript and began working on it. After two years of painstaking effort, he published a slim and affordable volume of the complete *Nāvanītakaṃ* in the original Sanskrit. He also wrote a learned introduction and a preface to the work. Some extracts from his preface are painful and moving at the same time.

> The … reason for neglect in its study by the Vaidyas, was its enormous size and high price, which a few could afford to pay.
>
> It was possible therefore that this *grantha,* one of the best researches into the state of Indian medicines, must have remained in obscurity for a still longer period, but for the attempt to bring it into the present form, as it lies before the readers. It was one of the several sources of information to scrutinise the fact that how such a valuable literature of our ancient ancestors went into decay …

> The main object of the present work is to furnish the Vaidyas with useful Ayurvedic work of ārṣa formulae and the way in which they were prevalent in the olden times …
>
> *This work is produced … with no other motive of self-interest* but with a view to make it accessible to all interested in Ayurvedic science. (Emphasis added)

Sri Balwant Mohan's volume was published in January 1925 by Mehar Chand Lachman Das, proprietor of the Sanskrit Book Depot in Said Mitha Bazaar, Lahore.

Colonel Bower, who had purchased the original manuscript of *Nāvanītakaṃ* from the unnamed Turkic Muslim treasure hunter, sold it to the Bodleian Library for a handsome amount. It still lies there.

6

Formulas and Techniques for Preparing Hair Dyes in Ancient India

Note

This is a companion essay of sorts to the chapter titled 'A Murder that Unearthed a 2nd-Century Sanskrit Manuscript on Ayurveda', found earlier in this work.

— 1 —

One of the ugliest sights that assaults the senses on a daily basis in urban India is a virulent form of mass hysteria masquerading as free expression and fashion: artificial hair colouring. Greying middle-aged men and women who dye their hair black (or apply mehendi, brown-red) is understandable. But that phenomenon became passé a long ago. What we now have is an insecurity-engendered epidemic that cuts across age groups and multicoloured genders: discolouring one's hair with shades that don't even have a proper name.

In malls and cinema halls, in restaurants, and on roads, it is common to see a repulsive explosion of oranges, yellows, blues, purples, pinks, greens, and the entire VIBGYOR spectrum atop people's heads. It is visual battering of the worst sort: the victims have no respite, the perpetrators have no remorse, and the assault isn't confined only to our eyes. It impacts our entire sensory and emotional experience because it overturns the fundamental notion of aesthetics. The subliminal message that these hideous hair colours transmit is this: ugliness is beauty.

This vile phenomenon is both the creation of and driven by ubiquitous, greedy corporate forces. The global market for the hair colour industry in 2022 was about $21 billion and is growing at 8.5 per cent CAGR (compound annual growth rate); the Indian market was valued at around $500 million and growing roughly at about the same rate.

Dire warnings from doctors about the health hazards of using chemically manufactured hair dyes and colours are naturally drowned in the relentless barrage of compelling advertisements from these hawkers of cancer and other fatal diseases.

Dyeing hair is almost as old as human civilization because it is wired to a fundamental human impulse that refuses to accept ageing. Ancient India, too, had evolved an astonishing range of recipes and techniques and procedures for preparing hair dyes. Like in the present time, the hair-dye industry has been a thriving business in India for centuries.

— 2 —

One of the earliest treatises that gives detailed recipes for preparing hair dyes is a delightful Sanskrit work titled *Nāvanītakaṃ*. Dating back to the 2nd century CE, the work is primarily an Ayurvedic compendium that also deals with a number of allied subjects.

Verses 1 through 27 in the tenth chapter of the *Nāvanītakaṃ* deal with the recipes for preparing hair dyes. What strikes us instantly is the intimate, detailed, and expert knowledge of a stunning range of plants, herbs, (organic) chemicals, and metals used for making hair dyes. Even more astounding is the manner in which it provides precise information for making a variety of concoctions and mixtures to produce specific results. A further nuance is also interesting to note: not all ingredients were used directly as hair dyes; some were used merely as dye-producing agents. However, the ultimate goal was the same: to produce deep black or blue-black hair dyes.

Like all traditional treatises or compendia related to worldly knowledge that were produced in India in ancient times, the *Nāvanītakaṃ* too invokes various Devatas and proclaims that using the hair-dye signals *maṅgalam* or auspiciousness, and that it aids in the attainment of the *puruṣārthas.*

The original Sanskrit term for hair dye is *keśa-rāga* (literally, 'hair colour'). This is also the title of the tenth chapter of the *Nāvanītakaṃ.* Unfortunately, the full text of the work is not available, and in many places, words, entire sentences, and even whole chapters of the original manuscript are unavailable.

The following were some of the recipes for preparing hair dyes in ancient India.

1. Boil (text missing) and oleander in sesame oil. This mixture, applied as nasal drops or an ointment, is an approved remedy for turning grey hair black.
2. A paste made of *prapauṇḍarika* (a variety of ginger) (text missing) and applied as a plaster, is a remedy for turning grey hair black.
3. Bamboo-manna, garden-nightshade, śatapuṣpa (*Peucedanum graveolens*), and sesame seeds, when applied to the hair, cause it to become as black as antimony. Antimony is also used in the preparation of Kohl.
4. Indigo, rock salt, and long pepper, mixed with water and ground into a paste when applied to the hair, cause it to turn black.

5. First, wash the head with chebulic and emblic myrobalans. Then prepare a paste of *alambuṣā* (*Sphaerantus indicus*) and indigo, and with it, while warm, anoint the head and leave it on for some time. The hair will not turn grey.
6. Collect the following: copper sulphate, *Musta* (*Cyperus rotundus*), iron sulphate, bile of a turtle, powdered iron, *danti* (*Baliospermum montanum*), *Sahadeva* (*Sida rhomboidea*), and *Bhṛṅgarāja*. Take one part of each, boiled with the oil of beleric myrobalan. This is a remedy for turning grey hair black, and if it is applied regularly as an ointment, it will prevent the hair from turning grey.
7. One *prastha* (about 10 kg) of the juice of bhṛṅgarāja, the same quantity of milk, and one pala (about 11 grams) of liquorice, boiled in onc *Kudava* (about 186 grams) of oil, will make even a crane turn black. Within a week, it will remove wrinkles and grey hair for 12 years. Within a month, it will do the same for one hundred years if administered as nasal drops.
8. Take two pala of the roots of *rāmataruṇi* (*Rosa alba*), one pala of liquorice, half a pala of *savaraka* (*Symplocos racemosa*), and 10 pala of the oil of beleric myrobalan. Boil it in the heat of the sun in an iron vessel for 10 days, and administer it as nasal drops. This will make grey hairs become the same colour as the large black bee.
9. One prastha of the juice of emblic myrobalan, the same quantity of ghee, and one pala of liquorice—all this together—should be boiled over a gentle fire. Its application as an ointment will give sight to the blind and black colour to grey hair. If it is continually administered as nasal drops, it will even restore a person's lost sight.
10. Take equal parts of no more than one emblic myrobalan from each of the three myrobalans, indigo, and blue lotus. Take also

the fruit of *piṇḍāraka* (*Vangueria spinosa*), antimony sulphide, roots of long pepper, and leaves of *sahacara* (*Barleria cristata*), and add a decoction of *Jamun* and soil from the roots of the Jamun tree. Grey hair will turn black.

11. Take the fruit of *Kakubha* (*Terminalia arjuna*) and two kudava of sesame oil, and boil the whole in the oil of beleric myrobalan slowly over a gentle fire. Administer it as nasal drops for 15 days. On the 16th day, the noble patient will have left no white hair, his scalp will be black, his face and eyes will look shiny, and all his hair will be of a deep dark colour, says Agastya, the best of teachers.
12. Take the three myrobalans, flowers of sahacara (*Barleria cristata*), *Jamun, Karśmarya* (*Gmelina arborea*), flowers of kakubha (*Terminalia arjuna*), kernel of the mango, and fruit of piṇḍāraka (*Vangueria spiñosa*), iron sulphate, flowers of *āsana* (*Terminalia tomentosa*), indigo, blue lotus, knots of the root-stalk of the lotus, antimony sulphide, black mould, powdered iron, two *kaptakärika*, two *S'ariva*, *Madayanti* (*Jasminum Sambac*), juice of Bhṛṅgarāja (*Eclipta alba*), and oil of beleric myrobalan. Mix all this with a decoction of *āsana* (*Terminalia tomentosa*) and let it stand unboiled for 10 days in an iron vessel. After this, boil it thoroughly over a gentle fire, and add to it one half as much of *shukta* (fermented rice water). This shukta should have already been kept in *Mudga* (*Phaseolas mungo*) and *Māsha* (*Phaseolus roxburghii*). Then, on the completion of the half month, having kept it well-protected in the meantime, administer this preparation. Having prepared one's body with the three myrobalans and dieting on *Kichdi*, one should use this oil as nasal drops in doses of one *shukti* (conch shell) at a time, with care and in a sheltered spot. If a person who has a head full of white hair takes one prastha of this oil as nasal drops, his hair will turn black.

— 3 —

The *keśa-rāga* section of *Nāvanītakaṃ* ends here. Clearly, there is abundant information on a range of topics, the chief of which is organic chemistry and botany. The minuteness with which our ancients studied plant life so early in our history and the kind of intense experimentation that they had undertaken are nothing short of awesome. This kind of in-depth study and practical application in an area that is non-essential to life—making hair dyes—is the icing on the cake.

Appendix

The keśa-rāga section lists a whopping 47 ingredients used in preparing various kinds of hair dyes as described so far. Only 45 ingredients have been identified accurately. The full list is given below.

- Sesame oil
- Bezoar, gallstone, serpent stone
- Solanum nigrum
- Dyer's indigo
- Long pepper
- Inknut, chebulic myrobalan
- Emblic myrobalan
- *Alambusha* — A sort of sensitive plant
- Calamine, carbonate of zinc, sulphate of zinc
- Nutgrass
- Green vitriol, iron sulphate,
- Iron powder
- Bile of a tortoise
- Croton plant
- *Sida rhomboidea* (or arrow leaf side)

- bhṛṅgarāja
- Balearic myrobalan
- Milk
- Liquorice
- Sprout of the Asoka tree
- *Lodh* tree (even today, it is an essential ingredient in making face packs and powders used in wrinkle treatments)
- Black iron
- Ghee
- Triphala
- Blue lily
- Indian prune
- Sulphide of lead
- Piper root
- Leaf of *nīlapuṣpa* (belonging to the *Verbesina* genus)
- Black plum or jamun
- Fruit of arjuna-vruksham
- Oil of beleric myrobalan
- Flower of sahachara (*kurinji* in Tamil; *karvi/kara* in Hindi)
- *Gambhari* — beechwood, white teak, etc.
- Flower of *kakubha* or wild lettuce, China lettuce, etc.
- The seed of mango fruit
- Knot on the lotus stalk
- Mud of the colour of a*njana* (lead sulphide)
- Wild brinjal
- Indian sarsaparilla
- Madayanti or mehendi/henna
- Flower of kino tree
- Extract or decoction of kino tree
- Black iron vessel
- Vinegar

7

The Delightful World of the Extinct *Mankhas*

— 1 —

In his English translation of the Jain text, *Uvasagadasao*, the German Indologist Rudolf Hoernle recounts a common sight that he witnessed in his travels in Bengal and Odisha.

> At the present day, beggars may be found in Bengal who carry pictures of such deities as Shitala, goddess of small-pox, or Olabibi, goddess of cholera; in Puri they carry pictures of Jagannatha.

The translation was published in 1890, and Hoernlé had evidently spent several years preparing the book.

His simple observation mentioned above evoked hazy memories of similar scenes that I had witnessed in my own childhood in various parts of rural Karnataka. I saw them at *jātrās* (fairs, melas) and *siḍi-utsavas (*special festive occasions and fairs). Men and women would be standing, squatting, or running behind people, beckoning them to see their picture-scrolls. The scrolls would be neatly bound and folded inside small wooden boxes, and the boxes, too, had intricate carvings on them. The picture-scrolls or *Paṭa* typically showed elaborate scenes from various Puranic stories drawn as snug little miniatures encased in panels. Not unlike the comic strips we are all familiar with. Except that these Paṭas had no descriptive text. In a way, these were the mobile equivalents of the renowned *Paṭa-Chitra* art form in Odisha. The men and women who displayed them in these fairs would unfurl the picture-scrolls and narrate the stories in animated detail, infusing impressive dramatic skills and narrative techniques. They didn't charge a fixed fee. I recall paying 50 paisa on one occasion. On its receipt, the artist blessed me with an elaborate devotional song dipped in rustic poetry invoking Shiva and Devi.

Little did I know back then that these were professionals, that their profession had a beautiful name, or that it indeed had a long and fabulous history.

They were called Mankhas.

Both Ananada Coomaraswamy and Dr V. Raghavan translate Mankha as 'picture showmen'. They were also known by other names: Gauriputraka, Kēdāraka, Yamapaṭaka, and Pratimādharin.

—2—

For countless centuries, Mankhas were omnipresent, not just in India but abroad as well. What began as an art form, practice, and profession of exhibiting scroll-pictures and paintings depicting different Puranic themes evolved into an invaluable cultural treasure.

Travellers to India from various countries were so awestruck and inspired by it that they spun off variations suitable for their own cultures. Over time, this art form traversed to China and other regions that had comprised the Brihad-Bharata. For example, as relatively recent as 1416, Ma Huan, author of the

Chinese work *Ying-yai Sheng-lan* (or *Yingya Shenglan*), describes this scene he witnessed in Java:

> There is a sort of men who paint on paper men, birds, animals, insects and so on: the paper is like a scroll and is fixed between two wooden rollers three feet high; at one side these rollers are level with the paper, whilst they protrude at the other side. The man squats down on the ground and places the picture before him, unrolling one part after the other and turning it towards the spectators, whilst in the native language and in a loud voice he gives an explanation of every part: the spectators sit around him and listen, laughing or crying according to what he tells them.

The Bali variant of the *Mankha* art form is known as 'Wayang Beber'. It was classified as a dramatic art. The artist who performs it is known as the 'Dalang'. He unfurls several sheets of cloth containing paintings of scenes from stories from the Ramayana and the Mahabharata. Each cloth is unrolled one by one, i.e., scene by scene, and the Dalang narrates the scenes using dialogue. Like so many such ancient art forms, Wayang Beber is also on the verge of extinction.

The art form was also popular in Persia. The meaning of the Persian word śūrat *khwān* is quite revealing: 'One who pictures the state of angels and men as to reward and punishment on the day of resurrection, and receives a remuneration for it from the bystanders.'

The picture or scene described above is a direct borrowing from the *Yamapaṭas*, which were wildly popular in India for several centuries, as we shall see. Interestingly, the word śūrat also means a puppet in Persian popular theatre, and *khwān* is the reciter or singer of the story performed by the puppets. Even more interestingly, the khwān begins the performance with an invocatory verse of an Islamic song known as the *rāk-ī-hindi*. The word *rāk* is a corruption of the Sanskrit word *rāga*. Thus, *rāk-ī-hindi* means 'Hindustani/Indian tune or song'. Both the manner and modalities used in enacting this art form were almost wholly imported from the classical Sanskrit theatre tradition, which begins with the *Nāndi* invocation and ends with the *Mangalam*.

The Mankha art form survived almost intact even during the British colonization of India. John Lockwood Kipling—Rudyard Kipling's father—describes his experience of watching the Mankhas in action in his travelogue, *Beast and Man in India*.

> One of the most popular of the pictures sold at fairs is a composition known as Dharmraj, a name of Yama, the Hindu Pluto, and also used broadly for Justice. The Judge is enthroned and demon executioners bring the dead to receive their doom. The river of death flows on one side of the picture and those go safely across who hold a cow by the tail, while others are torn by terrible fishes. Chitrgupt, the clerk or recording angel of Yama, considered to be the ancestor of the Kayasth or clerkly caste, sits in an office with account books exactly like those of a Hindu tradesman, and according to the record of each soul, punishments or rewards are given. For, as a popular native saying has it—'God looks out of the window of heaven and keeps account.' *Duts* or executioners torture offenders, while the blest sail upwards in air-borne chariots.

Kipling published this book in 1891, which happily corresponds with Rudolf Hoernlé's observations in Odisha and Bengal in 1890. Kipling was a teacher, traveller, and documenter of foreign societies, while Hoernlé was an indologist. Both witnessed the same India around the same period.

— 3 —

When we think about it today, consternation and melancholy strike us. The nonchalant manner in which we have squandered away Bharatavarsha's profound cultural imprint that had exercised such invisible suzerainty throughout a vast region of Asia is really unforgivable. That the squandering happened *after* 'independence' magnifies the extent and scale of the tragedy.

For example, today, Walang Beber is an endangered art form in Indonesia because Mankhas have become extinct in the very cradle in which they were birthed: Bharatavarsha.

This gradual decay and neglect followed by destruction proves another fact of Indian history: as long as the tempering, soothing, and motherly palm of Sanatana culture exercised its silent influence on alien cultures, they remained largely sober. Despite successive Islamic invasions in many parts of Southeast Asia, the intrinsic Sanatana clime remained unchanged there. Even Persia, which had been wholly Islamized centuries ago, continued to draw inspiration from Hindu culture and art forms. But the day India embraced something called secularism, the whole thing not only imploded but became irretrievable.

On this melancholy note, we shall explore the brief history of the lost cultural treasure of the Mankhas.

— 4 —

The earliest mention of mankhas occurs in Patanjali's *Mahābhāṣya* mentioning the display of paintings (*citra*) depicting Krishna slaying Kamsa. The literal rendering of the text is as follows: 'How in respect of the paintings? In the pictures, men see the blows rained down on Kamsa, and how he is dragged about.'

The clear inference is that the tradition of displaying these paintings in public, such as in exhibitions, fairs, etc., was already in vogue during Patanjali's time, and the Mankha art form was already a recognized profession.

Jaina Prakrt texts unambiguously define the term *Mankha* as a professional picture showman, and he is clubbed in the class of entertainers such as actors, dancers, storytellers, etc.

The *Bhagavati Sūtra* mentions the name of Gosala Mankhaliputta (also known as Maskari Gosala or Makkhali Gosala). The *Mankhaliputta* refers to the profession of Gosala's father, who was a Mankha.

A Sanskrit gloss describes Mankhas as *citraphalakavyagrakara-bhiksu-visesa* meaning a *Bhikshu* or mendicant who accepts alms by exhibiting pictures of deities that he carries with him. In general, there are copious Jain texts mentioning and even extolling talented Mankhas.

Long story short, by the post-Gupta era, picture exhibitions as an art form was flourishing, and it would retain this high position until the British colonial period.

Its evolution is actually a thrilling story by itself.

From exhibiting and narrating picture-scrolls showing Kamsa's pummelling at Krishna's hands, the focus shifted almost exclusively to something known as the *Yamapaṭṭaka* or Yamapaṭa. The Yamapaṭa showed elaborate picture-scrolls representing virtuous and evil deeds and the reward and punishment arising therefrom in *Yamapuri*, the abode of Yama.

Major Sanskrit literary works mention Yamapaṭṭakas, or picture showmen who painted Yamapaṭas.

In Vishakadatta's renowned play *Mudrārākṣasa,* dateable between the 5th and 9th centuries CE, Kautilya's spy, Nipunaka, disguises himself as a picture showman. He says that men earn their living by means of the same Yama who kills people. Then he enters Chandanadasa's home, carrying a scroll with figures of Yama painted on it. But before he enters, this is the dialogue he utters: 'I will enter here, show my pictures and chant my song (*yamapaṭaṃ darśayān gītāni gāyāmi*).' After his errand is over, he brings its report to Chanakya, saying in Prakrt, 'Spreading out the Yama picture scroll, I commenced my song. (*jamapadaṃ pasariya pauttohmi gīḍaim gaidyum*).'

Banabhatta's *Harshacharita* paints a descriptive narrative of picture showmen:

> Like those who depict *Naraka*, loud singers paint unrealities on the canvas of the air…. In the market street amid a great crowd of inquisitive children, he observed a *Yamapaṭṭaka* in whose left hand was a painted canvas stretched out on a support of upright rods and showing the God of Death mounted on his dreadful buffalo. Wielding a reed wand in his other hand, he was expounding the features of the next world, and could be heard to chant the following verses. (Verses omitted for this essay)

The prolific translator of Sanskrit literary works, M.R. Kale, in his notes on the *Mudrārākṣasa*, writes as follows: 'The exhibition of *Yamapaṭas* was one of the sources of making money.' Likewise, K.T. Telang's edition of the same play has this about Yamapaṭas: 'A series of representations of the exploits of Yama, something like the boxes of sacred pictures which are shown about to this day.' And Telang too gives a reference to the aforementioned passage in *Harshacharita.*

Writing in the *History and Culture of the Indian People,* the scholar N.R. Ray gives us quite a brilliant description of the Yamapaṭa and its various offshoots:

> *Yamapaṭas* were executed on textile scrolls and dealt with themes of a narrative-didactic nature, showing the results of Karma in

> the other world. Buddhaghoṣa, the celebrated Buddhist scholar … refers to a similar kind of painting to which he gives the name of *cāraṇacitra* which consisted of scenes of happy and unhappy destinies of men after death with appropriate labels attached to them and shown in portable galleries. There can be no doubt that these *Yamapaṭas* or *cāraṇacitras* are the ancestors, in form, meaning and presentation, of the *paṭacitras* that are widely current in Eastern India.

As mentioned earlier in this essay, like all else in Hindu cultural life, this tradition of a sub-genre of art too shows our unbroken continuity. N.R. Ray concludes his assessment on a sombre but profound note:

> No contemporary example of *Yamapata* or *charanachitra* … has survived to this day; but it was evidently a folk-art of ethnic and religious significance and of wide popular appeal, an itinerant school of deep and great educative value for the rural masses. (Emphasis added)

Next, the prolific and comprehensive scholar of Indian art and culture Stella Kramrisch wields her pen like a paintbrush when she writes,

> As permanent or temporary decoration, on the floors, on the walls and ceilings of private houses, palaces and temples, and in the streets, *paintings instructed and enlivened the mind of the public. Even religious teachers used painting as the most popular means of communication, that could be understood by the illiterate and the child.* There is a class of Brahmanical teachers, known by the name of Mankha. They make a (portable) framework upon which they cause to be drawn a variety of pictures, depicting scenes of good and evil destinies, of fortunes and misfortunes,

> and causing the labels to be inscribed: 'By doing this deed one attains this', 'By doing that, one attains that. Thus, showing different destinies, they wander about with these pictures.' (Emphasis added)

In the Vijayanagara era, picture showmen quite obviously received substantial patronage. In a short but valuable study of Vijayanagara paintings, C. Sivamurti gives us impressive details of how *chitrapaṭas* evolved during that period. While Yamapaṭas had retained their prominence, their model had branched out in various forms and innovations.

Jain chitrapaṭas, for instance, played an influential role, and perhaps for the first time, elaborate labels were inscribed under each scene. Some examples include the life of Rishabhadeva, the birth and life of Vardhamana Mahavira, etc.

The Hindu side displayed paintings of Yudhishtira's coronation, the love between Radha and Krishna, *amṛtamaṃthana,* etc.

We see a rather weakened continuation of the same (Vijayanagara) tradition even today in most temples in South India. The walls of these temples show an elaborate and scene-by-scene depiction of, say, the *Sthaḻapurāṇa,* the various *mahimās* of the presiding deity, and other stories.

— 5 —

Following the tragic destruction of the Vijayanagara Empire, the Mankhas preserved their art under the patronage of the Nayakas in South India. Thanjavur, Madurai, Kadapa, and Mysore, among others, sustained and embellished the art. In other parts of Bharatavarsha as well, Mankhas somehow managed to survive, painfully wheezing out their last breaths in, say, Maharashtra, Rajasthan, Bihar, Bengal, and Odisha.

What Rudyard Kipling's father saw and documented in 1890 was an art form that was in its death throes, impelled by the plunder-hungry marauders of his own native England. Once the pride of Sanatana society, Mankhas, like scores of similar artists, were hurtling towards extinction.

And when I encountered them in my childhood, they were standing on the verge of beggary, but their generational reverence for our deities and our sacred stories, and the memory of the profoundly devout manner in which they narrated their picture-stories wells up my eyes. Even as I conclude this essay.

They themselves weren't aware of their preeminence as the exalted inheritors of a hoary cultural treasure. Perhaps, that is the greater tragedy.

8

The Transmission of Sacred Education in Bharatavarsha: A Historical Journey

Prologue

As late as 1891, Dr Francis, a surgeon commissioned by the colonial British government, landed in Calcutta and jotted down detailed notes of his observations of our society and people.

The Indian National Congress had been founded six years earlier, and the third generation of the Hindu mind was being colonized by the tools fashioned in the thriving laboratory of deracination that Macaulay had established five decades ago. But it would take several more decades for this toxin to seep, infect, and permanently impair the Hindu cultural and social fabric.

The Hindu society that Dr Francis discovered was deeply, inextricably moored in its ancient roots. A mode of living outside this framework was not only unthinkable to this society but was also violative of its most cherished ideals and beliefs. And a defining feature of this society was sanctity and devotion in every domain: from waking up to sleeping, from birth till death, best exemplified by this immortal verse:

> *ātmā tvaṃ girijā matiḥ sahacarāḥ prāṇāḥ śarīraṃ gṛhaṃ*
> *pūjā te viṣayopabhogaracanā nidrā samādhisthitiḥ* |
> *sañcāraḥ padayoḥ pradakṣiṇavidhiḥ stotrāṇi sarvā giro*
> *yadyatkarma karomi tattadakhilaṃ śaṃbho tavārādhanam* ||

> You are my Atma (Soul), Girija (the Divine Mother) is my *Buddhi* (Refined Intellect), the Shiva Ganas (the Companions or Attendants) are my life-breath and my Body is Your Temple, My interactions with the world are Your Worship and my Sleep is the State of *Samadhi* (complete absorption in You). My walking is Your *Pradakshina* (Circumambulation); my Speech are Hymns in Your praise, Every work I do is Your *Aradhana* (Worship), O Shambhu.

Dr Francis noticed precisely this trait in the daily lives of Hindus around him. He describes the sanctity attached to *Snana* (ablution) as 'praiseworthy and purifying'. He marvelled at the seasoned ethics of the Hindus who swore upon the *Śāstra, Gaṃgājala, Sālagrāmaṃ, Tulasi* leaves, *Rudrakshi*, and *Agni* in disputes that were heard in the courts established by the British. Contrary to the prejudiced and vitriolic narratives about the 'depressed and ill-treated Hindoo women' spewed in British journals and newspapers, Dr Francis found that 'Indian girls are remarkable for their zeal in learning whatever they are taught'.

And then he indirectly discovered the secret of how such a society—ruthlessly plundered and impoverished by his own country—could still be so functional and harmonious, and how its people could still be so cheerful and forbearing.

The secret was its traditional educational system.

However, Dr Francis had witnessed only a sliver of this vast universe when he wrote: 'The natives of India are very fond of proverbs, and stories. The *Kuhani-wala* (storyteller) is always a welcome visitor in inns for travellers and wherever people congregate . . . they are highly popular.'

This educational universe is as timeless as Bharatavarsha itself.

The Essential and the Professional

From the earliest times, the Hindu civilization recognized two types of knowledge, broadly speaking: the essential and the professional. Its genius was rooted in the sublime and invisible manner in which it fused the two and achieved an unbeatable harmony both in theory and practice. Unlike the West, which considers essential knowledge and professional knowledge as opposing poles or as distinct from each other, the Santana mantra was synthesis.

In the Santana worldview, philosophical, spiritual, or Dharmic knowledge is essential knowledge. Professional knowledge is rather self-explanatory. The former encompasses the *Manōmaya* and *Vijñānamaya Kōśas*, ultimately leading to the Ā*nandamaya* Kōśa. The latter covers the *Annamaya* and *Prāṇamaya Kōśas* or the base existential planes.

From another perspective, professional knowledge can be loosely understood as civilizational (as elements that constitute the building and maintenance of the physical aspects of a civilization) whereas essential knowledge is cultural, leading to the spiritual and the philosophical. The former is *prakṛti* and the latter is *saṃskṛti.*

The Hollowing Out

The aforementioned understanding of this basic cultural fabric of Bharatavarsha was quite commonplace even six or seven decades ago. The Hindu society in general had retained this understanding on the subconscious plane because its overall cultural inheritance had infused it in its DNA, so to speak. However, the sort of divisive and deracinated ideologies that eventually became mainstream and acquired political heft have pretty much hollowed out this inheritance. Its vilest manifestation is the ongoing toxic narrative about something called a 'pure Dravidian stock', whatever that means. Education is the edifice on which this vile narrative rests. In turn, the edifice of this edifice is the selective historical claim that the lower strata of Hindu society were denied education.

But a truthful study of history clearly shows that the education that such toxic narratives refer to is *literacy*, not professional education. In fact, since the dawn of the Sanatana civilization, professions in India have progressively and systematically evolved, and they eventually touched the summits of expertise in grammar, skill, application, production, and artistry and aesthetics. The now-obsolete word 'workmanship' was a prized and un-poachable treasure in the hands of generational professionals. There's a deep-seated reason that Shah Jahan chopped off the fingers of the 22,000 artisans who had sculpted the Taj Mahal. This honed professional perfection was made possible by the much reviled 'caste system'. It is the same 'caste system' that enabled the spread of professional education across both space and time: across the vast geography of undivided Bharatavarsha and over hundreds of generations. Indeed, the town planning systems in pre-British India provide lived proof of what can be called the professional history of India.

However, the equation of education with mere literacy was the direct outcome of the British policy of destroying all professions and reducing experts to clerks and peons, slaving away their entire lives in the service of a foreign empire of pirates.

Likewise, on the other side, another spurious claim that the Brahmanas monopolized all sacred, i.e., essential, knowledge also deserves re-examination. But at this distance in time, this monopolization is largely a thing of the past in the sense that Vedic and sastric education is now freely available to the whole Hindu society, which is certainly a welcome development.

However, there are deep and wide historical currents even in this area that reveal vital clues to an important question: how essential knowledge was disseminated throughout Bharatavarsha for several millennia. The question is hugely significant given the fact that this dissemination occurred in a multi-pronged fashion; it was highly creative, diverse, and flexible in both method and expression.

This essay narrates the brief story of the journey of how essential or sacred education was transmitted throughout (undivided) Bharatavarsha—a country so vast with such difficult terrains—reaching the corners and crevices of lakhs of villages over countless centuries, during a period when communication and travel were not only tough but hazardous.

Chapter One: The Syllabus of Life and Afterlife

This essay began with the story of Dr Francis for a reason. In his time, he was just the latest in a protracted marquee of European travellers to India who noticed the intrinsic trait of Hindus described earlier. Another way to characterize this trait is this: although the teeming millions of Hindus that the British encountered were illiterate and impoverished, they were—in the clouded European view—astonishingly well-informed, had a profound outlook towards life, and were highly cultured. Ananda Coomaraswamy described these Hindus memorably:

'Scratch their skin, give them a bath and clothe them in finery, and they will be fit to rule a wise and just kingdom.'

Regrettably, in their unquenchable hunger for loot, till the very end, the British could never understand the source-fount of the culture that produced such refined people.

With the benefit of aeons of accumulated wisdom and a wealth of historical material, it is clear that our ancient Rishis, Gurus, and Acharyas relied on direct communication of essential knowledge and developed creative and malleable methods for its retention and transmission. Over time, these methods were systematized and through them, this essential knowledge reached even the last person in Hindu society. This is the profoundest working example of direct benefit transfer; that is, even the 'last man on the street' was imbued with sacred knowledge without passing through the rigours of scholastic education.

The Sanskrit term for knowledge is *Shruta*: that which is heard. Its direct translation in Tamil is befittingly *ke̱lvi.* In Kannada, the word *ke̱lu* means 'hear or listen'. The titanic scholar of Indian aesthetics, culture, and philosophy Dr V. Raghavan describes this inimitable and sagely system of Hindu cultural and sacred education with vivid imagery drawn appropriately from agriculture, the first culture:

> That our religious history has thrown up saints from among weavers, cobblers, potters, shepherds and Harijans *shows how widely the soil has been irrigated and fertilised by the country's spiritual engineers.* (Emphasis added)

This irrigation first occurred with the tradition of reciting the Ramayana, the Mahabharata, and the Puranas, the triad of our sacred literature. In fact, Bhagavan Veda Vyasa himself declares that he composed the Mahabharata to broadcast the distilled essence of the Veda to the world. We must remember that the Ramayana was originally *sung* and that it is a musical epic.

This sacred triad expounds on the secrets of the Veda by narrating stories of the lineages of august personalities, including Rajarshis and Rishis, who, through their deeds, showed how Dharma must be upheld in the mortal world to attain immortality. Then there are the familiar stories of the grand, delightful, and often bizarre sport of the Devatas and divine incarnations who come down to the earth and crush Adharma as a means of stamping the supremacy of Dharma. We also get a detailed, guided tour of the various celestial worlds, complete with the *Apsarās, K*āmadhenu, Kalpavṛkṣa, etc. However, even these worlds come with a warning: there is an expiry date for our stay there. Only the Devatas are permanent residents. Which is why our sacred literature tells us that these celestial worlds should not be our highest aspiration. The true dwelling of all human life is the inner world, signified by *ātmānanda*, which is indeed our natural dwelling. To this delectable and extensive feast of sacred literature are added incidental details of cosmogony, discussions on the nature of time, and substantial details of the sacred geography of Bharatavarsha.

This is a sweeping syllabus of both life and afterlife, a well-rounded and embracive education in the essential core of the eternal Dharma, *darśana*, *ācāra*, and *saṃskāra*. This essential knowledge includes a wide gamut of ancillary knowledge in its ambit, such as morals, ethics, ideals, values, and history. The ultimate purpose and intrinsic feature of this education was to prepare the human in his quest for ascent to *ātmānanda*. It didn't matter whether *ātmānanda* was actually attained; the goal made the quest meaningful and fulfilling.

This education was open to all and freely given because the givers considered it their sacred duty. It was true universal education.

It is because these vital roots have been chopped off that we today have a profusion of useless tripe crowned by something called 'personality development' and 'leadership'.

Chapter Two: The Methods

Broadly speaking, the most effective methods of teaching sacred knowledge included recitation, storytelling, and performing arts. The refrain of every Guru and Acharya in our tradition remains this: the sublime and regal philosophy of the Veda (*Prabhusaṃmita*) was transmitted to the common people through the stories of Itihasa and Purana, narrated in the tone and tenor of a friend (*Suhrutsammita*). In the poignant words of the late Pandita Vajapeyam Srirangachar:

> *The word of the Veda is akin to the command of an emperor.* Our job is to simply obey. There is no scope of questioning the why and how of the command. But the Puranas are wholly unlike this. They unravel to us the same secrets of Dharma as the Veda. However, *like a close friend, the Puranas understand our limitations and doubts and questions and discuss them threadbare.* They give us the detailed picture of virtue and vice, good and evil through stories and examples of real people. In this manner, they win over our mind and heart and motivate us towards right action. *The ultimate aim of both the Veda and the Purana is to elevate us. The difference is only in the method of instruction.* (Emphases added)

Indeed, the preface of every Itihasa and Purana unfailingly mentions that they were recited by *Sūta-paurāṇikas* to vast assemblages of people gathered typically at *Sattras* (*Yaga* and *Yajna*). In fact, this aspect of Puranic recitation is another area that shows Hindu cultural and social continuity. The popular surname Puranik itself indicates this in a living fashion.

Although the tradition of reciting Puranas and Itihasas has woefully dwindled, it continues to bind Hindu society to a good extent even today. In fact, the phenomenal success of dedicated spiritual TV channels like 'Aastha' owes to their telecast of Puranic discourses. The lament of the late great Vidvan, *Mahamahopadhyaya* N. Ranganatha Sarma, tugs at our hearts:

> The tradition of reciting and listening to Puranas has come down to us from ancient times in this sacred Bharatavarsha. In both villages and cities, it was common to witness Purana recitations in temple premises in the evenings. The thawing of this tradition in recent times is proving highly dangerous for the growth of our Sanatana culture. *It is equally a matter of great regret that our children do not have even a basic acquaintance of the Ramayana and the Mahabharata. A good section of contemporary Hindus have not even heard of great Bhaktas like Dhruva, Prahlada, Markandeya or Ambarisha;* they are ignorant of courageous heroes like Nala, Harishchandra, or Yayati; they know nothing about virtuous women like Damayanti, Anasuya, or Chandramati. This is the direct consequence of the decline of the tradition of Purana recitation and listening. *More alarming is the fact that even the educated class of Hindus show a wanton negligence towards Puranas. Some have even gone to the extent of hurling contempt against Puranas, 'We don't need your Purana!'* However, the truth is exactly the opposite of this attitude. When our ancients declared that the Puranas are part of the fourteen branches of learning, they weren't merely praising the Puranas. We must not forget the fact that the very purpose of the Puranas is to inform and educate the masses about the most essential topics related to both worldly knowledge and spiritual literacy. The stories narrated in the Puranas are extremely thrilling. The moral and ethical principles that one must learn from these are invaluable. *The philosophical tenets expounded therein in simple terms without difficult theories are worth contemplating throughout life.* Specialist topics such as *Yoga, Jyautiṣa* (astronomy), etc., that occur incidentally are essential knowledge

> for every person.... The sections on ācārasaṃhita (related to right conduct) and *dharmasaṃhita* (expositions on Dharma) are useful tools for sculpting cultured and ethical people. (Emphases added)

The destruction of the age-old social harmony of Hindu village life is concomitant with the erosion of this lived tradition of Puranic discourses and its replacement with television and now digital gadgets.

To fully quantify the magnitude of this loss, it is essential to briefly examine the awesome history of Bharatavarsha's cultural conquest, most notably of Southeast Asia. To invoke Dr V. Raghavan again,

> The evidence of numerous inscriptions establishes the continuity of this practice of [Puranic] exposition all through the course of Indian history; the wide provenance of these records shows that this machinery of popular religious education was active ... in Greater India [*Brihadbharata*] too.
>
> *If, without flame and sword, Hinduism spread over the whole of the Far East, it was possible because the Ramayana and Mahabharata*, through the oral expounder, the sculptor, and the dancer went forth in advance, clearing the way and conquering the peoples' imagination. As early as A.D. 600, Somasarman [presented] a temple in Cambodia the Mahabharata, the Ramayana and the Puranas, and provided for their daily exposition; a temple to Valmiki was raised in Campa by King Prakashdharman. (Emphasis added)

Likewise, Asit Haldar, a painter of the New Indian Renaissance, captivates our imagination in a simple line that profoundly ensconces the true spirit of Sanatana Dharma:

> The cultural expansion of India into greater India was mainly due to the spiritual fact that India always tried sincerely to

> get into the spirit of the cosmic reality and that she was never content with the surface value of life. *Our artist-philosophers have always preached the openness of life, though they never understood it in terms of material success.* (Emphasis added)

As this tradition of imparting sacred education evolved over the course of our history, it acquired wings and feathers and soared heavenward. With the eclipse of Hindu culture in North India under the dark orb of Islamic invasions, we have almost no records testifying to its original glory. However, South India has a considerable wealth of evidence showing the details of this sacred educational system. Indeed, a weighty hoard of inscriptions in the Tamil *Desam* is one of the best proofs disproving the Dravidian fiction that Tamil kings were not Hindus. In Dr Raghavan's words once again,

> The Pallavas, Cholas, and Pandyas knew the value of the Itihasa and Purana, and epigraphs found all over the peninsula show how these kings helped to … fulfil their mission of disseminating countrywide religious education…. *Thus, the practice of popular exposition of the epics and the Puranas has been handed down to the present day in an unbroken tradition.* Today, such expositions, though to a lesser extent, constitute one of the leading forms of popular religious education all over South India, especially in the Tamil country … the epic that holds the people enthralled is the Ramayana … hardly a day passes without some sweet-voiced, gifted expounder sitting in a temple, *matha*, public hall or house-front and expounding to hundreds and thousands the story of the Dharma that Rama upheld and the Adharma by which Ravana fell. (Emphasis added)

Even a century ago, few people in Tamil Nadu could have anticipated that a day would come when a 'Dravidian' ideologue would sinisterly name himself as Ravanan or that a sitting chief minister would mock Sri Ramachandra, asking the name of the engineering college he attended.

Chapter Three: The Sprawling World of Puranic Translations

Translations and episodic renditions of Itihasas and Puranas were brilliant vehicles for spreading our sacred education. The centrality of this phenomenon cannot be emphasized enough. The accomplices of the evolution and flowering of *Bhāratīya bhāṣā* are the translations of all the best works of Sanskrit.

While the Ramayana and the Mahabharata exist in every Bharatiya bhasha, their translators and poets have not only made sweeping interpolations and changes; in some cases, their versions have acquired an appeal that has remained more enduring than the original. The splendid *karṇāṭabhāratakathāmañjari* by Kumaravyasa has a delightful episode where Arjuna, disguised as a Sanyasi, elopes with Subhadra. Whereas this is absent in Veda Vyasa's original, its charm and attraction have made generations of people believe that it is indeed in the original Mahabharata. Countless plays, films, and songs have been produced based on just this episode. However, Kumaravyasa, Kamban, Tulasidas, et al. have uniformly venerated Valmiki and Vyasa and retained the original spirit of their culture-building literary creations. This point is the most effective and truthful rebuttal to the ideological merchants who purvey phoney theories like '300 Ramayanas'.

Temples, *Maṭhas*, *Ghaṭikās*, *Agrahāras*, and Travelling Gurus

On the structural plane, Maṭhas and temples became the fecund and glorious centres of sacred education. Other institutions resembling large universities of our own time included Ghaṭikās and Agrahāras. In fact, Maṭhas were the later-day manifestations of Āśramas and *Tapovanas* of the Rishis mentioned in ancient Sanskrit literature. As scholars have correctly pointed out, '*Maṭhas* were originally natural habitations in the form of mountain caves, which were later enlarged into structural buildings.' Consonant with the continuous stream of the tradition of spreading sacred education, Maṭhas naturally played a central part in the Hindu social and cultural life.

While there were Maṭhas for every sect in Hindu Dharma that taught their respective philosophies, the syllabus was a wholesome amalgam. The student was taught both tough philosophical texts and popular sacred literature such as *stotrams, bhajans,* poetry, songs, etc. Thus, upon graduation, the student could give discourses to both the scholarly tribe and the unwashed masses with equal elan. The other facet of some of these Maṭhas was the fact that their chiefs and acharyas were also travelling teachers, foraying into every corner of Bharata to spread sacred education. Thankfully, this tradition is still quite strong.

The phenomenal role Hindu temples have played as hubs of devotion and centres of cultural education needs an independent volume. Temples were the place where Itihasa and Purana were expounded, preserved, and propagated. They endure as the lifelines and the oxygen that sustain Sanatana society. In fact, temples are miniatures of the Hindu cultural universe sprawled across the globe. An ugly, unexamined, and dangerous notion that has imprisoned a vast swathe of the contemporary Hindu psyche is this: 'I am not religious but spiritual, and so I don't need to visit temples to prove that I am a Hindu.' The popularity of this notion actually reflects the impressive success of the soulless materialist discourse aimed at delinking Sanatana Dharma from its grandest physical expression, the Hindu temple. However, stalwarts like, say, Dr S. Srikanta Sastri gave us this brilliant exposition about what a temple exactly stands for:

> [T]emples occupied a prominent place from the perspective of education, fine arts, [reflected the] economic condition [of the kingdom] and social service … people had a firm belief and faith in the pious act of donating to temples. [Donors included] everybody from the monarch to the most ordinary citizen … temples were governed and maintained by a duly elected board. They distributed money, food grain, and seeds to farmers from the Deity's Treasury … [temples] were also engaged in moneylending … temples conducted various celebrations like *pakṣotsava* [fortnightly *utsavas*], *māsotsava* [monthly *utsavas*], *Brahmotsava*, and oversaw the distribution of the harvest derived from temple lands.
>
> Theatre and dance halls organised dramas during *Utsava* days in both Sanskrit and *Desha Bhashas*. Music and dance recitals offered as *Seva* for the Deity immensely enriched art forms like classical music, Bharatanatyam, and Vastushilpa [sculpture art]. Moral and spiritual discourses by learned scholars, Yatis, and such other eminences were drawn from the Vedic and Puranic lore thereby instilling and reinforcing Dharma among the pilgrims and others who visited the temple.
>
> *There were also lecture halls for imparting higher education in Veda, Vedanga, Medicine and other subjects* by teachers and scholars employed by the temple. Students were given free scholarship and boarding and lodging.
>
> Massive temples were secure like fortresses and contained an abundance of food grain, water and other supplies and provided shelter to refugees during wartime…. Because Hindu kings regarded temples as sacred spaces, they deferred harming or despoiling them even slightly even if this caution meant certain defeat in war. (Emphases added)

There is also a rough formula for understanding this phenomenon from a different perspective. Consider any town or village with an antiquity of at least 600 years and investigate its history briefly. The first feature that will become obvious is that it was originally a temple town. Since time immemorial, building a temple has been one of the first activities involved in the establishment of a new village or town. The temple was the cynosure and centre of the village's social activities. Once the temple was built, it would have its own annual utsava apart from the familiar Hindu festivals celebrated throughout the year. The village or town would have its own *Sthala-purana* and a Purana that described the *māhātmya* (glory) of the temple. Both were interlinked because their sources would be the same. The cultural history of South India is perhaps the most magnificent and detailed evidence of this fact.

The Cholas, for example, were among the most prolific temple-builders. Chola Aditya I blanketed almost the entire Cauvery Delta with temples, and kings of various dynasties who followed him also followed his precedent 'till throughout South India, no village or town was left without a temple, the visible symbol of the spread of Bhakti'. To cite Dr Raghavan once again, this was the resultant landscape of South India:

> The temple was also an art gallery, even as it was a hall for concert, lecture, or transaction of local affairs. The masterpieces of sculpture in the temples taught the entire mythology and the deeds of the gods to the masses.... All temples had paintings of religious themes.... All these show how art was harnessed for religious teaching in ancient India.
>
> The car-festival drew together the entire population of the locality. Such festivals in temples served as suitable occasions for religious discourses.

Chapter Four: Spreading Sacred Education through Performing Arts

Now we arrive at the final leg of this essay: how dance, drama, and music were used, perhaps as the most effective modes for transmitting essential education throughout the sacred geography of Bharatavarsha. As in other areas of India's cultural history, even this topic alone has enough sinews to sculpt a fine, independent work.

If the Puranas have been likened to *Suhrutsammita,* these arts have been likened to *Kāntāsammita,* i.e., imparting sacred knowledge in the endearing manner of persuading and winning over the beloved. This tradition dates all the way back to Bharatamuni himself, who clearly elucidates the educative, didactic, and religious usefulness of drama (comprising music, acting, poetry, and dance). Every aesthetician who followed Bharatamuni has adhered to his immortal dictum that drama and poetry teach the same lessons that the Vedas and the Puranas teach. There's a sublime reason why Rasānanda (aesthetic enjoyment) is known as the sibling of *Brahmānanda.*

In no particular order, we can mention a special class of wandering artists known as Mankhas (see the essay on Mankhas in this book) who toured various parts of Bharatavarsha, putting up exhibitions of religious pictures showing various episodes from the Itihasas and Puranas. They also carried painted scrolls displaying the glories of various *Avataras* and of our Devis and Devatas.

Most temples had their own drama troupes performing night-long plays during festivals and other sacred occasions. The story of how Raja Raja Chola gave substantial endowments to the drama troupe (comprising actors, singers, instrumentalists, percussionists, danseuses, etc.) dedicated to the Brihadeeshwara

Temple is perhaps the most lavish case in point. This endowment was typically known as the *Nṛtyabhoga.*

In general, this fount of divinity embedded in all our performing arts birthed countless rivers that watered our cultural and social landscape. The Yakshagana and Kuchipudi Bhagavatamu can be cited as two euphonious examples.

In its origins, Kuchipudi was an *Agrahara* in the fertile Krishna District of Andhra. The burst of devotion among its pious dwellers germinated an exquisite and enduring branch of Bharatiya *Natya.* Its influence was so magnetic that the Tamil country took inspiration from it and innovated the renowned *bhāgavata-mel̲a-nāṭaka* that flourished in Thanjavur, another fertile riverine belt. Its offshoots and variants became famous in Merattur, Uttukkadu, Nallur, Sulamangalam, etc. Its dramatic expressions gave us popular plays like *Prahlādavijaya, Uśāpariṇaya, Rukmāngada,* and *Mārkaṇḍeyacarita.*

The realm of music and devotional lyric was equally lush, with the Kannada country as its uncrowned monarch. Hundreds of thousands of *Devaranamas* composed by Haridāsas, Shaiva Vachanas, Padas, and Kirtanas have remained immortal. In fact, the school known as the *Dāsa-kūṭa,* founded by Achalananda Dasa, dates all the way back to the 9th century, during the Rashtrakuta era. Its later successors include the venerated Purandaradasa, Kanakadasa, Vijayadasa, Jagannathadasa, Sripadaraja, and Vyasaraja.

The concatenate atmosphere in the Telugu country was populated by the lovely blossoming of the *Sankirtana* tradition popularized by Tallapaka Annamacharya, his lineage, and that of his disciples. He was followed by Bhadrachala Ramadasu, one of the greatest Rama devotees, who composed and sang his Kritis from jail. The last summit of this tradition is undoubtedly Tyagaraja Swami. By his time, the whole Telugu country was exploding with Bhajana-Mathas—this was a later innovation of an existing tradition dating back to the Bhakti Movement. Dr Raghavan gives us its contours and impact:

> This school infused new life into the old path of devotion. *Bhajana* now developed on a large scale, and the visit to Tanjore and other centres, of performers of *Sankirtana* from the north, especially from Maharashtra, perfected the *Bhajana-Paddhati* which [were] maintained by a chain of *Mathas* in places big and small. (Emphasis added)

Harikatha was yet another extraordinary mode of spreading sacred education, especially in South India. It is one of the most singular, original, and unique gifts given by Hindu Dharma to the world of art. Its origins are in a Sanskrit art form known as *Akhyāna* mentioned by Bhojaraja. Harikatha is also known as *Kathākālakṣēpa*. Because the details of a Harikatha performance are quite well known, further elaboration is unnecessary. However, its impact on shaping the spiritual, moral, and ethical life of Hindu society in South India over the centuries has been truly extraordinary. In fact, until the 'company dramas' burst upon the scene, Harikatha was the most popular and effective vehicle for spreading sacred education in the nooks and corners of *Dakshinadesha*. But like so many such sublime art forms, Harikatha too, today stands on the verge of extinction.

Epilogue

We have scratched just the surface of an ennobling topic in this essay. Two awesome features of all these traditional modes of imparting essential education to Hindus must be mentioned.

The first is the fact that tradition was also popular across space and time because the Hindu society of those eras regarded tradition as the proverbial friend, philosopher, and guide. Above all, tradition was sacred. Questioning it in the vile 'revolutionary' spirit that is commonplace today didn't even arise.

Tradition was the root, and Hindus of that period were merely occupying a temporal branch that was naturally destined to break and fall down and merge with the cosmos. Tradition was the perennial river, its followers, streams of bubbles.

The disfiguring caused by the colonization of the Hindu mind is primarily responsible for regarding tradition and popularity as enemies. This is why the intrinsic and lasting value of such an education in essential knowledge has escaped us today.

The second feature is the fact that this education—in form, content, method, and expression—was free, accessible, flexible, creative, decentralized, institution-independent, and above all, duty-bound.

We have sadly preserved only the wrinkled skin of the once-rugged body of this national phenomenon of sacred education that gave us the spiritual strength and cultural resilience to withstand and triumph over sustained civilizational assaults of fatal proportions.

On the other side, our strides in professional education, as impressive as they are, deserve scrutiny on a fundamental plane: the loss we have endured in the bargain.

Note of Gratitude

I would be failing in my duty if I did not acknowledge my debt of gratitude to a galaxy of brilliant scholars and writers whose material formed the raw material for this essay. Foremost among them stands Dr V. Raghavan, followed in no particular order by Radhakumud Mukherjee, M. Hiriyanna, Ananda Coomaraswamy, A.K. Haldar, Rabindranath Tagore, Stella Kramrisch, and Shatavadhani Dr R. Ganesh.

9

The Rise and Fall of the *Dramma* in India

Except for the closed club of numismatics fans, the journey of currencies throughout history is either bypassed or ignored by the general reader. This negligence is unfortunate, bordering on criminal, given the inestimable value of the study of currencies, which is inseparable from the study of history. A straight line connects the rise and fall of currencies with those of empires. The volatile tyranny of Muhammad bin Tughluq presents the most eminent proof of this truth, at least in Indian history. A central cause of the chaotic collapse of his empire was his psychotic experiments with currency. By artificially hiking the value of copper and brass coins to the same level as gold and silver, he bankrupted his economy overnight.

Unlike the paper wealth of the contemporary world, currencies historically had real value, from the era of the classical civilizations of India, Greece, and Rome all the way up to the abolition of the gold standard.

In fact, much of the reconstruction of the history of the Gupta Empire owes to the extensive and in-depth study of its coins. Gold and silver coins of the Guptas were variously known as *dīnāra, suvarṇa, rūpaka* (from which the word *rupee* is derived). The Gupta Empire literally set the gold standard in the realm of coins and currencies. After its fall, the monetary stability and standardization that it had established took different trajectories in different regions of Bharatavarsha in the subsequent periods.

From the earliest times, currencies in India were variously known as kārṣāpaṇa, suvarṇa, purāṇa, *dhāraṇa, niṣka, vimśopaka, rati,* and *dīnārī.* Of these, the most enduring currency was the dramma.

Dramma is derived from the well-known Greek currency, *Drachma,* which originated roughly in the 6th century BCE. Ever since, it has travelled throughout the world. However, it is perhaps only in India that it acquired highly creative expressions and usages for more than 1,400 years.

The literal meaning of Drachma is 'to grasp'. Its original value was equal to a handful of arrows. With Athens emerging as a major commercial centre in the 5th century BCE, the Athenian Drachma became its supreme currency. In its original form, it was a silver coin weighing 67.5 grains or 4.3 grams. However, its journey from Greece to Bharatavarsha during the course of history eventually transformed it to roughly 84 grains or 5.92 grams.

The (ancient) Persian and Arab currency, *Dirham* too, comes from Drachma.

In India, the Dramma took on a life of its own as it travelled over both space and time. It was a widely recognized unit of currency in all major and minor empires throughout the country. It also underwent many minor name changes, its value fluctuated, and its destiny underwent major changes, as we shall see.

We notice the earliest mention of Dramma on some copper coins minted by the Yaudheya kings, who flourished in the 3rd century CE.

Coins were typically named after their issuers, i.e., kings. This was an ancient political custom whose intent and effect was to stamp the absolute supremacy of the *Chakravartin* or *Samrāt* or monarch over the territories that he had conquered. Non-recognition of his currency meant instant punitive or military action against, say, a rebellious chieftain or recalcitrant groups.

Apart from the Gupta Empire, we have the example of the 8th century currency named *kṛṣṇarāja* rūpaka (rupee), named after the Kalachuri king Krishnaraja who ruled in the 6th century.

Next, we have the *Srimad ādivarāha-Dramma* of the Pratihara king Mihira Bhoja I, who ruled from 836–85 CE. To trace the history of this extraordinarily durable currency, we need to visit a decrepit village named Siron Khurd near Lalitpur in Jhansi. The original name of this village was Siyadoni, once a flourishing commercial town under Pratihara rule. In 1887, an inscription was found here that mentions the *ādivarāha*-Dramma, and this was how it looked: a silver coin whose obverse was engraved with a beautiful carving of *ādivarāha* Swami, and the reverse has text summarizing the glory of Mahavishnu's *Varāha* Avatar. The other interesting fact is that Srimad *ādivarāha* was also one of the honorifics given to Mihira Bhoja I. Mihira Bhoja was one of the early Hindu monarchs who gave nightmares to the pioneering Arab invaders, who characterized him as a 'fearsome infidel with a large army and fine cavalry'. The Siyadoni inscription was engraved by his son, Mahendrapala I, in 901 CE.

For about two centuries, the *Ā*divarāha-Dramma was not only the staple currency of the Pratiharas but was prevalent in the entire region, roughly encompassing Madhya Pradesh, Uttar Pradesh, the foothills of the Himalayas, Rajasthan, and parts of Gujarat.

When we travel down to the Karnata-Desha in the same period, we spot a magnificent inscription in Soraba (about 90 kms from Shivamogga). It is magnificent for its innate virtue, and it moves us for the noble values that Hindus of that era abided by. Dated 991 CE, the inscription speaks of a loyal citizen named Katega. The king of that region Kakkala Deva had remained childless for several years. As the ancient Hindu dictum went, a childless king leaves behind an orphaned kingdom, defenceless and vulnerable to invasion and anarchy. And so Katega took a solemn vow to cut off his head and offer it to the Mother Goddess Gundadabbe so that his king might be blessed with a son. Lo and behold! A son and successor to the kingdom was born. When he heard this happy tiding, Katega stoically walked up to the soldiers of Kakkala's army, narrated his oath to them, and offered his head. The inscription describes how he reached *svarga* (heaven) through this virtuous act of self-sacrifice. The overwhelmed king, Kakkala Deva, personally visited his village and immediately granted 24 hera-drammas in Katega's honour.

We can next move to Konkana from Karnata-Desha. Here, we notice a stone inscription dated 1260 CE in Uran, now part of Navi Mumbai. Engraved by the Shilahara king Someshwara, it records a grant of 162 Paruttha-dramma coins. This amount was the fixed income generated from a garden in Konthalesthan in Chadiche village. It was given to the deity named Uttareshvara Mahadeva of Shri-Sthanak (Thane). The crux of the story in this inscription is in the name, Paruttha-dramma. These coins resembled the ancient Parthian Drammas (the Parthian Empire was an ancient Iranian Empire from 247 BCE to 224 CE). Today, the Parthian region roughly corresponds to the Khorasan belt.

Apart from this, other types of Drammas that were excavated in the Konkana region in the early 20th century were the coins of a variation of the Sassanian type of Dirhams. These coins were known as *Gadhia Paisa* or donkey-money in the local Konkan parlance.

Then, when we travel along the Konkana coast and reach Gujarat in 1296 CE, other interesting stories await us. Here, we see Sarangadeva of the Viradhavala (Vaghela) dynasty giving Vishalapriya-Drammas for various purposes, such as payment to horse-dealers, oil-makers, customs officers, and making grants to temples, for *Naivedyas,* and to pupils of *Gurukulas*. The Vishalapriya-Dramma was the coinage issued by his ancestor, Vishala-Deva.

A noteworthy feature in all of this is the fact that these currencies retained their names even after the original issuer and his dynasty disappeared from the scene centuries ago.

The final leg of this Dramma journey takes us to Kondavidu in the Andhra-Desa. Here we notice a benefaction made by Nadindla Goparasa Ayyangaru (Iyengar) in 1520 CE. The purpose of the grant was pious: Goparasa had faith that his bequest would enable the Vijayanagara Chief Minister Saluva Timma and his wife, Lakshmamma, to earn *punya.* Among other things, the grant provides for the following:

One damma on every bag of the following items produced in the region: onions, turmeric, fenugreek, cumin, mustard, new gunny bags, green ginger, lime fruits, and coconut.

Two dammas on every bag of the following items: jaggery, cleaned cotton, ghee, castor oil, dry ginger, iron and steel chisels.

Three dammas on every bag of mango jelly.

Four dammas on every bag of sugar, arecanuts, cotton thread, and betel leaves.

Six dammas on every bag of long pepper, pepper, sandal, cloves, nutmeg, mace, lead, tin, and copper.

It is significant that the word dramma has been transformed to damma in the Andhra-Desha by the 16th century.

With the total destruction of Hindu political power in northern India and the advent of the Mughals, the fortunes of dramma underwent a sea change. In the Mughal period, the word dramma had become corrupted as *Daam.* This is the popular Hindi word, which today exclusively means 'price', and not a specific unit of currency. In Akbar's reign, Daam had degraded in value, and instead of silver, he issued Daam-s in copper coins: 40 Daam-s were equal to one silver *Rupiya.*

We have other interesting sidelights as well. For example, for over seven centuries, the Karnata-Desha (Kannada-speaking region) had different Drammas such as Gara-Dramma, Daaya-Dramma, Hera-Dramma and Belliya-Dramma (silver Dramma*)*. These were widely used even in the late 16th century. The Tamil equivalent was the *Dirāmaṃ.*

Over the next three centuries, the Dramma witnessed a steep decline, and its linguistic form too underwent changes. In the Kannada and Telugu-speaking regions, it came to be pronounced as Dammidi. Its value had dwindled to just one-twelfth of an *Anna* (16 Annas made a Rupee. The Anna was demonetized in 1957). The Dramma or Dammidi had become the smallest unit of currency in the 20th century.

However, the word Dammadi itself hung on to dear life for two more decades. It was in vogue in Kannada and Telugu literature and cinema till the mid-1980s.

Now it only exists on printed paper and electronic media as a historical artefact.

10

The Story of a Spotless Poet Who Mortgaged an Alphabet in His Name

When William Shakespeare memorably declared through Polonius, 'neither a borrower, nor a lender be. For loan oft loses both itself and friend', he merely stated an eternal truth of worldly life. There's a reason moneylenders have been universally reviled since the advent of money in human civilization. Usury was among the main reasons why Jews were subject to such hatred. It is the same reason our own Marwaris, Gujaratis, Sindhis, and Settis are derided.

But we now live in an indebted era in which the global economic system actively encourages and abets people to entrap themselves in lifelong liability. Borrowing is no longer considered shameful. On the contrary, it has become fashionable to not only borrow but to renege on the loan. Epic defaulters have attained cult status as role models. Netflix even did a two-season documentary series detailing this sleaze by profiling select celebrity defaulters.

Changing attitudes notwithstanding, some elements in every society remain unchangeable because they are rooted in human nature. For example, the typical borrower subconsciously hates paying interest on the sum he or she has borrowed. According to this attitude, interest is 'free' money that the lender gets without doing any work. On his part, the lender might forgo the principal but is merciless in collecting interest. Interest is also the recurring chilli powder rubbed on the original wound called pledge: no lender will lend without taking collateral.

Like in all societies, the Hindu society too recognized the typical items that can be offered as collateral: land, house, jewellery, etc. However, when we excavate history, it yields a rich harvest of real-life stories that show the exalted side of moneylending in the Hindu society of the past.

This is one such story.

It is set in Sugandhapura or Sugandhavarti or Saundatti, 78 kilometres from Belagavi (Belgaum), 41 kilometres from Dharwad, 500 kilometres from Bangalore.

For nearly four centuries, Saundatti was helmed by the Ratta dynasty, a branch of the imperial Rashtrakutas. While the Ratta rulers were devout Jainas, they also patronized and nourished all Panthas. Their regime was elevated by prolific Basadi-building activity and refined by literature. Overall, the Ratta kingdom reflected the same ambience of all great Hindu empires: a society that was bound by piety and cultured by education and the arts.

An extraordinary Kannada inscription dated 3 July 1228 describes the atmosphere in Saundatti. It was ruled by the *Mahāmandaleśvara* (governor) named Lakshmideva. The inscription describes him as the 'delight of the sages and wise men'. He was as valorous as Rama and endowed with his virtues. He was assisted by a council of the most excellent and competent ministers and *Munis*.

Mallikarjuna was one such minister.

His son is the protagonist of our story. His name is Rudrabhaṭṭa, hailing from the Atri *gotra*.

From his boyhood, Rudrabhaṭṭa distinguished himself as a precocious student. He grew up to become well-versed in the 'best sciences'. But he was primarily renowned as a *Su-Kavi*—an outstanding poet.

This is how the inscription extols him: 'Rudrabhaṭṭa was the king of poets. From (Goddess) Sarasvati, he acquired excellence of speech. He may be compared in the excellence of his poetry with his illustrious predecessor of the same name: Rudrabhaṭṭa. He became an excellent poet in just six months after commencing his studies.'

The older Rudrabhaṭṭa is the renowned author of *Jagannātha Vijaya,* an epic narrative poem in the *Champu* style. He flourished in the reign of the Hoysala monarch, Vira Ballala II, in the 12th century.

Our Rudrabhaṭṭa's poetic prowess and prodigious learning earned him a grant of 18 villages from the Raṭṭa ruler. Life was obviously good for him, until it wasn't. It appears that overnight, his family was hit by a calamity. While the inscription doesn't give any details of the misfortune, it clearly says that Rudrabhaṭṭa was on the edge of bankruptcy. He approached a wealthy businessman in Saundatti, seeking a loan of one thousand gold coins. And this is where the full extent of Rudrabhaṭṭa's penury is revealed: he had nothing to offer as collateral.

What follows is what makes this story so profound. He told the businessman that he would offer *one alphabet in his name as collateral.* Henceforth, he would drop the letter *Bha* from his name. The letter would be in the lender's custody till his loan was cleared. Thus, from then on, Rudrabhaṭṭa was addressed as Rudraṭa by all the citizens of Saundatti. This was akin to grievous humiliation.

To appreciate the full significance of this, we need to transport ourselves back to the social and cultural milieu of that era. The surname Bhaṭṭa was held in reverence by the entire society. It was both a surname and an honorific. The person who had earned it had to necessarily embody *Pāṇḍitya* or *Vidvat* (scholarship) through both learning and spotless conduct. Thus, his surname itself was a lifelong reminder of this sacred vow. Those who wore it took it seriously.

And so, we can only imagine Rudrabhaṭṭa's deep anguish when circumstances forced him to pledge a letter in it, thereby deforming the exalted surname. In fact, there is intense meaning in the letter *Bha,* which means 'sun', 'light', 'radiance', etc. By choosing to pledge it, Rudrabhaṭṭa was, in a way, mortgaging the light of his scholarship. Which also opens another insight: that the Sanatana tradition regards the sale or trade of knowledge as a great sin.

Rudrabhaṭṭa could have chosen to pledge any letter in his name, but he consciously chose *Bha.* It would be a constant self-reminder of his indebtedness, which would be reinforced each time the people of Saundatti addressed him as Rudraṭa.

The eminent scholar of archaeology Professor S.K. Dixit makes a poignant observation about this extraordinary episode: 'Those were the days when the scholar's name was literally honoured.'

Equal credit of honour should go to the businessman who actually accepted the letter *Bha* as collateral and lent a thousand gold coins to Rudrabhaṭṭa. How does one encash an alphabet? And what does this tell us about the value system of our ancestors?

The story has a happy ending.

Rudrabhaṭṭa stoically bore the self-inflicted insult of his truncated name. Eventually, he returned the loan and 'got back' his alphabet and, thereby, his original honorific. The inscription describes the whole episode as his 'spotless achievement'.

I concur with my head bowed.

Postscript

We need to remember that this episode is not fictional. And because it is not fictional, it makes the crime worse—not including such character-sculpting episodes in our school textbooks. Even a 10-year-old student can flawlessly understand the value and ideal inherent in this episode. However, it appears as though our present educational system has been designed to inculcate immunity against virtue.

Part II
Colonial India

11

The Vijayanagara Empire or the Hindu Resistance to Islamic Expansion into South India

Preface

If the full and accurate story of the Vijayanagara Empire were narrated in the way it should be, this is the picture we get: the Vijayanagara Empire remains an extraordinary watershed event not just in Indian history but in the history of the entire world. Although it might sound trite, it merits repetition: that this empire is a magnificent and unbroken saga of inspirational indefatigability and grandeur sprawled over nearly three centuries. It was primarily founded and sustained with the explicit purpose of safeguarding Sanatana Dharma against Turushka incursions, a task it executed with aplomb. It is thus unsurprising that there is no sphere of Hindu life and activity that the Vijayanagara Empire did not touch and transform into gold. If Sanatana Dharma continues to survive in South India today, the entire credit for it still rests on the hulking shoulders of this empire of Dharma.

What Was Europe Doing?

The fact that the Vijayanagara Empire was one of the world's grandest empires cannot be emphasized enough.

However, the Eurocentric version of the history of Bharatavarsha feigns as though the Vijayanagara Empire did not exist. When we objectively delve into the annals of this version, it is clear that Eurocentrism remains an enduring curse, especially upon Hindu history.

Which elicits this question: forget world history, what is a summary history of Europe itself? This is the short answer: about an entire millennium of internecine wars fought by 'countries' as big (or small) as, say, Tamil Nadu, Gujarat, Karnataka, Kerala, or Telangana. All these were Christian countries. All were densely feudal, highly class-conscious, and ruled by absolute despots who obtained their monarchial sanction from a jealous Christian God. Colonial scholars of history, who were groomed in this atmosphere, issued grand and sweeping verdicts about Indian history.

To illustrate, let's pick a random year. Let's pick 1421.

In England, the nine-month-old boy 'King' Henry VI was coronated and, with it, inherited the bloody Hundred Years' War, a long-running sceptre that haunted his regime till 1453. Perhaps no other king of England witnessed such a conspiracy-fueled, war-torn, and strife-ridden reign. Cliques and factions constantly muzzled this monarch's nominal power. His over-ambitious wife, Queen Margaret of Anjou, wielded the real power behind the throne. Dukes and cousins were murdered with impunity. Peace and order were supplanted by palace intrigues. England lost both its dominance and its lands in France. A bloody civil war (the infamous Wars of the Roses) broke out just two years after the Hundred Years' War ended. An incensed plebian named Jack Cade became the practical epitome of civil revolt against the oppression of the masses by this power-intoxicated royalty. He mustered a 5,000-strong mob and threatened Henry VI himself. Courts became the watering holes of political conniving. The tattered reputation of Henry VI plummeted to its lowest when he was openly described as 'shy, timid, war-averse, passive and mentally unstable'. Henry indeed literally lost his mind—politely known as 'nervous breakdown' in contemporary parlance—several times during his rickety monarchy. In the end, 'having lost his wits, his two kingdoms and his only son', Henry VI died a prisoner in the Tower of London on 21 May 1471.

William Shakespeare has canonized Henry VI's infamy by dedicating an entire trilogy of plays that skewer this monarchical dishonour. To borrow a line from the bard himself, these plays were written not because Shakespeare loved Henry less but because he loved England more.

The Scene in South India

In 1422, the city of Vijayanagara, located 8,000 kilometres from London, witnessed the stately coronation ceremony of Devaraya II. He had ascended the throne just a year after Henry VI had taken power in England.

Famed as Prauḍha (erudite, great, mature) Devaraya, he was the greatest emperor of the Sangama Dynasty, which founded the Vijayanagara Empire. He inaugurated a reign spread over a quarter-century, marked by serial military victories, political and social stability, economic splendor and prosperity, and cultural and scholastic excellence. The full story of his glory has been rather eclipsed by the blinding dazzle of Sri Krishnadevaraya's flamboyance.

Devaraya II deservedly gets full credit for fully bringing all of South India under the Vijayanagara *Śvēta-cchatra* (the White Royal Umbrella, a symbolic accourtment signifying a powerful sovereign). At the height of his rule, the empire spanned

Gomantaka on the west coast and Odisha in the east and subdued the warring and recalcitrant Rajas of Malabar. Prauḍha Devaraya's reign also witnessed the high point of Kannada literature. It was the age of the Krishna-blessed poet, Kumara Vyasa, who composed the immortal *Karṇāṭabhāratakathāmañjari* or the *Kumāravyāsabhārata* or the *Gaduginabhārata.* Devaraya II was himself a poet of some merit who composed quaintly titled works: *Sobagina Sone* (The Drizzle of Beauty), *Amaruka,* and *Mahānāṭaka Sudhānidhi.* Another little-known fact about his rule is his encouragement of the fabled Kerala School of Astronomy and Mathematics. Its celebrated exponent Parameshwara was patronized by Devaraya II.

When Devaraya II left the mortal world in 1446, he had comprehensively transformed the Vijayanagara Empire not only as an indomitable political force but also as an aspirational climate in which both rulers and the people vied with one another to scale higher peaks of wealth, culture, and learning.

In 1446, the disastrous Treaty of Tours became public knowledge in England. Its seedy revelations emitted shockwaves throughout the island country. The infuriated masses learned that in 1444, Henry VI had secretly ceded Maine, a province in France then under British control, back to King Charles VII of France. But its backroom reality showed a far worse picture: it was not a treaty but a *dowry* that Henry VI had given to France solely in order to marry the fabled beauty, Queen Margaret of Anjou, niece of Charles VII. The outrage that this alleged treaty generated in England eventually led to a series of political murders, followed by the aforementioned revolt of Jack Cade.

And the year 1446 was 42 years before the Portuguese pirate Bartholomew Diaz sighted the Cape of Good Hope and half a century before another Portuguese pirate Vasco da Gama actually crossed it.

At the height of its power, the Vijayanagara Empire was perhaps the world's greatest economic magnet, which enticed these warring Europeans in droves. With some latitude, it can be said that the 15th and 16th-century Europeans came to India to trade primarily with Vijayanagara. We have their own testimony for it in the form of the glowing Portuguese accounts that consistently praise Vijayanagara as the greatest empire on earth and its capital as the most fabulous city in the world.

Yet, just three centuries later, we find a history book ironically titled *A Forgotten Empire* written by another European on Vijayanagara. No doubt it is a work celebrating the empire, but it is also highly reflective of the European mood of the 20th century. Robert Sewell remains perhaps the solitary exception among European scholars and researchers of Indian history who wrote a laudatory account of the Vijayanagara Empire.

But on the larger canvas, unless this backdrop of the comparative scenario of world history is kept in mind, a full grasp and appreciation of the Vijayanagara Empire and its enduring legacy will elude us.

The Picture in Uttarāpathā

If the story of the Vijayanagara Empire can be narrated in just one sentence, it is this: what began as a spirited and coalesced Hindu resistance against alien Islamic invasions birthed a grand civilization that showed the world what true Hindu unity could really accomplish.

But the prelude to the founding of Vijayanagara was scripted about 600 years earlier. With the first barbaric raid on Sindh by Muhammad bin Qasim. It is the familiar tale of the first brush of Hindus with Islam, known popularly but incorrectly as the Arab 'Invasion' of Sindh. It was not an invasion but a piffling incursion, not unlike the raid of Alexander. However, to the Hindus, Qasim's raid gave a putrid taste of what an Islamic war really meant in practice. Temple destructions, forcible conversions, cow slaughter, gang rape of women, mass enslavement of men, women, and children. Hindus of today who are unfamiliar with all these stand to suffer the same fate.

Around the same time that Qasim was ravaging Sindh, his Islamic compatriot Tariq ibn Ziyad had shattered the Christian empire in Spain and overwhelmed the Visigoth chief, Roderick.

The difference between the two incursions is notable. One was a comprehensive imperial victory of Islam at the southern tip of Europe, and the other, an unimpressive sally in a limited region in Bharatavarsha.

The motivation that powered both events was the same, but the outcomes were widely different. In the former case, the newly ascendant Abrahamism, Islam, had managed to clobber another ancient Abrahamism, Christianity. In the latter case, Islam could only manage to dent a relatively small Hindu kingdom.

Muhammad bin Qasim stayed in the Sindh region for about three years, but the real story begins after he left.

The moment he left, Hindus in Sindh launched a stiff resistance, began to reconquer their lost territories, and systematically expelled the alien Muslim 'governors' that Qasim had left behind. There is a momentous civilizational significance in this fightback and reconquest, which is noteworthy especially for contemporary Hindus: this was the voluntary and relieved return of thousands of Hindus to their *Matru-Dharma*— what is known today as *ghar wapsi*. There was no Vishwa Hindu Parishad or allied Hindu organizations that had to convince these forcibly converted Hindus to return.

This brings us to the other great myth of indian history: that the so-called Islamic conquest of Bharatavarsha was a cakewalk.

On the contrary, India was the toughest country for Islam to penetrate. It still is. In fact, Bharatavarsha is the only country in the world in which Islam met with its greatest failure. Among other things, one of the intents behind the Marxist project of distorting Indian history on an epic scale was to hide the truth of this Islamist failure. Even after countless jihads, invasions, and Islamic despotism spread over 800 years, this *Punyabhoomi* is still a Hindu majority. *Hindu-majority India is Islam's greatest failure.* We have a handy and recent example to verify the validity of this statement: how much of their Hindu past do the Yazidis still remember?

Hindus have preserved the core essence of their ancient Dharma almost intact. This did not happen by accident or by magic or by divine intervention; our ancestors literally spilled their blood, made incredible sacrifices, and fought back with the sort of grit and steely determination that, to today's Hindus, will seem like fiction. Boys as young as 13 or 15 held a sword in one hand and placed one leg in the grave, chanting this heroic mantra: *If we win, we reclaim and preserve our Dharma; if we lose, we reach heaven which is reserved only for heroes.* And all these men, women, boys, and girls died like heroes in defence of our Dharma. They died so that we could remain Hindus.

The next major and dark chapter in this story is the savage invasion of the barbarian Mahmud of Ghazni. But between Qasim and Mahmud, there is a period of about 300 years during which no alien Muslim invader dared to glance in the direction of Bharatavarsha. Even in this case, the truth that no 'mainstream' history book will dare to reveal is this: Mahmud of Ghazni could not establish an Islamic empire within the borders of Bharatavarsha. Like a crafty bandit outfitted with an army, all he could do was plunder large regions of India and scamper back to the safety of his citadel in Ghazni, Afghanistan. Even after his death, Bharatavarsha largely remained untouched by alien Islamic invasions for another century.

It was only after the second battle of Tarain in 1192 that extensive regions of north India came under direct Muslim rule.

This is the overall timeline that we get: 712 to 1192; 500 years. In other words, it took Islam half a millennium to gain even a foothold in Bharatavarsha. But once Muslim rule was formally established in Delhi, it gradually began to spread its tentacles throughout the country.

But from the Hindu perspective, the establishment of the so-called Delhi Sultanate marks the beginning of the Age of Resistance. It was the first time in the history of Bharatavarsha that Hindus lost freedom in their own *Mātrbhūmi*.

But entirely consistent with their perfidious flair, our secular 'historians' call this period as the 'Medieval Muslim period'. In reality, it must be called the Age of Resistance because, till the very end, what is known as the Islamic rule of India was a rule by fanatical foreigners who settled in India. It was not a rule by any definition of the term but an all-encompassing oppression of Hindus motivated and guided by the Islamic doctrine.

Another significant factor emerges from this history. Even as Islamic despotism took deep roots in Delhi, Hindus never gave up fighting. The five hundred-plus years of Muslim rule starting from Qutub-ud-din Aibak till Aurangzeb are dotted with brilliant sagas of freedom struggle waged by our Rajas, chieftains, and generals, big and small. There is no Muslim ruler who did not face the brunt of this freedom struggle waged by Hindus.

And the rise of the Vijayanagara Empire is the greatest and most successful epoch of this ceaseless resistance offered by Hindus.

The Backstory of Dakṣiṇāpatha

Even as the Delhi Sultanate consolidated its power over large parts of north India, none of the early sultans ventured in the direction of Dakṣiṇāpatha or southern India. It was considered extremely risky and dangerous.

But it was Ala-ud-din Khalji who first braved this risk and became successful. At the start of the 14th century, both Ala-ud-din Khalji and especially his general Malik Kafur stormed Dakṣiṇāpatha and left behind a gruesome trail of devastation. For the first time, Hindus in South India got a hands-on taste of a full-scale Islamic invasion from which they had been immune so far. The experience was so terrifying that, for nearly 70 years, they were unable to even come to terms with it. Lament. Denial. Dejection. Despondency. An overall sense of doom. This describes the state of the Hindu psyche in the aftermath of the Khalji ravage.

The scene in southern India at the onset of Malik Kafur's invasion was quite pathetic, to say the least. Four major Hindu empires were constantly fighting with one another: the Sevuna at Devagiri, the Kakatiyas at Warangal, the Hoysalas at Dvarasamudra, and the Pandyas in Madurai. If the blunt truth must be told bluntly, these four Hindu empires had plastered themselves with disgrace. They had failed the Hindu populations that they were supposed to protect and govern. Even if two of these empires had joined hands, there is little doubt that Malik Kafur would not only be beaten back but would have perhaps been killed in battle. On the contrary, Ramachandra, the foolish Sevuna king of Devagiri, actually aided Kafur against his own Hindu brethren in the south.

As a consequence, in one extensive sweep, Kafur burned hundreds of temples in this vast region–Warangal, Belur,

Dvarasamudra, Srirangam, Chidambaram, Madurai, Rameshwaram, and almost the whole of Malabar, including Cochin, Travancore, and Kozhikode, and looted prolific amounts of wealth.

Madurai, especially, suffered the worst atrocities. In fact, eventually, a Muslim governor named Jalal-ud-din Ahsan Shah established something called a Madurai Sultanate. I have narrated this complete story in my monograph titled *The Madurai Sultanate: A Concise History*.

The following is a summary of this torrid tale of the virgin wreckage of Hindus in South India: when Malik Kafur had finished his desolation, Hindus in the whole of Dakṣiṇāpatha were left leaderless and defenceless. Quite obviously, these barbaric Islamic invasions deeply impacted the Hindu psyche in ways that the contemporary Hindu mind finds it hard to fathom. The very foundations of their Dharma were shaken. Even worse, the last great Hindu emperor of South India, Hoysala Vira Ballala III, was brutally assassinated by the so-called sultan of Madurai. His body was skinned, straw was stuffed into it, and his dismembered head was paraded at the city gates. With that, the Hoysala dynasty was extinguished.

Gangadevi, the queen and wife of Kumara Kampana—the gallant son of the Vijayanagara monarch Bukkaraya—graphically describes the situation in Madurai in her famous epic poem, *Madhurāvijayam*. It does not make for easy reading:

> O King! The city, which is called Madhurapuri for its honeyed loveliness, has now become the city of cruel beasts; it now lives up to its earlier name of Vyaghrapuri, the city of tigers because humans don't dwell there (anymore).
>
> Those temples of Gods, which used to reverberate with the sacred melody of the mridangam, now echo the dreadful howls of jackals.

> In the Agraharams of our city, huge columns of smoke emanating from the scared Yagnas used to rise up and reach the skies amid the sacred Vedic chants but alas! today those selfsame Quarters send up wretched stenches of meat roasted by the Turushkas; the Vedic chants are today replaced by the beastly cacophonies of drunken hoodlums.
>
> During the days of Pandyas, our women used to bathe in [river] Taamraparni, whose waters turned white from the sandal-paste applied to their breasts. My lord! Now she's coloured only in red from the currents of blood flowing into her from all the cows slaughtered by its wicked occupiers all over the country.
>
> O King! I cannot bear to look at the countenance of those Dravida ladies who were bounteously endowed with beauty. Ravished horribly by the scourging Turushkas, these delicate women now sport lifeless lips and exhale hot breaths, and their abundant tresses that have come undone are painful to the eyes. I don't have the words to describe the suffering and dishonour painted on their faces, which know neither redemption nor protection.

While these brutal Islamic invasions terrorized Hindus in South India, they did not endure this suffering and humiliation like cowards. On the contrary, they were waiting for an opportunity to extract vengeance against these hated Turushkas from Delhi.

All they needed was solid leadership.

That leadership was slowly emerging behind the scenes.

Towards the end of the reign of Vira Ballala III, the royal family of the Hoysalas knew that their power had irretrievably declined and that they were fighting a losing battle against these Turushkas from the north. In a conveniently overlooked episode of Hindu history, during the last days of Vira Ballala III, prominent members of his Hoysala family effected a silent transfer of power into the hands of five unassuming brothers;

they are renowned as the Sangama Brothers. Over time, their family came to be known as the House of the Sangama.

The Rise and Rise of the Sangama

Just three years before his death, Vira Ballala III coronated his son Virupaksha Ballala (or Vira Ballala IV) as his successor in the historic city of Hosapattana. A few months later in the same year, he also elevated the Mahāmaṇḍaḷēśvara (grand governor) Vira Hariyappa Odeya as the caretaker of a substantial territory of his empire. Likewise, he divided his empire among various Nayakas (leaders) and Odeyas (lords, masters, chieftains). It was both a literal and symbolic presage of the transfer of power from a fading dynasty at the dusk of its former glory.

Hariyappa Odeya would eventually emerge as a great frontline warrior who fought against Islamic forces under the leadership of the Sangama Brothers.

Vira Ballala III had truly shown great foresight when he spotted the Sangama Brothers, who had taken the sacred vow to safeguard Sanatana Dharma against the Turushkas. This bloodless transfer of political power from the Hoysala dynasty to the Sangama Brothers is both unique and unprecedented in the political history of India.

The sacred vow of *Hindūdharmarakṣaṇa* taken by the Sangama Brothers was the profound consequence of Vidyaranya Swami's inspiration and guidance. His younger brother, the distinguished Sāyaṇācārya, joined this extraordinary Yajna. Their combined efforts firmed up the spiritual foundations of this rising empire, set the blueprint for its administration, and sculpted its social and religious policy. By any measure, the Vijayanagara Empire was a Dharma-Rajya. Vidyaranya Swami and Sāyaṇācārya ensured that no Vijayanagara ruler ever forgot the foundational purpose of the empire: it was explicitly founded to act as the custodian of Sanatana Dharma in southern India against attacks by the unclean, savage, and barbaric Turushkas. The day it forgot this founding purpose was the day it was overwhelmed by the Bahamani rulers.

The establishment of the Vijayanagara Empire in 1336 was an epochal and exciting event, even in its own time. After the foregoing bloodless transfer of Hoysala power, its officials and commanders seamlessly merged with the House of the Sangama and wholeheartedly supported the cause of Sanatana Dharma.

The leadership that Hindus in South India had so desperately wanted had now finally emerged.

The five Sangama Brothers–Harihara, Kamparaya, Bukkaraya, Marappa, and Muddappa–took the blessings of the Sringeri Shankaracharya and launched an all-out campaign to expel the despicable Turushkas in South India and liberate Hindus. With Vijayanagara as the capital, the brothers took charge of the four divisions of the empire: Bukka in the centre, Marappa in the west, Kamparaya in the east, and Harihara in the northwest. Gomantaka was helmed by Muddappa. In this new administrative setup, the Vijayanagara rulers took extreme caution to leave the Hoysala and the Tamil traditions undisturbed. Vira Ballala III had divided his empire into three major divisions, with a capital in each. His chief capital was Dvarasamudra (Halebidu). To the north was Hampi, and Thiruvannamalai was the southern capital.

A fact that no 'mainstream' history book on the Vijayanagara Empire mentions is that Vidyaranya Swami was also a seasoned warrior and a military strategist who directed the liberation efforts against the Turushkas. His whole personality and his inestimable legacy remind us of the famous Sanatana dictum:

> Agrataścaturō vēdāḥ pṛṣṭataḥ sahasram dhanuh |
> Idam brāhmam idam kṣātram śāpādapi śarādapi ||
> The four Vedas are in the forefront, a thousand bows (and arrows) at the rear;
> We are well versed in both Brāhma (spiritual power) and kṣātram (valour);
> Be it in imprecating a curse or wielding the arrow.

The legendary D.V. Gundappa paints a highly evocative miniature that brings out this ennobling personality of Vidyaranya Swami:

> Six hundred years ago, the spirit of brāhma in Sage Vidyaranya, instead of becoming a vocation of supplication, was transformed into a courageous endeavor and contributed to the rejuvenation of the Vedas. However, *the renunciate life of this glorious eminence did not culminate in passivity but instead, radiated the light of steely valour, and whose Vedanta instead of becoming dry recitation, directly became the cause for the Hindu civilisational overhaul.* (Emphasis added)

The fact that this glorious legacy of Vidyaranya Swami has all but been erased is a grisly reflection of the climate of the last century. Treating Vidyaranya Swami—literally, the Forest of Knowledge—as if he were a mere twig counts as an unforgivable crime against the Sanatana civilizational memory and our cultural inheritance.

The Decimation of the Madurai Sultanate

One of the initial campaigns of the Sangama Brothers resulted in spectacular success. This was against Ala-ud-din Shah II or Sikandar Khan, the Muslim governor ruling Madurai. It is both a thrilling and riveting episode in Hindu history.

Bukkaraya appointed his son Kumara Kampana to lead the expedition, and the son proved more than worthy of the task. In a series of superb, unstoppable victories, Kumara Kampana first quelled the recalcitrant Sambuvaraya, the chieftain of Tondaimandalam. In fact, the episode of Sambuvaraya's obstinacy sheds light on the stupidity and myopia of all such Hindu rulers. Sambuvaraya was a minor chieftain with pretensions to royalty. Instead of voluntarily subduing his ego and joining the larger cause of defending Hindu Dharma, he opted for war against a fellow Hindu, thereby shedding greater volumes of Hindu blood. We notice the same theme in the case of another chieftain belonging to the Vanyaraja dynasty.

After quashing both chieftains, Kumara Kampana marched against the Muslim ruler at Madurai. En route, he crushed the Muslim prefect at Samayavaram, located about six miles from the sacred *Tirthakshetra* of Srirangam. This brilliant military engagement was frontally led by the extraordinary Brahmana commander Vira Gopanarya, who clobbered the Turushka prefect and slaughtered him. The liberation of Srirangam sent waves of delight throughout the Hindu community. Vedanta Desika, the great exponent of Viśiṣṭādvaita, was so elated at this splendid victory and so profoundly moved by Gopanarya that he composed laudatory Sanskrit verses in honour of this great warrior. The verses were inscribed on the walls of the Ranganatha temple in Srirangam. Some excerpts follow:

> [H]aving smashed the Turks with their ranks full of upraised bows, he reinstalled Ranganatha in his own town … and worshipped again with all rites. Such is the mirror of fame of Gopanarya.
>
> ….
>
> [T]he Brahmana Gopana, brought to his own royal capital Srirangam, having cut down with his might the Turkic army.

> Mingling Srirangam with the earth of the *Krtayuga*, he reinstalled Vishnu along with Lakshmi and Mahi, and like the lotus-born Brahma, worshipped him with all the rituals.

Kumara Kampana next marched straight into Madurai. Ala-ud-din Shah II was now completely isolated and stood no chance before the onrush of the Vijayanagara army. He offered a feeble resistance but was quickly overwhelmed and slaughtered in a short battle.

The thrilling liberation of Madurai from the clutches of the cow-eating Turushka ruler sent waves of ecstasy throughout Hindus in Dakṣiṇāpatha. He had been resolutely crushed, and the fabulous Meenakshi Sundareshwara Temple had been reclaimed. Its stately doors leading to Kailasa itself were reopened for the first time in half a century, and this is how the Hindus of Madurai celebrated the aeonian triumph:

> During these Mahomedan days, in the Virodhi Samvatsara of the Salivahana Saka, the general of the King of Mysore, named Kampanudiaver, a native of Karnata, having conquered the Mahomedans, took possession of the kingdom of Madura. He opened the Siva and Vishnu temples, which had been locked-up throughout the country. He opened the Shiva temple at Madura; and obtained a personal view of the god. The general, seeing this grand sight was glad. He struck his eyes and with great piety made the customary offerings; he gave many villages to the temple, and many jewels and established ordinances for the regular performance of worship. The general, his son, and his son-in-law gave many jewels to the Siva and Vishnu temples, and ordered the sacred services to be conducted. *Kumara Kampana had saved the honour of the land; and there is no wonder that the people call him by the name of the province from which he hailed—Kampana of Karnataka.* (Emphasis added)

Madhurāvijayam, or the reclamation of Madurai, established the House of Sangama as the new unchallengeable Hindu empire, which had sprung out of the ashes of Turushka depradations. The vengeance that Hindus had been clamouring for all along was finally consummated.

By 1378–80, all traces of the Islamic menace in the Vijayanagara territory had been eliminated. The new empire safeguarding Hindu Dharma soared over South India like a massive protective fort with imposing towers and vigilant turrets, and Hindus willingly gave the Sangama Brothers their complete loyalty.

The history scholar Dr Saletore captures this epoch in stirring prose:

> It must be remembered that the indefatigable sons of Sangama threw upon the enemy a united front; and this concerted action had the double effect of silencing all opposition and of annihilating the forces of Islam, which took two and half centuries to combine again against Hindus. *The one objective of the Sangama sons was the preservation of Hindu independence in South India.... Vijayanagara stood as the visible embodiment of the national resistance to save the southern enclave for the Hindus and keep it free from being over- run by the Muhammadans.* (Emphasis added)

The common people realized that the honour of their homes and the destiny of the country were safe in the hands of the descendants of Sangama.

Thus, after nearly 70 years of terrible humiliation during which the whole of South India had been defiled by Islam, Hindus had finally burst out from the earth and heralded a glorious new era. The Vijayanagara monarchs instilled a fresh surge of confidence in Hindus and inspired them to win freedom from the alien rulers in order to protect their dwellings, women, and children and to preserve their ancient dharmic heritage unhindered. At the height of its glory, the Portuguese traveller Domingo Paes wrote the following about the Hindus of that era:

> In the Vijayanagara Empire, there were the finest young Hindu men to be ever seen or could be seen. And *among all of them, I did not see a single man who would act like a coward. Theirs was a tradition of courage and duty*. (Emphasis added)

Indeed, it is one thing to defeat the invading forces of Islam, but it is entirely another thing to sustain the victory for centuries. This is perhaps the greatest legacy and gift of the Vijayanagara Empire to the Hindus of South India. As long as it was at the helm, no Muslim ruler from the north dared to glance in the direction of South India. For about three centuries.

In fact, the Bahamani Muslim kings, the sworn enemies of Vijayanagara, lived in constant dread of Vijayanagara. It is said that for an entire year after Sri Krishnadevaraya's death, the Bahamani Sultans refused to believe that he was really dead. They believed that even his ghost had the power to defeat them.

Sanatana Cultural Rejuvenation

Copious legends narrating the remarkable military victories, the well-oiled administration, and the splendid wealth of the Vijayanagara Empire are quite well known. What is lesser known is the role of the empire in rejuvenating and renewing Sanatana Dharma in a comprehensive sense.

A grand and spirited revival occurred in all realms of Hindu culture, including art, music, literature, poetry, painting, philosophy, traditions, customs, and social etiquette. This revival was so pervasive and far-reaching that the successors of Vijayanagara—the Nayakas, the Palegars, etc.—sustained it till the Westminster-style of Indian democracy extinguished these princely states, thereby halting their cultural continuity. The Vijayanagara legacy is still visible throughout South India, and Hindus exhibit it subconsciously in their daily lives—for example, in their social life, forms of worship, celebration of festivals, and undertaking *Tirtha-Yatras.* The roots of the Mysore Dasara, a festival with global stature, are embedded in the Dasara celebrations that were initiated during the Vijayadashami festival in the era of the House of Sangama. In fact, there is a direct connection between the *Mahanavami Dibba* in Hampi and the Mysore Dasara. That is a period spanning half a millennium.

Finally, the singular role played by the Vijayanagara Empire as the greatest embodiment of Hindu resistance to alien Islamic invasions is this: recall the fate of Sanatana Dharma in north India. Not a single Hindu temple of the classical period survives there.

12

The Mughals and the Nehrus: A Tale of Two Durbars

Preface

National rot obviously begins at the top of the government apparatus and seeps, infects, and corrodes before finally consuming the country and the society that created the government. In plain language, it consumes people.

But the national rot begins not with a nebulous entity called government; it begins in the innermost recesses of the people manning it. People who willingly darken these recesses by slaughtering their consciences. This holds true for functional governments built on the foundations of honesty, integrity, transparency, and a demonstrated concern for the well-being of citizens.

But how do we grasp the phenomenon of governments founded on the most corrosive impulses of our base instincts? That is, 'governments' whose edifice comprises fanaticism, unprovoked cruelty, wanton violence, unquenchable rapacity, heinous depravity, and unmitigated persecution of their own innocent citizens even in peacetime. The 'governments' of Muslim empires throughout the world ever since Islam acquired state power are the best, lived illustrations of this phenomenon.

Needless to say, Muslim empires that ruled various parts of Bharatavarsha were no exception to this.

These Muslim empires did not establish 'governments' in any real meaning of the term, both in theory and practice. They were unchained despotisms and unbridled tyrannies. The administrative structures they set up were primarily meant to satisfy these objectives: the lifelong enjoyment of no-holds-barred depravity, the personal extravagance of the sultan, the ceaseless expansion of Islam, and the persecution of non-Muslim subjects.

Francois Bernier, the 17th-century French physician who travelled to India and wrote graphic accounts of his experiences travelling in Aurangzeb's empire, gives a revealing observation of the character of Mughal rule in India: '*The Great Mughal is a foreigner in Hindustan. To maintain himself in such a country he is under the necessity of keeping up numerous armies, even in the time of peace*' (emphasis added).

Writing two centuries later, the British bureaucrat W.H. Moreland makes this astute observation: '[T]here was no independent aristocracy, *for independence was synonymous with rebellion, and a noble was either a servant or an enemy of the ruling power*' (emphasis added).

However, Professor K.S. Lal gives us a near-perfect assessment of an Islamic 'government' when he writes,

> [I]n the Islamic state, Delhi was not the capital of the empire; it was Quwwat-ul-Islam. *The king was not the ruler of the people; he was Amir-ul-Mauminin, 'the conqueror of infidels and shelterer of Islam.'* The army was not the royal army; it was *Lashkar-i-Islam.* The soldier was not a cavalry man or infantry man; he was *Ahl-i-Jihad. The law of the state was not any secular or humanitarian law; it was Shariat, the law of Islam. The state was not an end in*

> *itself, like the Greek state, but a means of sub-serving the interests of Islam.* Conquests were made, shrines were broken, captives were taken, converts were made - all in the name of Islam. The raison d'etre of the regime was to disseminate the Islamic faith. (Emphases added)

Under such a system, what goodness, what virtue, what sublime values, what ideals, what philosophy, what education, and what elevating art and literature can flower? In fact, empires founded on this feral ideology can only be founded after first destroying these ennobling aspects of life. They can only be sustained through brute force, even in peacetime, because the fear of a more ruthless usurper is a clear and present danger that faces the ruling sultan. As the Islamic history of India repeatedly shows, the usurper was often the sultan's own son.

Muslim rule set back Bharatavarsha by its concomitant duration of *eight* centuries. But there is a more fundamental side to this national misfortune. A diligent researcher will find abundant historical evidence—from Islamic sources themselves—to show that *this rule corrupted the ethical and moral framework of Indian society* in unfathomable ways with far-reaching consequences. It is a curse that has not only persisted till date but has been exacerbated almost to the point of no return.

We notice the unbroken legacy of this profligate corruption in perhaps the most vital areas that impact our daily lives: governance, administration, and the judiciary.

In fact, we can trace chilling parallels between the dissolute administrative and scrofulous judicial systems of Muslim empires and those of the Congress governments after independence.

To explore these parallels, this essay considers the Mughal administrative system and its judicial setup as the model that the

Congress adopted, perhaps subconsciously. The reason for this selection is straightforward: the Mughal Empire is *still* regarded as a showpiece of religious tolerance, syncretism, liberalism, magnanimity, magnificence, and good governance.

This essay is largely exploratory, and it would be a national service of sorts if a researcher or scholar expanded this theme into a full-length book.

Parallel 1: A Regime of Foreigners

From the time Iltutmish consolidated his grip on the so-called Delhi Sultanate up to Aurangzeb's blood-soaked reign, all sultans stuffed their administration with alien Muslims, who broadly belonged to two classes.

The first class, which poured into India from Central Asia like an unceasing swarm of locusts, included adventurers, freebooters, (former) aristocrats whose careers had been wrecked at home, relatives of the sultan or his clan, and sundry mercenaries looking to make fortunes via shortcut.

The second class comprised foreign Muslims or their descendants who had already settled in India and had been serving in various capacities in the sultan's administration.

W.H. Moreland writes as follows about the administrative demographics of Akbar:

> The [administrative] Service was not by any means confined to men of Indian nationality, and *in Akbar's time it was predominantly foreign. Akbar himself was a foreigner*—the Omrahs consist mostly of adventurers from different nations who entice one another to Court.... Blochmann gives a list of all such appointments to ranks about 500 horses. (Emphasis added)

Here are some numbers that quantify Moreland's observation: *70 per cent* of senior officers in Akbar's administration came from Muslim families who had accompanied Humayun from Afghanistan. Akbar rewarded and promoted them after he became the sultan. Of the remaining 30 per cent, *more than half* were Muslims, both Indian and foreign. The remainder were Hindus.

In the 40 long years of his reign, Akbar appointed a grand total of *21* Hindus in his administration. Of these, 17 were Rajputs. These appointments were part of his shrewd move to consolidate his hold over Rajputana. The remaining four Hindus included the following: Birbal, Raja Todar Mal and his son, and finally, a Khatri official whose name is unknown.

We notice an eerie similarity in how Nehru chose his favourites. The extended circle of his advisors, friends, and people he looked up to mostly included foreigners.

Edwina Mountbatten tops the list for a different reason.

During the 17 years of his unmuzzled prime ministerial regime, the Soviet and Chinese embassies in Delhi had a field day. For a comprehensive and eyewitness history of how this played out in real life, Sita Ram Goel's *Genesis and Growth of Nehruism, How I Became a Hindu,* and *Nehru's Fatal Friendship* are highly recommended.

Apart from Nehru's fascination with Soviet Russia and Maoist China, a survey of his record as prime minister elicits a rather straightforward question: why couldn't Nehru find a single Indian architect to build factories, townships, cultural, and educational institutions? What compelled him to import the American architect Joseph Allen Stein to design and build sprawling complexes in the Lodi Estate area, which houses the India International Centre, Ford Foundation, UNICEF, Worldwide Fund for Nature, and the India Habitat Centre.

Other buildings that Stein built in India include the Durgapur township, IIM Kozhikode, Triveni Kala Sangam Arts Centre, and American Embassy School.

We notice the same trait of alien imports during the regime of his daughter, Indira Gandhi. In fact, she outdid her father's Communist addiction by packing her Prime Minister's Office with hardcore Communists. The fact that P.N. Haksar wielded frightening levels of power is well-known, but what is now forgotten is how he directly took orders from the Kremlin. The whispered tales of Soviet suitcases landing directly at her official residence deserve a separate chapter in the recent history of India.

On another front, Prime Minister Indira Gandhi was constantly anxious not to upset her powerful British friends in England. They repaid her affection by arranging a whirlwind, pan-England tour for her in December 1978. The tour had an underlying purpose: England gave Indira Gandhi an international platform to rehabilitate her image, which was in tatters after the Emergency. The personal friends she most trusted were foreigners: the American journalist and photographer Dorothy Norman (wife of Edward A. Norman, the son of an early Sears & Roebuck businessman), Margaret Thatcher, British novelist Barbara Cartland, former Opposition leader of the British Parliament Michael Foot, and Louis 'Dickie' Mountbatten.

Cut to Rajiv Gandhi, and the foreign element takes on a sinister dimension. His wife is an Italian by birth, and her close friend Ottavio Quattrochi was a ubiquitous figure in Rajiv's regime. In those days, it was pretty routine to read news reports and exposes that invariably mentioned the scary clout that Quattrochi's European and American friends exercised in the corridors of South Block. The Bofors scandal was undoubtedly the most horrific manifestation of the extent of foreign penetration into the Indian government.

However, public discourse in India has largely overlooked an equally chilling incident, which is significant on a very sensitive plane: the plane of national self-respect and the morale of our defence forces. This was Rajiv Gandhi's misadventure in Lakshadweep in December 1987. On 26 December, a 17-year-old Rahul Gandhi alighted on the shimmering beach from an orange-white Lakshadweep administration chopper with four of his buddies, all of them in jolly party mode. Funded by the Indian taxpayer. The chopper departed, only to soon return with another fresh batch of his buddies. They joined Rajiv, Sonia, Sonia's mother, their Italian relatives and other foreigner friends, Amitabh Bachchan, and a few others in Rajiv's close circle. The finest brands of alcohol flowed like the luscious waters of the Arabian Sea even as the revellers fattened themselves on the sumptuous food paid, again, by the Indian taxpayer. But the grotesque climax of this abhorrent drama of casual impunity against the Indian citizen was the use of India's premier warship the *INS Viraat* as if it were a private taxi. For 10 full days. Imagine that you're the captain of *INS Viraat*, and you witness this flagrant soirée of entitled dynasts playing out before your own eyes. Imagine serving foreigners who have total access to such a sensitive naval infrastructure—access granted by the prime minister himself. Imagine what that scene does to the morale of your junior officers and seamen.

It is only the fixed deposit of the countless years of the *tapasya* of our Rishis that helped Bharatavarsha survive Rajiv Gandhi.

Cut to Sonia Gandhi, who was widely regarded as the super prime minister during the two terms of the Manmohan Singh government from 2004–14. We observe an entirely new and spooky magnitude of the foreign element in India's government.

If Nehru and Indira Gandhi had Soviet advisors and Italians ran amok in Rajiv Gandhi's tenure, Prime Minister Manmohan Singh was superseded by an unconstitutional and treacherous body called the National Advisory Council (NAC). A random name comes to mind: Jean Dreze. Why was this Belgian—whose name no one had ever heard before—given such disturbing levels of access to the highest offices of the Indian government? Essentially a federated network of anti-India and anti-Hindu NGOs, most members of the NAC have proven links with international breaking-India forces. The damage that this single institution has inflicted upon India has been enormous and irreparable.

Overall, the parallel with the Mughal administrative setup is as clear as daylight. Even if it is unjustified, the Mughals at least had a reason to stuff their administration with foreigners. Islamic kinship and tribalism were tremendous bonding forces in that era. Besides, like all their preceding Muslim rulers, they too realized that tyranny and oppression were the only means to maintain their power in an alien land populated by a majority of Hindus.

What excuse did the Nehru dynasty have?

This brings us to the second parallel.

Parallel 2: Character and Qualifications of the Foreign Elements

What was the basic character, mindset, and motivation of these foreigners who were allowed by the Nehru dynasty to acquire such fearsome power?

For the answer, we turn to the next parallel with the Mughal empire. Once more, Moreland furnishes the answer:

> [Alien Muslims] came to Akbar's Court in search of a career, or at the least a livelihood; if the search was unsuccessful, they

> withdrew, while success meant the attainment of military rank, administrative functions, and remuneration, sometimes in the form of a cash salary, and sometimes by the grant of the whole or a portion of the revenue yielded by a particular area.

Here, the unstated fact is that alien Muslims came into India because one of their own, the Mughal, was ruling in Hindustan. The easiest and shortest route to success was to typically enlist in his army and hope to rise up the ranks. But there were other routes as well.

One of the most popular routes for these alien Muslims to secure a job in the Mughal Empire was to find a patron who would introduce him to the sultan. If the sultan *liked* the candidate, a formal appointment letter was granted. The emphasis is on the word 'like' because there was no test of fitness, and no educational qualification or work experience was sought. No rules were set for increments or promotions, and as Moreland writes, 'everything was based on whim and loyalty and intrigue'.

Mirza Ghiyas Beg presents the most high-profile example of this foetid system. A migrant from Teheran, Ghiyas Beg, contemptuously known as a donkey-seller, came to India with the help of a merchant named Malik Masud. Masud was also a noble in Akbar's court, and he introduced Ghiyas to the sultan. With a combination of chicanery, seasoned flattery, and intrigue, Ghiyas quickly rose to the rank of the *divan* (treasurer) of Kabul. He was also the father of an extremely beautiful daughter named Mehrunnisa, more popularly known as Nur Jahan. He was also the grandfather of Arjumand Bano, alias Mumtaz Mahal. Ghiyas Beg's children inherited his skills at subterfuge and seedy politicking. Most notably, his son Asaf Khan (Jahangir's brother-in-law) and Nur Jahan held Jahangir in their thrall by constantly getting him drunk and drugged on opium. When Asaf Khan died, it was revealed that he was the second wealthiest man in the Mughal Empire only after the sultan.

Although not to the same extent, the Nehru dynasty too sustained its power by creating and nurturing a durbar. The process quite obviously began with Jawaharlal Nehru. His immediate and extended family, relatives, ideological buddies, and his yes-men were unilaterally awarded with plum posts and lucrative business opportunities. Prominent names include Indira Gandhi, Vijayalakshmi Pandit, Krishna Hutheesing, B.M. Kaul, Padmaja Naidu, V.K. Krishna Menon, M.O. Mathai, R.A. Kidwai, the Thapar dynasty, Khushwant Singh, and Jayanti Dharma Teja. While Ghiyas Beg had married off his daughter to Jahangir and his granddaughter to Shah Jahan, the slick talker Jayanti Dharma Teja enveloped Sanjay and Rajiv Gandhi's youthful years akin to a scheming uncle. He sponsored Sanjay's apprenticeship at the Rolls Royce factory in England and entertained Indira Gandhi's sons in palatial French chateaus. He gifted their mother exorbitant mink coats from Moscow.

On her part, Indira Gandhi vastly enlarged this durbar and stuffed it with truly lethal elements. The Emergency gave the nation a full taste of the scale and depth of their villainy. Reading the late journalist Janardhan Thakur's classic *All the Prime Minister's Men* is akin to entering a rogues' gallery populated by Indira Gandhi's courtiers. It is a shocking and frank litany of their misdeeds. The extent to which Bansi Lal, V.C. Shukla, D.K. Barooah, Yashpal, R.K. Dhawan, N.D. Tiwari, Siddharth Shankar Ray, Navin Chawla, Mohammad Yunus, Rukhsana Sultana, and Ambika Soni went evokes disbelief in the minds of the current generation. Except that all of it is true. Although the book has historical value and we're distant from that era, it still is a chilling read for the central message it delivers: of how close we had come to losing our hard-won freedom from colonial rule at the altar of Emergency.

Dhirendra Brahmachari was another courtier who ran a parallel government. Thakur's book characterizes him as 'Indira's Rasputin'. Today, not even a trace of the memory of Dhirendra Brahmachari remains. It is rather hilarious to notice that Google classifies him as a 'teacher'. It was Nehru who invited this charismatic 'teacher' from Bihar to teach Yoga to Indira Gandhi so her health could improve. Dhirendra Brahmachari's ascent was swift. Within a decade, he had emerged as a much-sought-after powerbroker. And for about two decades after that, he became a power centre in his own right. He had bypassed the Indian government by ensnaring the person of the prime minister herself. The Shah Commission report on the Emergency uncovered that he had illegally purchased a Maulle-5 aircraft for private use and had paid for it in US dollars. But the definition of 'private use' is where the real story lies. Of the 213 trips that he had logged till the Janata government seized them, 123 were used for practice sessions. The practitioners were Sanjay and Rajiv Gandhi and Dhirendra Brahmachari. At the peak of his clout, he had carved out a sprawling independent 'Yoga Republic'. It was his private Xanadu, named Aparna Ashram, in Mantalai, Jammu. Spread over 126 acres, it was a deluxe *adda* for every vice on earth. Inside, he had his own airstrip, hangar, zoo, apple orchard, rose garden, vegetable garden, a private swimming pool, and a seven-storey mansion. Cabinet ministers grovelled before him. Bureaucrats courted him. Officials of powerful MNCs kept him in their good books. Weapons dealers were buddies with him. Starting with almost nothing, Dhirendra Brahmachari had built up a colossal empire in a comparatively short period, solely owing to his permanent status as a powerful courtier of the Nehru clan. Does this remind us of Asaf Khan?

After becoming prime minister, Rajiv Gandhi continued the durbar tradition. He packed his court with his Doon School buddies, businessmen friends, assorted elements, and Sonia Gandhi's Italian worthies.

Journalist Tavleen Singh's eponymous book, *Durbar,* is a tell-all, intimate expose of the inner workings of the Rajiv and Sonia durbar. It is the first-hand account of a former inmate of this durbar, and it makes one queasy and disillusioned. Like *All the Prime Minister's Men,* but with lesser intensity, this book too evokes a familiar question within us: exactly what kind of leaders did our people entrust the nation to?

The durbar culture that the Nehru dynasty spawned is also deeply disturbing on a larger political and national canvas. The history of the last seven decades shows how all democratic institutions, rules and procedures were meant only to subserve this durbar.

The same history also reveals that several constitutional amendments were made because the Nehru dynasty found some original provisions pesky. The First Amendment—i.e., curbing the scope of the original Article 19 dealing with freedom of expression—is a classic example of this.

As the discussion so far shows, those who kowtowed to and supported the dynasty were suitably rewarded. However, the durbar culture could not acquire such deep roots, nor could it have had such longevity without first transforming a spiritual civilizational state into a socialist quicksand. Creating a durbar culture simultaneously creates a sprawling ecosystem of middlemen—brokers, fixers, pimps—who sustain it and cocoon the ruler. About six decades ago, the former Communist agent Philip Spratt correctly prophesied the long-term cancerous consequences of the socialist malaise that was injected in the 1955 Avadi Session of the Congress party:

> When the resolution on the socialistic pattern was passed at Avadi, an important Congressman compared it to the Emperor Akbar's Din Ilahi. Socialism, he said, is Nehru's personal fad, which will quickly be forgotten when he passes from the scene. It seemed a shrewd judgement at the time, *but it overlooked the attraction of socialism for a ruling party of hungry careerists.* (Emphasis added)

The licence-quota raj, which flourished after this session, is polite-speak for a well-oiled and ruthless system of fixers who paralyzed the economy for private profit.

Which brings us to the third parallel.

Parallel 3: An Administration of Flunkeys

The third and the final parallel between the Mughal and Nehru dynasties belongs to the realm of administration. It is here that the poisonous flower opens its petals in full bloom. The nucleus is the dynasty, and the petals are the dynasty's protection. This is as far as the analogy takes us. In the Mughal and Nehru dynasties' schemes of things, the petals are attached but can be replaced, detached, or re-attached based on whim, cunning, ruthlessness, utility, servility, and dispensability.

Under the Mughal dispensation, the sultan was heir to his officers at all levels. In practical terms, this meant that official positions and the fortunes derived therefrom could not be passed on generationally. For example, a *Mansabdar*'s son could not automatically become a Mansabdar after his father's death. And the father's death could occur for any reason, ranging from rebellion, embezzlement, or even beaming a wrong glance at the sultan. The Mansabdar would then be stripped of his rank, and his whole family would be literally thrown on the streets—

his wives would become slaves and servants overnight and his children would be blinded, sold, or slaughtered. But if the mansabdar somehow managed to remain unharmed and died peacefully, and the sultan recognized his service, life would be slightly better for his progeny. In Moreland's words, 'the most that could be hoped for was that enough would be left for the maintenance of the family, and that the sons would be given a start in consideration of the father's services'.

The Nehru dynasty followed a modified version of this system. If we dig out the media and scholarly archives for about six decades, several common themes emerge. One notable theme is the manner in which civil servants of varying seniorities were made to 'disappear'. Likewise, judges who went against Indira Gandhi during the Emergency were superseded, harassed, and punished in creative ways.

On the other side, pliant and loyal bureaucrats and judges were guaranteed generational rewards. The case of notorious Chief Justice A.N. Ray is a study in judicial infamy. At the height of his sycophancy, he would frequently telephone Indira Gandhi's personal secretary to 'seek advice' even on mundane matters. It appears that he had literally followed Indira Gandhi's explicit demand for a 'committed judiciary'. That precedent has ever since grown into a hydra-headed monster.

Now we come to administration proper. The first element in this area was economic administration.

One of the singular features of Akbar's revenue administration was the minuteness of the organization he maintained. To a large extent, credit for envisioning and implementing this system should ideally go to Raja Todarmal and Birbal. Everything in his empire that had the potential to yield money was identified and milked dry.

The only parallel to this Akbaresque system in recent history is Indira Gandhi's administration. In the late 1970s, a former chief minister of Karnataka was once questioned by the media about his role in officializing corruption in the state. His answer: 'I am helpless. That woman [Indira Gandhi] in Delhi knows the minute details of every ministry and department and the exact amount that she could squeeze from each for "party funds".'

The other similarity in the realm of economic administration is perhaps one of the most corrosive forms of oppression. In the Mughal Empire, administrative position and influence primarily emanated from landholding. The sultan typically distributed *jagirs* of various sizes to his bureaucrats. They in turn had to deposit a fixed sum from the revenue yielded by the jagir into the empire's treasury. However, an officer possessing even a large jagir could deposit a small sum simply because the land itself would not yield much. There is ample evidence to show that murders and intrigues were rife among bureaucrats vying for lucrative jagirs. In plain language, a fertile jagir was akin to a lifetime income guarantee scheme. The bureaucrat had to simply secure his position for life and do no other work.

Such a system obviously birthed and sustained corruption and oppression on an industrial scale. Bureaucrats routinely sent false accounts of revenue to the Mughal treasury. The fraud began right at the time of the allotment of the jagirs. Those who sought profitable jagirs first 'booked' a powerful courtier in Agra and got their allotment. The courtier would then receive a perpetual cut from the revenue that the *jagirdar* concealed from the sultan.

The Nehruvian similarities in this area are eerie. The socialist system that Nehru birthed and further strengthened after the Avadi Session created a nationwide ecosystem of fixers and brokers; these were the real engines that ran the government.

This ugly reality was affirmed by Rajiv Gandhi's famous admission that only 15 paisa in every rupee allocated by the government reached the common man. For decades, there was a broker at every level, from deciding ministerial berths down to the appointment of the last clerk.

Which brings us to the next similarity.

In 1611, William Hawkins, a high official of the East India Company, was appointed as a commander of 400 directly by Jahangir. This powerful position also got him the prized jagir of Lahore. Jahangir's courtiers were naturally inflamed. In his *Voyages,* Hawkins narrates his extremely bitter experiences with Jahangir's crafty *Vazir*: '[The Vazir] continually put me off with grants in places where outlaws reigned, and when I was given a *jagir* at Lahore, I was soon deprived of it on some pretext.'

This mirrors the sort of bureaucracy that the Nehru dynasty created. There are copious real-life stories of how this system worked in which corrupt *babus* ganged up against an honest officer (or someone who was outside their closed clique), made his life miserable, and eventually drove him out.

In order to flesh out this point in greater detail, we can look at Moreland's description of Akbar's *babudom*:

> In order to rise, an officer needed readiness of speech, plausibility, and the capacity for carrying on, or at least withstanding intrigue.... Akbar, like other rulers, was surrounded by men of this type. They preferred to remain at Court, and a province or a jagir served mainly to replenish their resources; *they were less concerned to promote the prosperity of their charges than to keep things quiet, to see that complaints did not reach the Emperor's ears, and meanwhile to amass, or to spend, as much wealth as could be collected under these conditions.* (Emphasis added)

Replace 'Akbar' with the Nehru clan and 'men of this type' with, say, the 'Lutyens gang', or the 'Khan Market gang', in the foregoing description and see how it fits perfectly like a glove. The history of the last seven decades proves this point.

The unscrupulous system of postings and transfers, the auctioning of bureaucratic positions, the brazen trading of official favours that used to routinely occur in the closed clubs of Delhi—these are the Nehruvian equivalents of the Mughal administrative system described by Moreland, Hawkins, and others. If journalists could lobby for ministerial appointments and act as scribes for various Congress-friendly lobbies, how different is it from the Mughal system described so far? There is a historical reason why such tremendous furore erupted from the entitled, legacy Nehruvian courtiers when the Narendra Modi government cracked down on the Delhi Gymkhana Club in 2020.

Moreland's other characterization of the Mughal courtiers is also worth exploring further: 'They preferred to remain at Court, and a province or a jagir served mainly to replenish their resources.' Several variants of the Nehruvian durbar's courtiers and their extended families belong to this category.

The first included the powerful office-bearers of the Congress party who held no constitutional position. Stories are legion of the frightening clout that they wielded both on the government and the party. In the journalistic annals chronicling Indira Gandhi's regime, such office-bearers were described variously as '[fund] collectors' and 'executioners'.

The second included influential civil servants who remained permanently anchored in Delhi and acted as the Nehru dynasty's water carriers and trouble-shooters. Some were even adept at image management—dropping hints to friendly media and sending hostile feelers to unfriendly media.

To understand the third category, we need to return to Jahangir's sultanate. Unlike Akbar, Jahangir believed in frequent transfers of his officials. But in practice, this translated into increased exploitation of the people by the transferred officials: make hay while the sun shines because the official didn't know how long his tenure would last in a particular jagir. Thus, if the Nehruvian bureaucrat accidentally landed a 'plum posting' and was uncertain of his longevity there, he would loot on a far more epic scale than his predecessor.

The fourth and final category in the Mughal administration was a generic post titled *Ahadis*. The Sultan or his immediate family chose Ahadis with great care and caution. They were essentially positions of extreme trust. Some Ahadis managed the Sultan's gigantic household. Some guarded the harem; others took care of provisions, fruits and vegetables; some accoutred the Sultan and his family members; others guarded his archives; and the most trustworthy of them took care of the kitchen. The name Pratibha Patil instantly comes to mind in this context. To the nation's eternal disgrace, she was *gifted* India's presidency by a grateful Sonia Gandhi in recognition of her long years of culinary service.

Arguably, the worst parallel between the Mughal and the Nehru dynasties is the manner in which both ran India aground, chiefly through maladministration. Moreland once again gives us a tragic but lucid and accurate assessment:

> [T]hese officers administered the [Mughal] Empire, and the fortunes of the masses … were in their hands. The questions of real economic importance regarding the great men of the Empire, and indeed of India taken as a whole, concern the many rather than the few. *What qualities were brought out among the successful officers by the system which has been described? Could*

> *it be counted on to produce administrators who would have the good of the people at heart, or did it tend to equip the country with exploiters rather than cherishers of the poor?* (Emphasis added)

For just a sliver of the answer to Moreland's question, we can take a random incident that occurred in April 2021. A haughty IAS officer barged into a wedding in Tripura and physically vandalized the venue, thrashed the marriage party, and behaved in a manner that shames even hardened goons. He is a creature of the oppressive Nehruvian bureaucracy. He is the contemporary equivalent of the *Subedars*, Mansabdars, Jahgirdars, and *Qazis* who inspired pure terror among the populace in the Mughal period.

Epilogue

The deeper we dig, the more odious the parallels. The sheer volume of available historical material is enough to compile a comprehensive research work showing how the Nehru dynasty inherited the worst elements of the Mughal dynasty and oppressed Indians in an era of freedom far more effectively than centuries of foreign rule had ever done.

13

Bengali Arrack and Bouleponge in the 17th-Century Mughal Empire

Jahangir, Roe, and Beer

Thomas Roe, the artful Britsh ambassador in Jahangir's court, did not take a long time to ensnare the Mughals' affections. It owed it to a rather spiritual reason. One of the hinges upon which the art of diplomacy rests is the diplomat's acuity in grasping the vices of his target. With Jahangir, it was liquor. Rivers of it. Which Roe brought to his court and his *ghusal-khana*. An incessant supply of red wine conquered Jahangir, whose name literally means 'world conqueror'. Roe then tutored the Badshah in the subject titled, 'What beere (beer) was? How made?' On his part, the Mughal joyously allowed himself to be coached in the fine art of brewing British beer. Swimming happily in this sea of alien spirits, Jahangir gave permission to the East India Company to open a factory in Surat. It would be blessed and protected by the Mughal Empire.

Jahangir was not the first, nor would he be the last of the Sultan-sized alcoholics who are ubiquitous in the annals of the Muslim history of India. He was an epic representative and an inheritor of this drunken tradition dating back almost to the history of Islam itself, notwithstanding its doctrinaire prohibition against liquor. In fact, unhinged binge drinking is one of the most prominent markers of the Muslim history of mediaeval India. The sultans swam in these perfervid, spirituous waters. Their cupbearers, politely known as the nobility, were also their uninhibited playmates. The alcohol and aphrodisiac industries constituted the two major economic engines of Muslim empires in India, especially the Mughal Empire.

In Jahangir's time, the alcohol industry had exploded into epidemic proportions, a fact recorded by all the early European travellers and businessmen who had trickled into India. Their forays, too, had seedy and unflattering sides. Boorish manners, rowdy behaviour, Christian fanaticism, morbid drunkenness, and an unhygienic lifestyle topped the list. They introduced a shocking range of deadly venereal and other diseases into India.

Much before Jahangir took over the throne in Agra, the Portuguese had devastated Malabar, and their Christian inquisition had reduced Gomantaka into a wasteland populated by thousands of Hindu dead bodies and shattered temples. The Dutch had also made impressive inroads in areas as widespread as Bengal, Cholamandalam, Malabar, Surat, and Sri Lanka. The British and the French joined this Indian party slightly later.

Without exception, all these European actors left behind copious and extravagant records of their experiences in India. With India and Indians.

Broadly speaking, these records cover three major commercial theatres of that era, which were fabled for their wealth and business activity: Bengal, Machilipatnam, and Surat. Bengal and Surat, especially, were in the thrall of the Mughal Empire. These European chronicles, travelogues, reminiscences, and even official reports vividly describe life in these thriving regions. The dominant feature of this life was something known as the Muslim social culture. While ambassadors like Thomas Roe describe the sociopolitical, economic, and geographical details, lower-ranking officials, captains of ships, merchants, solo adventurers, and missionaries supply supplementary details that are raw, earthy, and eye-opening. Overall, the whole corpus reveals a rather comprehensive panorama of what Indian society had become under Mughal rule.

Heart of Darkness

This essay has selected just one pixel from the foregoing panorama for the briefest examination: the sprawling liquor industry.

The European side of these chronicles should also be weighed uniformly because they unwittingly but clearly betray information about the sort of human vermin that sailed on these occidental ships.

The lowest-ranking seamen and deckhands were dregs of their native societies. Their lifestyle included bawdy behaviour, manic alcoholism, rampant whoring, deranged violence, and street hooliganism. Their captains typically exhibited a willful blindness towards this criminality but stepped in to whip them into submission only when these excesses became intolerably excessive. Punishment was meted out as a last resort. Punishment was given because the criminality hurt business. Punishment had its cynical genesis in money, not conscience. Joseph Conrad's acclaimed literary classic, *Heart of Darkness*, is perhaps the most brutal and also the most accurate depiction of this conscience-free colonial plunder, whose inseparable accomplice was wanton mass murder.

Muslim Society during Mughal Rule

The middle and upper echelons manning the European ships naturally interacted with their counterparts in the Muslim society of the Mughal Empire. Their experiences with this society made them want more of it.

Then there were the pious chroniclers as well. For much of its history, it was mandatory for every vessel of the East India Company to have a chaplain on board. Accordingly, a ship named *Benjamin* that sailed from Gravesend, England, in the late 17th century carried a chaplain named Ovington, who travelled extensively in Western India. The following is a slice of his eyewitness account of the typical behaviour of the upper-class Muslim society of the Mughal period:

> [T]he Mahometan Principles indulge an extraordinary Liberty [in the matters of] Women, [they] strictly prohibit the tasting of . . . Liquor. The Moors [Muslims] here, as in other Kingdoms, practise the Use of Concubines, according as their Fortunes and Abilities can reach . . *they fancy not only an impunity to themselves, but something of Merit, by propagating the number and increase of the Faithful.*
>
> ...
>
> In the Families of Men of Fortune and Estates, some, ... notwithstanding their prophet, thro' whose prohibition they are restrain'd from wine, will yet privately be as licentious therein... and many of them take the liberty of mixing dutra [dattura] and water together to drink, without any privacy or fear, which will intoxicate almost to madness, when they gulp it freely; and this sometimes puts them beyond their Native tender Deportment, and forces them upon suddain [sudden] Bold Attempts. 'Tis commonly observ'd concerning this Herb Dutra [Dattura], that whatever Humour [temperament or emotion] prevails in any person at the time of his drinking it to Excess, that Temper continues with him in the highest pitch, 'till the inebriating quality abates. If he is Melancholy, he is then rais'd to the utmost degree of Sadness; If Amorous, he is all Love and Flame. (Emphasis added)

When the European guests of these wealthy Muslim elites had their first taste of this depraved enjoyment, they found it similarly addictive and simply couldn't get enough of it. They quaffed down generous draughts of this Dattura-induced intoxicant and indulged in identical behaviour. Ovington, the pious chaplain, writes in an alarmed but restrained tone:

> The English and other Europeans sometimes in their pleasant Frolicks, are pleased to divert themselves with these gay Humours and strange Actions, by taking a cheerful [cheerful] Draught or two of this Liquor.

But this drink stood no chance before the mother of them all: the fabled Bengali Arrack (spelled in the primary European sources as Arak, Arac). It was the absolute monarch of alcohol in the Mughal Empire. Its Goan cousin stood on a slightly lower rung on the ladder, which led to arrack suzerainty.

Bengali Arrack and Bouleponge

European travellers, including Ovington, describe how the said Bengali arrack was made: it was distilled from rice and sometimes from toddy, 'the juice of a tree'. But there was a more potent variant of the Bengali arrack. This was a compound liquor prepared by distilling black sugar mixed with water. Large chunks of the bark of the Babul tree were then added to this liquid and stirred continuously before it was finally distilled. It was known locally as Jagrey Arak (Jaggery Arrack). This formidable potion was drunk by Europeans in the quantity of what is today known as a 'shot'. And they were permanently hooked.

Indeed, Bengali arrack captured the European imagination like a tsunami, and they began making creative experiments with it. An august variety of innovative and new brews burst onto the scene in a rather short span. The indisputable leader of these brews was something known as Bouleponge, a head-spinning concoction composed of Bengali arrack, molasses, and nutmeg mixed with lemon juice and water. The drink Bouleponge is the Dutch word for punch (as in rum punch). The word actually signified an utensil in which this vinous liquid was brewed, and the drink was named after the utensil. Interestingly, *bowle* is still the German word for punch.

Bernier on Bouleponge

In the latter half of the 17th century, the famed French traveller and physician Francois Bernier witnessed the devastation that Bouleponge had wreaked in Balasore and its surrounding regions in Bengal.

The second Anglo-Dutch war had erupted in Europe, and its outcome in Bengal witnessed the complete halt of both Dutch and British fleets in the Bay of Bengal. Their respective, jobless crews dived into barrels of Bouleponge and began to die like flies. When the war was over after a year, the dismayed captains of the ships found that they were 'unable to put their vessels to sea'. There was simply not enough crew strength. And so, the captains were forced to bring them into obedience and discipline by passing the following strict orders:

Crew members should henceforth drink less punch/ Bouleponge

A blanket ban on visiting whorehouses, which had resulted in a calamitous outbreak of venereal diseases

Complete prohibition on getting daily supplies of Indian tobacco from local dealers

A total clampdown on drinking Bengali arac

Bernier declares his verdict on Bouleponge: '[I]t is pleasant enough to the taste, but most hurtful to body and health.'

Despite this, the Bengali arrack maintained its supreme reputation for almost more than half a millennium. This was thanks to the sprawling alcohol addiction of the Sultans and their Subedars, Manasbadars, amirs, and other nobles.

Toddy

The next drink measured in terms of its popularity and potency was the ubiquitous toddy. In Ovington's words, this is 'Palm-tree Juice, which the Moors as well as Europeans drink plentifully'. He testifies to its power as follows: '[I]t is so strong that that it turns the Brain immediately.' He also expresses some compassion for the European sailors who have no option but to drink it because 'no Malt drink is made in India'. In the same breath, Ovington sketches a rather coarse picture of what toddy did to these low-rung European sailors:

> Several Europeans pay [with] their Lives for their immoderate Draughts, and too frankly Carousing these chearful [cheerful] Liquors, with which *when once they are inflam'd, it renders them so restless and unruly that . . . they fancy no place can prove too cool, and so throw themselves upon the ground, where they sleep all Night in the open Fields,* and this commonly produces a Flux, of which a multitude die. [Emphasis added]

Flux was the word for diarrhoea or dysentery.

Closing Notes

Clearly, the foregoing narrative unravelled itself when just one pixel of the sweeping historical panorama of the 17th-century

Mughal Empire and European trading incursions into India was investigated. It is also an insightful revelation.

On the Indian side, it is a sure shot testimony to the historical truth that the Mughal Empire was primarily a force for India's downfall and for the disintegration of its society spread over an incredibly large geography.

On the European side, it unambiguously demonstrates the uncivilized and unscrupulous character of a people who eventually began to define and teach us civilization, culture, manners, and even the proper method of eating food.

14

The Sanatana Conception of Skin Colour and the Unresolved Problem of Racism

William Blake's *The Little Black Boy* is still an important poem for historical, cultural, social, political, and religious reasons. A general assessment of the poem shows that it was Blake's attempt at course correction, in a way. Its historical context is also significant—it was written by a White Englishman at a time when skin colour-based racial supremacy and discrimination were peaking.

Blake's poem ostensibly talks about the futility of discriminating against people based on skin colour, but its underlying theme is the beneficence of the 'Male Christian God' because as the Black boy in the poem says:

> When I from black and he from white cloud free,
> And round the tent of God like lambs we joy.

It is clear that the poet feels for the Black boy. Yet he doesn't forget to assert the fact that the White English boy, who is the master (race), is condescending to 'love' the Black boy. The last two lines of this pathetic poem hammer home this point. It is the sorry lot of the poor Black boy to 'shade' the White boy.

from the heat till he can bear,
To lean in joy upon our father's knee.
And then I'll stand and stroke his silver hair,
And be like him and he will then love me.

The last line is chilling: 'And be like him and he will then love me.' Blake's macabre poem is one of the more egregious literary proofs demonstrating the Biblical origins of white racism. Its greatest success happens to be the generationally deracinated Hindus who continue to seek approval from the White man, desperately trying to be like the White man so that 'he will love me'.

But this phenomenon goes far beyond the spiritual and cultural detritus caused by the psychological grip imposed by racism. It has led to genocides across the globe, and we can leave it at that.

Every country and culture has historically taken pride in what it regards as its highest ideals and values, which in turn shape its civilization and culture. By this yardstick and going by the verdict of history, it is reasonable to conclude that skin colour was the highest civilizational and cultural 'ideal' that the White race could take pride in for more than three centuries. Indeed, this pride has made a perverse, backdoor entry into India. The phenomenal sales of skin-lightening products reveal more than the Black colour that they supposedly conceal. This insane rush to out-white the White skin has accelerated after independence. Our cultural downfall couldn't have been swifter or more tragic. Almost every chronicle and travelogue written by Europeans makes this uniform observation about the unanimous Indian attitude towards White skin—we associated White skin with a specific ailment. *Leprosy.*

Which brings us to the crux of this essay: how important was skin colour in ancient Indian thought and culture?

The answer: zero. Here, it is important to take a wholesome view rather than a reductionist or isolationist view of the subject.

The notion of associating colour with specific human traits such as good and evil holds negligible or no significance in the Sanatana philosophical framework. The Hindu *Darshanic* system has no place for a rather juvenile question that continues to vex Western minds: the so-called 'problem' of eternal evil. In the Vedantic view, both good and evil are seen as emanating from the same source. They are two sides of the same coin. The so-called problem of evil is merely another expression of an immature mind. It is the consequence of looking at the world from a *Dvandva* (duality, separatist) perspective. The famous story of Prahlada illustrates this best. When his wicked father, Hiranyakashyipu, asks him to show Vishnu, Prahlada confidently says, '[H]e's within you; I seek him through love while you seek him through hatred.' The backstory to Hiranyakashyipu's hatred for Vishnu is both instructive and logical. He is originally Jaya, the former gatekeeper of Vishnu's abode, Vaikunta. Jaya's arrogance, which stems from his proximity to Vishnu, begets a curse from the Rishis. He falls into the evil realms and is born as an Asura, a demon. This birth is his atonement. The force that reunites him with Vishnu is his own son, Prahlada. This extraordinary story works on multiple layers and has made it immortal. We can also analyse this story from a mundane perspective: evil corrupts good, and the harder it fights with good, it ultimately becomes good. The source of evil lies within us, in the *ariśaḍvargas*—the 'Six Deadly Enemies', namely *kāma* (lust), *krodha* (anger), *lobha* (avarice), *moha* (possessiveness), *mada* (arrogance), and *mātsarya* (jealousy).

Thus, when we understand skin colour-based racism from this philosophical standpoint, it becomes clear that using mere *colours* like black and white to denote behavioural and cultural attributes is a product of the same ariśaḍvargas. In other words, racism is the outcome of ariśaḍvargas systematized by an inferior culture and imposed upon other cultures through the brute force of arms. The outcome of dispassionate argument and serene deliberation leads to acceptance, not strife. This is the method of the Hindu debating traditions of śāstrārthas and *vākyārthas.*

In several of his essays in *The Dance of Shiva,* Ananda Coomaraswamy severely condemns Western critics of Indian art for holding the ill-informed view that Indian sculptures were not artistic because they were dark, black, had 'many arms' and therefore were 'hideous and grotesque'. A major element in this pseudo-criticism emanated from the Western prejudice of associating black with evil. We can also consider the famous phrase 'black magic', a Christian concept, which has wholly evil connotations.

But to be more specific, there is not a single text in the whole corpus of Sanatana literature that inherently treats the colour black as evil or inauspicious. There is ample evidence to the contrary.

Why Bhagavan Veda Vyasa or Valmiki Maharshi chose to portray Rama, Krishna, Draupadi, Arjuna, and Hanuman in their respective colours is best known to them, but it certainly has nothing to do with the superiority of their skin colour.

The fact that the word 'Krishna' means 'black' is common knowledge. It is derived from the Sanskrit root *Krush*, which means 'to attract', 'to rub', etc. The word ākarṣaṇa or attraction is also derived from the same root. Its other meaning is the colour black. Therefore, the word Krishna means one who attracts, one who is capable of attracting, and so on. Clearly, the Mahabharata, the Bhagavata, and the Puranic lore perfectly delineate this fundamental character of Krishna: there was none who escaped his charms.

The literal meaning of the word 'Arjuna' is 'white', 'clear', 'of the lightning', 'of milk', etc. One of Arjuna's 10 names also happens to be Krishna, which is an apparent contradiction. But the contradiction is resolved when we go beyond stifling and superficial notions of colour. Thus, when we recall the aforementioned root, *Krush,* we see that Arjuna is described as an extremely handsome and attractive man, i.e., ākarṣaka. Hence the synonym, 'Krishna' for Arjuna, too.

Interpreted purely in terms of skin colour, the contrast here is rather interesting and profound. 'Black' and 'White' are placed side-by-side. They are close friends and confidants. They are master and pupil. Krishna, the master, shows his pupil a cosmic vision of himself, and the pupil realizes that all contradictions are merely allegations and emanate from the embodiment of divinity that is Sri Krishna. He realizes too that all of Creation itself is nothing but *kṛṣṇa-līlā*, the cosmic sport of Sri Krishna. This is the core philosophical strength that forged the Hindu civilization and its cultural and social values. This strength is why Hindu society finds it easy to synthesize apparent dichotomies. It is also why we subconsciously detect perfect order amidst seeming chaos. It is also the secret of our astounding survival and periodic renewal in spite of the unimaginable trauma that we have undergone.

And this is exactly the opposite of Western thought, which regards black and white as eternal, irreconcilable foes—*colour*, of all things! But let's accept this childish point for a moment and see what emerges.

Black also has connotations of mystery, which again is entirely consistent with the conception of the character of Sri Krishna in the Mahabharata. His words and deeds appear rather mysterious and inexplicable, but they always culminate in upholding

Dharma. But tom the *tamasic* minds of the West—the most recent example is Wendy Doniger—Krishna is an evil character because he gave us the Bhagavad Gita, a book that, in her view, is a manual of war.

Basic laws of physics also serve to illustrate our point further. White disperses colours, while all colours merge themselves into black. Sri Krishna, as the human incarnation of the 'Eternal Cosmic Consciousness' symbolizes this black. In his life, which is an unfurling of a cosmic play of his own authoring, Sri Krishna showed the cosmos to two people: his foster mother Yashoda and his friend and disciple, Arjuna.

However, the Christian God is a jealous male inaccessible even to his own son, Jesus Christ. He is an object to be feared. His alleged commandments infuse pure terror in the hearts of his own followers. Sri Krishna can be our friend or our foe, but he is always accessible. And what applies to Sri Krishna is also applicable to Shiva, who too is portrayed as having dark-coloured skin. Or to *Kāḻi*, the feminine aspect of the same cosmic reality.

'Black' and 'dark' are fundamentally two different things. The West continues to advertise its philosophical darkness by associating it with a mere colour. The birth and popularity of a dangerous organization called 'Black Lives Matter' in the United States hold an important lesson for us. It is the outcome of the historical phenomenon of colonial racism, which remains unresolved. Government legislation like affirmative action has taken American society only so far because the roots of racism have not been fully eradicated. In the case of racism, the roots lie in mada or arrogance or what is known as the superiority complex. Unfortunately, neither the Christian doctrine nor the post-Christian intellectual tradition of the West has the philosophical solution to overcome this malaise.

15

Sri Chamarajendra Vedaratnamala: The Immortal Garland of Sacred Sanatana Literature

— 1 –

Vijayanagara, the indomitable Hindu fortress in southern India, was founded on a simple but brawny vow: never again shall another Malik Kafur or Muhammad bin Tughlaq defile our temples and our women and slaughter the sacred cow. It was a sacred *Sankalpa* that the entire Hindu society made for itself. To discharge this vow, the empire was organized as a highly militarized state for two reasons. One, because it was the need of the hour. Two, because the genius of its founders realized that only valour can safeguard virtue, i.e., Kshatra protects Dharma. In fact, the Vijayanagara Empire can be likened to the Great Hindu Wall of South India. In a series of brilliant essays, Vidvan Rallapalli Anantakrishna Sarma brings alive the climate of Vijayanagara during the regime of Sri Krishnadevaraya. Just as we casually discuss the latest movies and books in coffee shops and restaurants, the people of Vijayanagara passionately discussed the prowess of various wrestlers in the city and the valour of fabled generals and commanders in the empire.

The Vijayanagara Empire was in fact the *last* great empire embodying the classical Sanatana Renaissance in an all-encompassing sense. It produced little if any original work matching the standard of, say, the Gupta period because its focus was renewal, rejuvenation, and preservation. We observe this signature in all its small and great endeavours and accomplishments—in art, painting, prose, poetry, drama, sculpture, temple-building, social structures, and the economic system. The emphasis throughout was on maintaining continuity. In the devastating circumstances in which the Vijayanagara Empire arose, the continuity of centuries of tradition was what gave it the moral authority to rule with an iron fist for so long.

Nowhere is this stamp of rejuvenation and preservation more pronounced than in its immortal service towards reinvigorating the very foundation of Sanatana Dharma—the vast corpus of its Vedic lore. The empire's service in this realm is truly epochal and unrepeatable. Its roots can be traced to the vision of Vidyāraṇya Swami, the spiritual inspiration behind the Vijayanagara Empire. However, the lion's share of credit for fulfilling it goes to his talented younger brother, Sāyaṇācārya. The great monarch who supplied the resources and the steely protection necessary for such a mammoth endeavour was Bukkaraya. He deservedly shares equal credit for its success.

The incredible brother-duo assembled an extraordinary team of the topmost Veda vidvāns in the Vijayanagara Empire and undammed the Tungabhadran flood of spiritual energy and scholarship required for this mammoth aeon of Sanatana renewal at its most foundational level. The final result of this prolonged churning was the nectar named *Vedārthaprakāśa*, popularly known as *Sāyaṇā-bhāṣya*, or Sāyaṇācārya's commentary on the Vedas. In the words of a cultural treasure of our own time, Shatavadhani Dr Ganesh,

> *The Vedārthaprakāśa was the highest summit of Hindu achievements in the medieval period.* The commentary encompasses all the four divisions of all the four Vedas leaving not a single word unexplained. This majestic feat is truly *na bhūto na bhaviṣyati*—never before, never since.... When we recall the fact that *apart from Sāyaṇācārya, no one till date has written another commentary on all the four Vedas without missing a single syllable, we immediately realize the immeasurable value of Vedārthaprakāśa.* The work was the very crux of the Vijayanagara Empire. (Emphases added)

Truer words were never spoken. Indeed, the *Vedārthaprakāśa* has become the undisputed and de facto authority for *unambiguously* realizing the secret of the Veda.

—2—

Five hundred years later and in vastly altered circumstances, another Hindu kingdom was helplessly facing the democratic axe of dharmic extinction. Weakly perched on the last legs of its very existence, it attempted a similar endeavour driven by the same Vidyāraṇyan vision. This was the Hindu Kingdom of Mysore, which had become independent after the fall of the Vijayanagara Empire but retained its ancestral umbilical cord of culture and tradition.

Its last illustrious ruler, Maharaja Jayachamarajendra Wodeyar ascended the royal throne in 1940. It was an era of rapid, alarming, and multipronged erosion of Sanatana Dharma. The Hindu community across the globe owes an unrepayable debt of gratitude for his singular service to Dharma in both quality and volume, given his short-lived tenure as maharaja.

The contrasting irony can't be crueller: while Sāyaṇācārya envisioned, authored, and completed the Vedārthaprakāśa and decisively asserted the revival of Sanatana Dharma, Jayachamarajendra Wodeyar attempted to preserve Sāyaṇācārya's legacy in a desperate era when India was in a vulgar haste to embrace the political system of her colonial oppressor. Sāyaṇācārya was successful because he had combined within himself the best qualities of Brāhma and Kshatra. Plus, the Hindu civilizational climate in his time pulsated with this warrior-spirit. Hindus of his period were tightly fused into a society—different organs of the same body, multicoloured threads of the same fabric. However, in Jayachamarajendra Wodeyar's time, each organ of this Hindu body was rebelling against the others, chasing the illusion of an independent body for itself. Kshatra was scattered, and Brāhma had eroded almost to the point of no return. Thus, we need to exercise caution before blindly extolling the sort of democracy we have adopted. It has come at the cost of Brāhma, Kshatra, and Dharma. So, whenever we read and hear things like the 'festival of democracy', we need to recall the fact that celebrating this festival is akin to celebrating the loss of Dharma.

Maharaja Jayachamarajendra Wodeyar's punctilious attempt at preserving Sāyaṇācārya's legacy was the first and the last of its kind done anywhere in the world at that time. After more than seven decades, it remains unreplicated and unsurpassed and will be so, perhaps for all time. In its underlying ideal, impulse, and inspiration, it compares favourably with Sāyaṇācārya's feat because, for those who are sincerely interested in the pursuit of Vedic education today, Jayachamarajendra Wodeyar's bequest is still the lifeboat they must depend on.

This bequest is the majestic 36 volumes of the *Rg Veda Samhita* published under the auspices of the Jayachamarajendra Vedaratnamālā (literally, 'Garland of Vedic Pearls'), a division of the Jayachamarajendra Granthamālā (literally, 'Garland of Books') publications.

Consistent with the Vedic spirit, it was envisioned not as a publishing endeavour but as a *Kratu,* a sacred yajna. After just seven years, it bore the *yajna-phala* (fruit of the yajna): 36 volumes exceeding 25,000 pages.

It couldn't have been otherwise because Maharaja Jayachamarajendra Wodeyar was the last great inheritor of the Vijayanagara legacy to occupy the ruler's throne of the Hindu Kingdom of Mysore. A throne that was later lustily usurped by the Gandhian opportunists of the Congress party. Ever since, Tipu Sultan's proxy lineage, disguised as Congressmen who bear Hindu names, has had a field day.

This essay narrates the story of Maharaja Jayachamarajendra Wodeyar's aforementioned yajnạ. It is the story of the making of the Jayachamarajendra Vedaratnamālā.

— 3 —

In a manner of speaking, the story of the Jayachamarajendra Vedaratnamālā is as transcendental and timeless as Bharatavarsha itself. Its foundation is the throbbing of the ages. Its origins are traceable to the qualifications for a king prescribed in the Dharmasastra and Rajyasastra corpus. Only Bharatavarsha regards the Rajyasastra as a Dharmasastra. To be more accurate, Rajyasastra is a subordinate or subset of Dharmasastra. A prime qualification prescribed for a ruler was the primacy placed on broad and deep learning, wide experience, and wise counsel. The contrast cannot be underemphasized: the mark of a powerful sultan was measured by the mountains of infidel skulls that he had piled up; the distinction of an enlightened maharaja was measured by the number of scholars, poets, and sages his court attracted. The word 'enlightened' is conspicuously absent in almost all Muslim rulers of India.

The Wodeyar dynasty, for most of its existence, remained anchored to this *Rajya-Sastric* dictum. Purely in the context of this essay, we can trace this precedent to the cultural renewal that was inaugurated by Krishnaraja Wodeyar III in the first half of the 19th century.

A few years after Krishnaraja Wodeyar III ascended the throne, the British snatched the political and administrative reins from him, essentially neutralizing his power. But instead of lapsing into depression and self-pity, this noble Wodeyar regarded the loss of political power as a profound opportunity and unleashed a wave of Sanatana cultural renaissance. Art, painting, literature, music, dance, and sacred learning were central to this enterprise.

All his successors, including Jayachamarajendra Wodeyar, dutifully beautified and built upon the edifice of this cultural revolution. It acquired an especial resplendence during the refined tenure of the *Rajarshi,* Krishnaraja Wodeyar IV, the predecessor of Jayachamarajendra Wodeyar. The golden age of Kannada learning, language, scholarship, and literature that began at the start of the 20th century witnessed its most enduring and prolific outpouring during this rajarshi's regime. It was clearly not a coincidental phenomenon.

Thus, Jayachamarajendra Wodeyar's immemorial service in the form of the Vedaratnamala was the uninterrupted Gangetic transmission of this Sanatana-duty-bound DNA.

— 4 —

However, when he ascended to the endangered throne of the Mysore Kingdom in 1940, the Vedaratnamala initiative was nowhere on the horizon. It was awaiting a Sankalpa, and it came from the visionary penance of, befittingly, a Sanyasi.

His name was Shilpa Siddhanti Shivayogi Sri Siddhalinga Swami, the Jagadguru of the Nagalinga Maṭha.

Over a considerable period, the Nagalinga Maṭha shared a close bond with the Wodeyar family. But now, in a climate of tumultuous political uncertainty, Jayachamarajendra Wodeyar consulted him for solace, peace, and solution. At the end of one of the meetings, the Swami said: no matter what the womb of the future holds, the regime of Your Highness will become truly immortal if he translates the entire corpus of the sacred Vedas along with its correct meaning and offers it to the public.

This was not just a piece of advice or suggestion, but an *Upadesha,* a sacred discourse. The following is the gist of his Upadesha.

> The Veda is the bedrock of every philosophical school and sect that ever arose in Bharatavarsha. If Dharma has to be truly rejuvenated in the contemporary age, it must recover its base, which unarguably, is the Veda. Only then will national progress occur in its real sense. The Veda is the kernel from which the ruler will derive the authority to turn the minds of his people away from Adharma and inculcate in them the lesson that Dharma is real national service. The Veda expounds this sacred truth and thus steers the country on the path of Dharma.
>
> Therefore, if the Veda is made easily accessible to the masses and its meaning is lucidly and unambiguously explained, the whole country will be sanctified.
>
> This hallowed *Sankalpa* has been living within me for a long time.

Jayachamarajendra Wodeyar immediately plunged into work and set in motion a train of practical steps that would enable the ultimate realization of the Swami's Sankalpa. He decided to singlehandedly sponsor the initiative, no matter what it took or however long it took.

But to understand the full significance of the Maharaja's contribution, we must visualize the overall clime of that period. A one-line description suffices: in the 1940s, the social and cultural atmosphere in the Mysore kingdom had already been poisoned by a nascent strain of intolerance, precisely against our Vedic heritage. This was the product of the toxic politics of colonialism, communism, and Dravidianism, which actively sought to divide Hindu society.

The litterateur, Dr S.L. Bhyrappa, in an understated manner, sketches the contours of this climate in his pathbreaking novel, *Vamshavruksha.* One of the protagonists, the historical scholar Sadashiva Rao, is repeatedly humiliated by his own university when he requests their support for his project of writing the comprehensive Hindu cultural history of Bharatavarsha. His superiors and the university administration tell him, 'just do the work for which we pay you *coolie*'. The term *coolie* means 'wages' but is typically used in the context of the wages paid to railway porters, construction labourers, etc. This is the state of affairs in Mysore after less than a decade of rule by the government of independent India. The same Jayachamarajendra Wodeyar, now bereft of political power, provides generous patronage to Sadashiva Rao.

From start to finish, Siddhalinga Swami acted as the spiritual mentor and guide of the Vedaratnamala. Work began in earnest on an auspicious day in 1940.

The first step was to assemble a team comprising only the topmost Vidwans drawn from a variety of specializations: Veda, vyakarana (grammar), nirukta (etymology), siksha (phonetics), and allied subjects. This team was headed by the Veda Vidvān, *Ghanapāṭhi,* 'Brahmasri' H.P. Venkata Rao, who was appointed as the general editor and chief translator and elevated to the high rank of *Āsthāna Vidvān* (Court Scholar). Indeed, Vidvān H.P. Venkata Rao merits a separate chapter.

— 5 —

The musicologist, reviewer, art critic, and prolific collector of rare music records V.A.K. Ranga Rao once memorably declared his contempt for 'holders of big university degrees with acronyms prefixed and suffixed to their names'. In his view, such degrees armed their holders with errors. In other words, V.A.K. Ranga Rao was expounding on the approach, method, value, and robustness of the scholarship of our traditional pandits. In fact, till the blind rush to acquire and treat a PhD as a marker of omniscience, this quality of scholarship had been regarded as authoritative.

Āsthāna Vidvān 'Brahmasri' H.P. Venkata Rao belonged to this standard of traditional scholars. Like thousands of such scholars, he too would have lived and died in obscurity but for the Jayachamarajendra Vedaratnamala volumes. His life is an archetype for all traditional scholars of the era. They had become the generational victims of an educational system where Sanskrit pandits and Vedic vidvāns had been reduced to becoming clerks serving the exploitative bureaucratic apparatus set up by the colonial British.

H.P. Venkata Rao underwent rigorous traditional *pathashala* training and distinguished himself as a *Ghanapāṭi* of eminence in *both* the *Rg* and *Yajur Vedas*. However, this education did not fetch him a livelihood. So, he was forced to take up and pass the British-mandated Intermediate and Sub-Overseer examination in the English language. He also sat for and cleared the Revenue Higher Secondary examination and landed a job as a revenue inspector and sub-overseer, i.e., basically supervising tax collection on behalf of the British government.

However, each day spent in government service only heightened his melancholy. Eventually, his cultural roots triumphed, and he quit the job that was keeping him away from his cherished Veda.

Vidvān H.P. Venkata Rao opted for the hard life amidst adverse circumstances. He started afresh and began copying, in elegant handwriting, our sacred literature from old manuscripts written on palm leaves onto paper. It was an intensive and demanding task that called for multifaceted expertise. A thorough knowledge of the Devanagari, the 'old' Kannada and Telugu scripts, and a solid command over these languages were the entry-level qualifications. He rendered several of our sacred texts into English as well. Unlike photocopying, which faithfully spits out both junk and value, this work had to be not only beautiful but error-free. Even a misspelling meant that he had to rewrite the entire sentence or page afresh. In this sacred journey, H.P. Venkata Rao copied lakhs of *granthas* in letters that resembled pearls. One grantha is 32 letters set to the *Anushtubh* metre. His fee was four rupees for 1,000 granthas. This sum was not bad for that era. However, given the demanding qualifications and the sheer ardour involved in the job, it was practically dirt-cheap. We cannot help noticing the sad irony: a formidable ghanapāṭi being reduced to a mere copyist, notwithstanding the fact that he regarded the work as a pious calling. The same comment is applicable to another towering Vidvān, Motaganahalli Subrahmanya Sastri—Venkata Rao's contemporary who worked on the *Granthamala* project—who was paid two rupees for translating 1,000 slokas.

Those who have seen Vidvān Venkata Rao's alluring handwriting have written glowing testimonies about how its elegance surpassed that of even printed texts. These copies were preserved at the Mysore Oriental Library.

Siddhalinga Swami's fortuitous acquaintance with Vidvān Venkata Rao was the exact moment that crystallized the landmark Vedaratnamala volumes. On Swami's recommendation, Maharaja Jayachamarajendra Wodeyar appointed H.P. Venkata Rao as general editor for the volumes at a rather generous remuneration.

Venkata Rao soon set to work. He formed a team entitled *Vēdavimarśana Vidvanmaṇḍali* or Committee of Vedic Scholars. Venkata Rao's immediate deputy was a scholar named Vidvān G.N. Chakravarthy. The Vyakarana Vidvān (Scholar of Grammar) 'Brahmasri' Lakshmanacharya was in charge of the grammatical nuances of the *Rg Veda Samhita*. In all, the initial core team comprised nine scholars. It was a remarkable mix of the topmost scholarship required to translate the *Rg Veda Samhita* into Kannada and English. Scholars of this core team included the following: G. Vishnumurti Bhatta, H. Gangadhara Sastri, Srinivasa Sastri, Hittavalli Biliranga Jois, Hittavalli Devara Bhatta, Venkataramanachar, S. Ranganathan, Puttur Anantakrishnamachar, and S. Sitarama Sastri.

Apart from this core team, scores of unnamed scholars assiduously laboured to translate this sacred initiative into reality. In the true Hindu spirit, they requested to remain anonymous.

— 6 —

A major contributor to the pace, success, and quality of the Vedaratnamala volumes was the inward attitude of its scholars. This attitude is what truly fulfilled the vision of Siddalinga Swami and brought Maharaja Jayachamarajendra Wodeyar's Sankalpa to fruition. The phrase *sanctified conviction* best describes it. Indeed, attitude, more than approach, makes all the difference between success and timelessness. To the team of the Vēdavimarśana Vidvanmaṇḍali, this was not merely a project or just another work of scholarship. Anybody who is acquainted with even rudimentary Vedic learning can testify from experience as to the profound impact it leaves on a person's life. Apart from the profound knowledge it imparts, Vedic learning has an intrinsic value that one realizes. It is something that cannot be fully articulated in words. It is what our tradition calls *Anubhavaika Vedya*—realization through experience. And here was a team of first-rate scholars and Vidvans whose life-breath was the Veda. We notice a glimpse of this attitude in the introduction written to the Vedaratnamala volumes:

> Although we have presented such a vast amount of material regarding the Vedic corpus, one must not conclude that its study is full or complete. Much remains to be said and written. We have examined only a droplet of the infinite ocean called the Meaning of the Veda. This sacred work has gone on for thousands of years by lakhs of Vidvans [throughout history]. All of them have attempted—according to their abilities—to expound on the Meaning of the Veda with the aid of primary texts and reliable commentaries. *But none of them spoke with the authority that they had uttered the final word on the Meaning of the Veda. Thus, we merely regard it as our duty to perform this sacred task in the service of humankind. Whether it has met with success or fulfilment is for Ishwara to judge.* (Emphasis added)

In this context, it is pertinent to draw a contrast. *Mahāmahopādhyāya* Hanagal Virupaksha Sastri had the following to say about the approach of Western scholars towards our sacred lore: 'Yes, they also learn our Vedas but do they have *Pujya Buddhi* (reverence) towards it?'

The singularity of the Vedaratnamala volumes becomes more distinctive when we compare them with similar work done by other *saṃsthānams* (princely states) of the period. Baroda, Kashmir, Travancore, Kashi, and other states in the Maratha region did publish valuable work in the Vedic and Sastric realms. However, these were largely piecemeal in nature. The Chamarajendra Vedaratnamala was and remains the only work that was undertaken in a rigorous, systematic, disciplined, comprehensive, and time-bound fashion.

As we have narrated earlier, the Vedaratnamala relies on and is entirely faithful to Sāyaṇācārya's commentary on the Vedas, titled *Vedārthaprakāśa.* The introduction to the corpus of Vedic literature in the very first volume runs up to *400 pages.* It is a complete education in all aspects of the Veda. It also provides exhaustive reasoning for using Sāyaṇācārya's commentary as its basis. It is backed up by incontrovertible evidence, the strength of tradition, and rigorous systematization. Following Sāyaṇācārya's hallowed footsteps, the Vedaratnamala has evolved a twelvefold structure, which can be summarized as follows:

1. 25 chapters (or sections) that provide a preparatory background for approaching Vedic learning. This also forms the preface.
2. An exhaustive introduction to Sāyaṇācārya's *Rg Veda* commentary, which is 'mandatory for any attempt to derive the accurate meaning of the Veda sans errors of omission and commission'.
3. The meaning of each mantra of the *Rg Veda* is explained. Then, each *sukta* is taken up individually, and its *maṇḍala* (book), *anuvāka* (a division of Vedic mantras), *aṣṭaka* (a common term for the eight portions of a saṃhitā), *adhyāya* (chapter), *varga* (part or division), *ṛṣi* (name of the Rishi who realized the mantra), *chandas* (metre in which the verse

is composed), devatā (the deity), and the number of the *Rk* are given.

4. This is followed by the *saṃhitā pāṭha* (textual rendition of the mantra with the proper intonations) displaying the *svara* marks in 'large font to facilitate easy reading'.
5. Next is the *pada pāṭha* or word-by-word rendering of the mantra, likewise with svara marks.
6. This is followed by the Sanskrit text of Sāyaṇācārya's original commentary.
7. Word-by-word meaning of the mantra in simple Kannada is given next.
8. After this, the full meaning of the mantra is explained in Kannada, titled *bhāvārtha* or essence of the mantra.
9. This is followed by a simple English translation of the mantra.
10. The section that follows this is titled 'Special Meaning', describing the special or unique meanings of the mantra in certain circumstances.
11. Next is a section titled 'Distinctive Topics'. This contains prolific explanations of hundreds of terms in the *Rg Veda* mantras classified according to their common usage, special meanings, relationships with other words, and changes in their meanings when used in other mantras. This section also describes some *upākhyānas* (episodes or stories) and topics related to Devatas and yajnas. If this was not enough, it also expounds in detail the opinions of Western scholars and puts them in their rightful place.
12. The final section is entirely devoted to grammar. It is faithful to Maharshi Panini and also uses the expositions of other renowned Sanskrit grammarians.

The volumes are rounded off with a detailed alphabetical index of the Rg Vedic mantras.

A whopping 62 authoritative source texts have been listed by the Vedaratnamala team. This is, of course, a partial list.

— 7 —

The first volume of the *Rg Veda Samhita* was published in the *Sarvajit Samvatsara* on the āśvayuja śukla *daśami* or 24 October 1947, two months after India attained political freedom.

The profound yajna continued with the same intensity, devotion, and pace. The result was that in less than a decade, 25,000 pages spread over 30 volumes of the *Rg Veda Samhita* were offered to the public. They became one of the greatest treasures that the Wodeyar dynasty bestowed upon Karnataka and the global Hindu community. The 36th and final volume was published in 1961, marking the completion of this mammoth yajna. The total corpus runs up to 32,000 pages.

Maharaja Jayachamarajendra Wodeyar personally oversaw various aspects of this devout penance. He offered valuable suggestions with respect to both aesthetics, content, and execution. Without sacrificing quality for speed, he simultaneously engaged four printing presses in Mysore and distributed among them this staggering volume of manuscripts: the Sharada Press, Vinayaka Printing Press, Shakti Electric Press, Chamundeshwari Electric Press, and Panchacharya Press. The presses, too, regarded this as sacred work, created special types for the volumes, and brought out elegant volumes. Only the topmost quality paper was used with Calico binding. Hundreds of families in Karnataka who have preserved these first editions still regard the collection with justified pride.

Notwithstanding the substantial expenditure involved, the *Rg Veda Samhita* volumes were sold at a heavily subsidized price. If this was not enough, Jayachamarajendra Wodeyar donated hundreds of copies of the volumes to various libraries, educational institutions, mathas, and individual vidvans and scholars. The profound descriptions of *dāna* (charity) narrated in our Dharmasastras found their 21st century embodiment in Jayachamarajendra Wodeyar. It is not an exaggeration to say that he had subordinated his royal crown at the *vedayajñavedi*—the altar of this mammoth Vedic yajna. And as it should, it turned out to be his crowning glory.

Unfortunately, the sweeping changes that independence wrought put a permanent halt to the remainder of this yajna: publishing similar volumes on the other three Vedas.

From another perspective, we can confidently declare that the Jayachamarajendra Vedaratnamala volumes are the most authoritative counters to Max Mueller's translations of the Vedas.

Along with the Vedaratnamala, Jayachamarajendra Wodeyar also sponsored the translation and publication of 24 Puranas. He had engaged 19 Vidvans for the task. The total corpus of the *Jayachamarajendra Granthamala* stands at a magnificent *2.5 lakh pages*.

Epilogue

Speaking on the 100th anniversary of Maharaja Krishnaraja Wodeyar III, the eminent Kannada poet D.R. Bendre recounted how he met a German scholar in Pondicherry who lavished praise on the Vedaratnamala volumes and eulogized the munificence and dedication of Maharaja Jayachamarajendra Wodeyar. Then, Bendre wistfully noted how even this praise from White-skinned Westerners failed to wake up the Kannada people to this priceless cultural treasure languishing in their own backyard.

The same cultural negligence and apathy is reflected in the fact that apart from litterateurs like A.R. Krishna Sastri, Anantarangachar, and others, *not one* Kannada literary eminence, editor, journalist, or newspaper or magazine has deigned to write a single word about the Jayachamarajendra Granthamala. It was as if it didn't exist.

Part III
Postcolonial India

16

The Partition of India Is a Virgin Field for Creative Fiction

— 1 —

> *There is a whole school of American Jewish writers who spend their time damning their fathers, hating their mothers*, wringing their hands and wondering why they were born. This isn't art or literature. It's psychiatry. These writers are professional apologists. Every year you find one of their works on the best-seller list. *Their work is obnoxious and makes me sick to my stomach. I wrote Exodus because I was just sick of apologizing*—or feeling that it was necessary to apologize. (Leon Uris) (Emphases added)

More than 60 years ago, Leon Uris uttered these words of defiant courage in the face of a pervasive pusillanimity that had already engulfed America much before its establishment was formally seized by the woke ideology. His words stand as a beacon of light and as an eternal reminder that truth has few friends. His classic novel *Exodus* is still relevant not only because of Uris' abiding conviction in Israel and the Jewish cause but because it is a contemporary showcase of that other truth: that literature (or generally speaking, art) is an extraordinarily powerful—and in many cases, an unerring key—for understanding history, civilization, and culture in the most native sense: through real people.

We find a philosophical echo of the truth of Leon Uris' words in the preface to Dr S.L. Bhyrappa's explosive literary phenomenon 'Aavarana'. On another occasion, while he was responding to a question on whether he didn't feel scared to write such a no-holds-barred novel, Dr Bhyrappa said, 'my view of literature is that it is a quest for truth, and if I don't tell it even now, I think my life will be meaningless. The freedom of expression that our Constitution guarantees to us implicitly includes the freedom to tell the truth.' [Paraphrased]

This, in my view, is one of the simplest formulas for the conquest of fear.

On the level of pure passion, the angry lament of Leon Uris applies a 100 per cent to post-Independence Indian literature about the Partition of Bharatavarsha. It was one of humankind's greatest tragedies, engineered by the alloyed forces of two Abrahamisms. Literary works based on the Partition are akin to textbook definitions of Uris' fury about Jews: a mass of textual apologia for Pakistan and an attempt to induce civilizational amnesia in the present tense.

Here are a few quotes that illustrate the global impact of the *Exodus.*

> Two months after the tenth anniversary, a novel was published in America that changed the public perception of Israel and the Jews. *Exodus* by the Jewish US ex-marine Leon Uris became an international publishing phenomenon, the biggest best seller in the United States since *Gone with the Wind.* Both the novel and the subsequent movie thrust Israel into the lives of millions, and with it initiated a new sympathy for the young country. (Jill Hamilton: *God, Guns and Israel*)
>
> *[Exodus is] an antidote to the public silence of American Jews.* . . . Something fundamental changed among American Jews as a result of the book. (Mathew Silver) (Emphasis added)

> *[The effect of Exodus] is so extraordinary that I wanted to go and fight for Israel, even die,* if need be, for Israel. Israel spoke to the need I had as a young black man for a place where I could be free of being an object of hatred. I did not wish I were Jewish, but was glad that Jews had a land of their own . . . (Julius Lester) (Emphasis added)

— 2 —

The fact that not a single work of literary fiction about the Partition strikes our memory is enough to tell the tale.

Until recently, the late Khushwant Singh's eminent apologia titled *Train to Pakistan* was lauded as the best novel on the subject. However, even in his own lifetime, Khushwant Singh had earned wide notoriety for being a grade-A sycophant of the Nehru dynasty. He was among the handful who had endorsed Indira Gandhi's Emergency. Reading *Train to Pakistan* makes it clear that it is a pamphlet of pseudo-secularism disguised as literature. But thanks to its author's political leanings, it reigned unchallenged for decades as the unquestionable Koran of the Nehruvian literary establishment.

Then there is Qurratulain Hyder's voluminous Urdu novel *Aag ka Dariya* (River of Fire). It is ambitious in scope but expectedly secular in its tenor and ideology. The fact that she chose the fall of the Nanda dynasty to begin her epic mound of selective interpretation is quite telling. Her central thesis, which is rather familiar, is couched in the words of a character named Kamal: 'The Indo-Muslim life-style is made up of the Persian-Turki-Mughal and regional Rajput Hindu cultures. So, what is this Indianness which the Muslim League has started questioning? Could there be an alternate India?' To put it mildly, this single titbit conveniently buries the centuries' long oppression of Hindus under alien Muslim regimes.

Next, we have Yashpal's Hindi novel *Jhoota Sach* (False Truth). This is a Communist Comrade's rendering of the Partition through the tainted spectacles of Marxist class warfare.

While Bhisham Sahni's *Tamas* is not as brazen as the rest, it too treads the path of secular safety. Nowhere does it mention the root cause of the Partition of India—the unilateral demand for a separate Muslim nation that emanated from the community.

But the undoubted granddaddy of all Partition 'literature' emerging from India is Salman Rushdie's *Midnight's Children*. It does contain some flashes of intellectual honesty, but as a whole, the work is clearly tailored to British sensibilities. The Booker Prize is the clearest proof of this.

The near-unanimous 'conclusion' of all these works is this: no one person, one community, or one ideology is to blame for the Partition. We're left to wonder whether all of humanity in India suddenly decided to plunge into genocidal insanity that was not driven by anything. V.S. Naipaul, in his majestic *Beyond Belief,* supplies a near-perfect analysis:

> *It was Muslim insecurity that led to the call for the creation of Pakistan.* It went at the same time with an idea of old glory, of the invaders sweeping down from the northwest and looting the temples of Hindustan and imposing the faith on the infidel. *The fantasy still lives; and for the Muslim converts of the subcontinent it is the start of their neurosis, because in this fantasy the convert forgets who or what he is and becomes the violator* . . . the new state was intended to be a triumph of the faith, a stake in the heart of old Hindustan . . . to . . . most of the Muslims of the subcontinent *the state that had been won out of India came as a kind of religious ecstasy, something beyond reason,* beyond quibbles about borders and constitutions . . . at the very beginning the new religious state was touched by the old idea of plunder. (Emphases added)

And so, the aforementioned kind of 'literature' woven around the Partition, as Uris said, makes us sick; it makes us hate our parents; it makes us ashamed of ourselves; and it incites us to disown our own heritage. It depresses us because it prevaricates.

While I am no fan of prescriptive literature, it must be said that when the author chooses a contemporary theme, honesty, not audience and ideology, must drive it. Creative liberty is not an excuse for lying. Interpretation cannot become a Persian rug to hide evasiveness.

— 3 —

As a historical event, the Partition was the savage triumph of a virulent fanaticism that had lost its imperial power but had never given up its messianic quest to reclaim the same brute power that is needed to sustain this fanaticism. It reclaimed it partially in the form of Pakistan, a usurped geography named after a religion, and after reclaiming it, it set about permanently erasing the historical markers of this geography.

As a theme for a profound literary exploration of the Partition, the story should actually begin with the alien Islamic invasions of India and not the clever-by-half trickery of *Aag ka Dariya,* which begins with the downfall of the Nanda dynasty. Or, if an author lacks sweeping erudition and scholarship in history, the story can begin with the death of Aurangzeb because the modern roots of the Partition, most clearly, were planted during that period.

Seventy-five years have elapsed since the Partition of India. This interim has also been highly eventful, and it provides fertile ground for a dispassionate and truthful literary exploration of this civilizational tragedy.

In the Sanatana tradition, poets and litterateurs are seated on the same high pedestal as the Rishis. The Partition is both an invitation and a challenge for present-day creative writers to test their prowess as to how best they can elevate themselves to this high pedestal.

Dr S.L. Bhyrappa pioneered this path with his *Aavarana*. If a 10th of that summit is reached, it is sure to capture the imagination of at least two generations, apart from being a massive commercial success.

17

Wanted: A Body of Creative Work on the 1962 Nehruvian Debacle

One of the passages that gnaws at my emotional universe like flies around an open, untreated wound occurs in Brigadier John P. Dalavi's *The Himalayan Blunder*, an unacknowledged classic that rips apart Jawaharlal Nehru's betrayal of India in excruciatingly brutal detail. The passage occurs at the very beginning of the book. Dalvi returns to India after being released by China, which had held him as a prisoner of war for seven months. This is the reception he gets:

> We landed in Dum Dum airport in Calcutta on May 4, 1963. We were received cordially, appropriately. But the silence there was disquieting. I realized later. We had to prove we weren't brainwashed by Chinese ideology. We had to prove we were still loyal to India. My own army maintained a suspicious distance. *The irony cannot be harsher: this treatment from a country, which for more than a decade had brainwashed itself into holding the Chinese baton wherever it went.* (Emphasis added)

The rest of the book is basically a blow-by-blow, fact-based enlargement of the trajectory of Nehru's fatal misadventure that culminated in Dalvi's humiliation. But Dalvi was not alone. Hundreds of his comrades in the Indian army had been sacrificed by Prime Minister Nehru to China in cold blood. But Dalvi's distinction lies in the fact that, as a survivor and victim of Nehru's treachery, he mustered the courage to unmask the great man's betrayal in all its nakedness. Dalvi's book endures to date as a fine model of national service. The service is twofold: one, as an honest soldier, Dalvi paid a posthumous tribute of pride and honour to all his fellow soldiers who were killed for no fault of theirs. Two, as a writer, he has exhibited the highest standards of intellectual integrity by allowing raw facts to narrate a contemporary story.

If the eminently preventable dishnour of India in 1962 was shameful, its aftermath was truly loathsome. In spite of receiving a relentless flood of well-deserved nationwide condemnation, Nehru showed absolutely no remorse. Which was entirely consistent with his personality. Indeed, Nehru's contemporaries as well as his honest critics have repeatedly observed how his upbringing, social circle, and personality traits were modelled after autocratic mediaeval nawabs and the worst of British colonial administrators. His younger contemporary, the fine scholar Sita Ram Goel, gives perhaps the best assessment:

> I view *Pandit Jawaharlal Nehru as a bloated brown sahib, and Nehruism as the combined embodiment of all the imperialist ideologies*—Islam, Christianity, White Man's Burden, and Communism—that have flooded this country in the wake of foreign invasions. (Emphasis added)

The history of Muslim rule in India reveals the fact that no nawab ever felt guilty of committing the most heinous atrocities against his own people. While Nehru did not commit atrocities in the strict sense of the word, the outcomes of most of his plans and actions were nothing short of atrocious.

This nawabesque streak in Nehru impelled him to hunt for a scapegoat to palm off his Himalayan blunder, whose cost was a loss of India's self-respect and precious territory to China. His long-time comrade and prized sycophant V.K. Krishna Menon had already been primed and fattened for more than a decade. India's humiliation at Chinese hands—entirely engineered by Nehru's woolly headed love of Maoist China—was the perfect excuse to lead this lamb to slaughter. It is precisely for this reason that Sita Ram Goel originally titled his work *Genesis and Growth of Nehruism* as *In Defence of Comrade Krishna Menon.* Krishna Menon paid the price for Nehru's addiction to power.

But the dried blobs of this rot did not end even after Nehru died in 1964. When John Dalvi published *The Himalayan Blunder* in 1968, Nehru's daughter and India's prime minister, Indira Gandhi, instantly banned it. It was also one of the most long-lasting bookbans in the Congress' tradition of stifling freedom of expression.

A recent work on the 1962 war is Shiv Kunal Verma's *1962: The War That Wasn't,* a splendid volume cum expose on the topic. A short poem by an army officer named Harji Malik included in Verma's work makes for painful reading:

> We died, unsuccoured, helpless
> We were your soldiers, men of bravery and pride
> Yet we died like animals, trapped in a cage with no escape
> Massacred at will, denied the dignity of battle
> With the cold burning flame of anger and resolution
> With the courage both of the living and the dead,
> Avenge Our unplayed lives,
> Redeem the unredeemable sacrifice
> In freedom and integrity
> Let this be your inheritance
> And our unwritten epitaph

The real villains of the 1962 debacle, starting with Nehru right at the top, followed by his extended family, including Brij Mohan 'Bijji' Kaul, Pran Thapar, et al., not only escaped unscathed and unpunished but were actually *decorated*. One Watergate scandal was enough to snuff out the political career of a sitting American president. But national calamities like 1962, the Emergency and Bofors, all of which were inflicted by members of the same bloodline, did not claim their offenders. This phenomenon is a perverse version of the Christian doctrine, which claims that Jesus died for the sins of mankind. In this case, countless Indians died for the sins of one dynasty.

The more shocking fact is how *little* all these sins against the Indian nation and the Hindu civilization have been documented. As a conciliatory exception, the Emergency has been documented fairly well, but in terms of the volume of output, spread, reach, and effectiveness, it still leaves a lot to be desired.

As far as 1962 is concerned, the material is so paltry that it is almost non-existent. At most, we have less than 10 books, half of which are truthful and reliable. And these are non-fiction works. *Till date, there has been no work of fiction in any genre narrating the dark truths of 1962.*

The 1964 Hindi movie *Haqeeqat* is an unclothed apologia for Nehru's blunder. *Haqeeqat* meaning 'reality', is actually a shameless saga of onscreen violence inflicted upon patriotic Indians. It is both an inversion and a perversion of reality. A little-known fact about the movie is that it was 'assisted' by Nehru's government, and Chetan Anand (Dev Anand's brother) promptly dedicated it to Nehru! The heavy hitters in the team of *Haqeeqat* were committed ideologues devoted to the Communist church called the Indian People's Theatre Association: Chetan Anand, Balraj Sahni, Kaifi Azmi, and his wife, Shaukat Azmi. The last two are the parents of Shabana Azmi.

Cut to the same timeline elsewhere in the world. The stirrings of the Vietnam War began around 1955. For the next two decades, the world witnessed one of the bloodiest genocides inflicted by America upon a tiny nation and a proud, ancient civilization. As American militaristic meddling in Vietnam escalated after the US Congress gave Lyndon Johnson sweeping powers, the US public began to see what the 'war' was really about.

Long story short, the sheer volume of material surrounding the US invasion (dressed up as usual as 'liberation' and a fight against communism) of Vietnam is enough to fill several large libraries. Excluding news reports and journalistic works, we find an almost inexhaustible treasure of literature on Vietnam: non-fiction, novels, short stories, poems, plays, feature films, short films, television series, and documentaries that explore Vietnam from every conceivable perspective.

We have a whopping 165 books directly related to the Vietnam War. Wikipedia gives us a list of hundred-plus films made on the topic. It is a genre-transcending repertoire that includes monster Hollywood hits like *Platoon, First Blood, Full Metal Jacket, Forrest Gump, Apocalypse Now*, and the extremely macabre *Forced Entry.* The 1979 blockbuster *Apocalypse Now* is notable for deriving its inspiration from Joseph Conrad's classic, *Heart of Darkness.* The eerie parallel between Conrad's novel and the film is based on 'heart of darkness', which is defined as Western-style colonial capitalism.

Now cut back to India during the same period. Two vital facts emerge.

The first: to our eternal shame, Nehru's government actually *supported* the Communist Bloc's offensive against South Vietnam, which for centuries had been a part of Brihad-Bharata.

The second: the mid-1950s was also the period during which Communist China was leisurely, clandestinely cooking its recipe for the ensuing invasion of the Himalayas. However, Nehru's lust for communism had blinded him to repeated and farsighted warnings from a range of stalwarts, including Sardar Patel and Rajagopalachari.

Today, all of this and more material is readily available in the public domain. The India of today is no longer ruled by the Nehruvian inheritors of the British colonial regime, whose hallmark was censorship. Besides, the internet and social media have completely shattered the gates and dissolved the walls surrounding access to information and its dissemination.

Yet, even 60 years after Nehru's 1962 blunder, no compelling creative work has emerged on this vital chapter of recent Indian history. The contrast with the copious amounts of creative output produced in the US about Vietnam is both chilling and shameful.

In a limited sense, American interference in Vietnam was simultaneously an act of domination and imperialism and a reflection of the insatiable hunger of its military-industrial complex. But it was definitely *not* an act of national betrayal on the part of the American presidents who were in office during that era. Nehru's Himalayan blunder was.

Sadly, its gravity has somehow escaped the attention of our artists, writers, playwrights, and filmmakers. If the subject is treated well, it has all the makings of a modern epic. This phenomenon of creative silence over such a serious issue has a parallel in another essay featured in this book: a paucity of literary fiction about the Partition of India.

And like that topic, we await a talented artist to pick up the Nehruvian betrayal of 1962. It is an urgent national need and a creative challenge.

18

Stability as a Metaphor in the Downfall of Indian Cinema

— 1 —

'Binge watching' is a term whose popularity has soared in direct proportion to the detonation of the OTT epidemic. The first usage of the word *binge,* recorded in A.B. Evans' *Leicestershire Words, Phrases and Proverbs* (1848), was as a dialectical verb meaning, 'to soak in water a wooden vessel, that would otherwise leak; to tighten up; putting hot water into a churn to make the wood swell before putting in the milk'.

A.B. Evans, the headmaster of the Market Bosworth Free Grammar School, also supplies another delightful connotation of binge: 'A doyed a-bingein' [i.e., died binging] is a not uncommon comment on the death of a drunkard, implying that his constitution was not strong enough to stand the process of making himself drink-proof.'

By 1854, binge was used both as a noun and verb to almost exclusively mean 'soak up alcohol, drink heavily'. In fact, the Kannada-ized English word 'tight' has retained the original connotation of binge, i.e., heavy intoxication. Some phenomena are universal cultural constants.

Around World War I, the usage of 'binge' extended to gluttonous bouts as well. Fast forward 70 years, and the term *binge-watching* trumpeted its appearance in 1996, the gilded age of videotapes and the dawn of DVDs in America.

A year later, Netflix was born as a DVD rental service.

Fifteen years since, binge-watching has been transformed into a contemporary idiom in what is known as popular culture, and OTT has globalized binge-watching and Americanized Indian cinema by asphyxiating it.

On the consumer side, the ongoing binge-watching frenzy evokes Somerset Maugham's terse but eerie description of the visuals of those infamous Chinese opium dens of the early 20th century:

> It is dimly lit. The room is low and squalid. In one corner a lamp burns mysteriously before a hideous image and incense fills the theatre with its exotic scent. A pig-tailed Chinaman wanders to and fro, aloof and saturnine, while on wretched pallets lie stupefied the victims of the drug. Now and then one of them breaks into frantic raving. There is a highly dramatic scene where some poor creature, unable to pay for the satisfaction of his craving, with prayers and curses begs the villainous proprietor for a pipe to still his anguish.

Maugham has painted in prose a compelling miniature of addiction. Without stretching the analogy too far, the 'villainous proprietor' in our context can be likened to faceless and impersonal technology, which literally pushes the binge-watching fix in gazillion packets of zeros and ones at lightning speeds right down into our palms.

The global OTT streaming market is currently valued at $140 billion and is racing ahead roughly at a CAGR of 15 per cent. The spinoff or ancillary market that it has spawned is the movie and web series review industry, which has created thriving niche media houses and wealthy individual reviewers. These are substantial, if not undeniable, economic indicators of the extent of normalized binge-watching.

Even without making any value judgements about the binge-watching phenomenon, there exists an eminent case for examining the course of a recent social and cultural trajectory.

Chalo, Picture Dekhne Chalte Hai!

'Going to the movies' (*chalo, picture dekhne chalte hai*) used to be the ubiquitous indicator, mostly denoting an event involving family or friends or both. To a large extent, it still is, and it cohabits with the rapid and pervasive incursions made by OTT. But the haste with which all film production houses across the world are scurrying to hawk their goods on streaming platforms barely weeks after the theatrical release tells a separate story.

In pre-liberalization India, movie-watching involved deliberate planning, budgeting, and project execution. The first victims of the post-liberation era were the drive-in theatres. These were not merely movie-watching expeditions but a gamut of sensory experiences one used to boast about. Single-screen theatres were felled next, and the ensuing consequences are familiar to most of us living in the regime of multiplexes.

But the underlying social impulse or outlook towards cinema had remained the same for decades: apart from being just another form of entertainment, cinema was simply a pastime or an enjoyable hobby at most. Among other things, technology, globalization, and wealth generation at unprecedented levels have altered this social and cultural landscape in a far-reaching fashion.

Two other intrinsic forces were at play as well.

The first was that the middle-class India of the pre-liberalization era actually frowned upon watching movies excessively, regarding them as corrupting, if not debasing, influences. This sociocultural attitude has proven to be one of the most durable civilizational inheritances, having its origins almost at the dawn of drama.

Every Dharmasastra treatise unequivocally and unanimously warns about the tainting influence of drama and reserves severe condemnation for actors. Likewise, every text on statecraft, including the *Arthashastra*, recommends unleashing spies to invigilate the behaviour and lifestyle of actors and track their movements.

Spilling well into the 19th century, Europe also had punitive laws punishing actors who entered a village or town on the grounds that they would corrupt the morals of fine young virgins belonging to respectable families. For centuries, actors were forbidden from receiving sacraments unless they abandoned their immoral profession. A phrase that I heard in my childhood about actors emanated from the perceptive tongue of a run-down *kirana* shop owner. It has stayed with me: '*Yeh sab log toh bade kothe ke randi hai.*' (All these people are whores inhabiting opulent brothels.) It might sound harsh and vulgar, but recent revelations from Bollywood have unambiguously proved that reality trumps even the vulgarest imagination.

The pre-liberalization era in India also boasted an impressive talent of truly well-informed and rather erudite reviewers who were able to place both a specific movie and cinema overall in proper perspective. It is still a treat to read those archives. The standard of movie reviews published in South India was truly exceptional and remains a collector's delight. Filmmakers were justifiably terrified of these critics.

There was also a non-filmy side to this. It was only on rare occasions that filmmakers and film stars were called upon to discourse on issues beyond films—on everything from the GDP to Mangalyan.

Woven with the first was the second force. This was the class that comprised both filmmakers and refined connoisseurs. It correctly regarded cinema as an art form and an aesthetic experience. This was not merely an outlook or an academic approach that this class had consciously cultivated. It was the natural flow of a millennia-old aesthetic tradition that they were proud to have inherited, imbibed, and then infused into their cinema.

The essence of the two aforementioned forces is that a healthy balance and stability were maintained. Propagating agitation, promoting extremism, and pushing toxic Leftist ideology using cinema as a cloak was still nascent. That propaganda would come much later, as we shall see.

— 2 —

Stability was the bedrock of Indian cinema, like it was of all our art forms. Stability was what produced hundreds of eminently watchable family dramas that were not only commercially successful, but some also became classics. Stability is what prevents movies with repetitive themes from becoming tainted with staleness. Stability was what disbarred the ennui that comes from over-familiarity.

Stability was the bedrock of Indian cinema because it had its durable roots in the Indian aesthetic tradition itself. It birthed the hundreds of Ramayanas and Mahabharatas and derivative literature and art over several millennia, sprawled across the entire sacred geography of Bharatavarsha in multiple languages.

Poor A.K. Ramanujan, who wrote his masterly nonsense titled *300 Ramayanas*, failed to grasp this fundamental truth of the Indian aesthetic tradition.

The erosion of stability is perhaps the single largest contributor to the near-comprehensive destruction of Indian cinema. Stability is also a great, contemporary metaphor for the decadal decline of Indian cinema. Its most visible manifestation is what is known as Bollywood.

But to understand how things plummeted to this nadir, we need to go to the very origins.

— 3 —

The Indian aesthetic tradition is as ancient as India. It dates back to its seminal formulation by Bharatamuni in his *Nāṭyaśastra.* The encyclopaedic treatise, datable at least to 200 BCE, still commands sway over all our performing arts, including cinema. The *Nāṭyaśastra* has almost singlehandedly birthed our aesthetic tradition, and few treatises have had such a decisive and shapely impact over an entire culture in the spatiotemporal realms. In fact, every aesthetician worth his mettle invokes Bharatamuni with reverence and takes extreme care not to violate his foundational principles.

Anandavardhana, the extraordinary aesthetician of the 9th century who mined the *Nāṭyaśastra* and unearthed the eternal principle of *Dhvani* (aesthetic suggestion) in his epoch-making classic *Dhvanyaloka* gives us what is essentially a commandment:

> santi siddharasaprakhyā ye ca rāmāyaṇādayaḥ ||
> kathāśrayā na tairyojyā svecchā rasavirodhinī ||

This is the essence of this verse: works like the Ramayana contain *Siddha-Rasas* or established aesthetic elements. The artist who exhibits undue libertinism in his work violates Rasa.

A millennium later, A.C. Bradley, the celebrated British aesthetician, pretty much echoes Anandavardhana when he says: 'If an artist alters a reality so much that his product clashes violently with our familiar ideas he may be making a mistake.'

A general way to think about Siddha-Rasa is to regard it as a foundational tradition that has evolved specific principles and rules via trial and error, experiment, and experience after passing through aeons of filtering processes. As in culture, so in aesthetics. Tradition is the river that feeds, nurtures, and sustains culture, and tradition is not 'created' by one person, one institution, or one book. As Shatavadhani Dr R. Ganesh memorably says:

> Indian literary [i.e., aesthetic] theory is mainly codified in Sanskrit. However, it is applicable to all genres of literature produced in all languages. Anchoring itself to universal experience, it steers clear of social, economic and political theories that change by the day. *Transcending sectarian biases, it provides insights into art that are experientially verifiable.* (Emphasis added)

To axe or weaken tradition based on individual whims, ideologies, politics, or what 'feels' currently trendy is to drain out the source of this perennial river. This engineered drought cannot be undone. The ancient, sacred river Saraswati, a great fount of Hindu civilization, dried up aeons ago, and we have to today content ourselves with mere academic research about it. Memories, not *life*, are all we are left with.

Immortal works of literature like the Ramayana, Mahabharata, and the Puranic treasure-trove have inspired countless retellings and derivative renditions—in part or in full—not only because they are immortal but because they have intrinsic beauty, and beauty is also malleable in a profound sense.

But it was only in recent times that two perverse phenomena have occurred almost in parallel.

The first was the deplorable growth of writers, artists, dramatists, and filmmakers twisting and distorting not only this priceless literary heritage but deliberately tampering with the original itself. The Telugu Communist writer Ranganayakamma's poisonous (literally) *Rāmāyaṇa Viśavṛkṣaṃ (Ramayana, the Poisoned Tree)* is one of the most egregious specimens of this category. It is the literary equivalent of E.V. Ramaswami Naicker's political rowdyism against Sanatana culture and society. Girish Karnad's serial incursions into our Vedic and Puranic lore belong to the same category. A more recent work is Chitra Devikaruni's *Palace of Illusions*, which has Draupadi sexually lusting after Karna in her fantasy. The less said about M.F. Hussain's filthy 'paintings', the better.

Retellings have always existed, and our past writers did take liberties. The Kannada poet Kumaravyasa's *Karṇāṭabhāratakathāmañjari* is suffused with such creative latitudes. Another recent example is K.V. Puttappa's *Sri Ramayana Darshanam,* imbued with enormous liberties. The most recent example in this line is Dr S.L. Bhyrappa's classic *Parva,* which takes extraordinary deviations from the Mahabharata. But all these poets and writers have stayed scrupulously true to the spirit of the original. Mountebanks like Ranganayakamma, Karnad, et al., became irrelevant in their own sordid lifetimes.

The second phenomenon is the widespread epidemic called 'interpretation'. This term is a code word for the calculated massacre of the finest traditions of Indian aesthetics. 'Interpretation' is actually a political hoax masquerading as literary criticism. Almost every such 'interpretation' uses theories and terminology imported from disciplines other than aesthetics. The ostensible *process* is aesthetic critique, but the ultimate *goal* is political.

In this scheme of things, you take an imported Western theory of sociology or anthropology, which claims that the only defining principle of the Hindu social organization is 'caste'. This premise is then transformed into a sub-theory that claims that caste is the root of all the ills plaguing this society. That oppression is the primary function of this 'caste system'. Then you recruit a hired cultural mercenary from the same Hindu society and award him or her the certificate of an 'art expert' or 'literary or cinema critic'. The grateful mercenary ransacks our epics and Puranas and miraculously finds exactly those elements that are deemed to 'prove' the aforementioned theories of Western sociology. And so, characters like Guha, Sabari, Vali, Shambuka, Karna, Ekalavya, Sita, and Draupadi become pawns servicing this ideology. From that first spurious step, the path to deifying a wife-stealer and serial rapist like Ravana can be trodden with swift ease.

This 'interpretation' malaise was the aesthetic accessory to the destructive spread of Marxism in India. When we grasp this root, a lot of answers regarding the downfall of Indian cinema will unravel on their own.

'Interpreting' our literary corpus using prisms other than aesthetics had the other calculated outcome: destroying standards. How confident would you be if a puncture fixer used his expertise to diagnose the heart condition of your loved ones? And if something like that happened in real life, both the puncture fixer and the hospital would face criminal charges. But this has exactly occurred in the realms of art, literature, and cinema. But how was it accomplished?

The Theory! The Theory!

First, posit a theory that things like aesthetics are outmoded and irrelevant in the contemporary world.

Get enough academicians and intellectuals to propagandize it.

Begin a 'movement'. This is a code word for using art, drama, literature, and cinema as vehicles to peddle political ideology.

Start a slew of 'literary' magazines and journals where the theory is both dressed up and disgorged periodically.

Offer the prospect of a promising career to young aspirants in the field.

That's how you build armies of the Faithful generationally.

Here is a sample of how this destruction of standards occurred.

In a meeting of the All India Progressive Writers Association held on 9 April 1936, the Hindi writer Premchand thundered thus:

> It is the duty of Indian writers to ... develop an attitude of literary criticism which will discourage the general reactionary and revivalist tendencies on questions like family, religion, sex, war and society and to combat literary trends reflecting communalism, racial antagonism, sexual libertinism.... *It is the object of our Association to rescue literature from the conservative classes* ... to bring the arts into the closest touch with the people ... as well as lead us to the future we envisage.... *Till then Indian literature had been dreamy and unrealistic. The progressive writers for the first time brought it down to earth.* (Emphases added)

The naked tenor of messianism oozing from this quote is breathtaking. What is also clear is the casual manner in which terms and phrases are thrown around as if they are settled truths. Terms like 'reactionary', 'revivalist', and 'conservative classes' have no universally agreed definitions and can be easily challenged on several grounds, the foremost of which are logic and history. So what were those 'literary trends?' And what was the 'literature' that these progressive writers wanted to 'rescue'? From one perspective, these 'literary trends' were the mien and the standard of literature that these folks aspired to create but couldn't.

The so-called 'conservative' charge that Premchand hurls is precisely rooted in our aesthetic tradition. In the domain of literary or aesthetic criticism, the universally accepted method, followed for unbroken centuries, was denoted by a lovely term: *sahrudaya samīkṣa* or *sahrudaya vimarśana*. It translates as '*appreciation* by a refined connoisseur'. Appreciation is an embracive term that includes pointing out defects as well. The standards involved in this appreciation primarily include the aforementioned elements of *Rasa* (feeling, emotion) *Dhvani* (suggestion), *Aucitya* (propreity), and *Vakratā* (turn of the phrase, embellishment, etc). These are universal aesthetic principles unaligned with language, country, genre, and art form.

As long as both our filmmakers and critics adhered to these tenets, we got classics like *Maya Bazar, Navrang, Satya Harishchandra*, and *Thiruvilayadal.*

— 4 —

Rajashekhara, the Sanskrit dramatist, poet, and aesthetician who flourished in the 9th and 10th centuries, dedicates an entire chapter in his classic *Kāvyamīmāṃsā* treatise describing the environment that a poet (broadly speaking, an artist) must cultivate for himself. The kind of standards that he mentions in the chapter by itself offers a mirror to the ruin of what passes off as art, literature, drama, and cinema today. A similar example is Kshemendra's *Kavikaṇṭhābharaṇa,* another illustrious work on aesthetics.

Poets and aestheticians of excellence deliver the following essence: at least a scintilla of culture and refinement is indispensable for anyone aspiring to be a poet or artist. The list of subjects that they all recommend includes but is not limited to the following: classic works of literature, prosody, grammar, the 64 arts, lexicography, logic, and life experience. An artist who is not equipped with these qualifications is endowed with *Vyutpattimāndya*—the broadest meaning of this term is 'cultural penury'.

Today, cultural penury is exactly what we notice in the most visual and composite of all art forms: cinema. Actually, 'cultural penury' is an extremely mild term to characterize the filth that is being rapidly churned out, especially on the OTT conveyor belt of perversion. Depravity, soullessness, and nihilism are being actively *promoted* in the name of cinema. All these are being dictated by a vile soup made up of wokeism, megalomania, and demonstrable insanity on the part of elite production houses and armies of deranged writers and directors.

What are the topics that our contemporary filmmakers select? They mostly revolve around crime, sex, more crime, and even more graphic sex. Of late, the ugly on-screen march of the LGBT+ ideological brigade has only worsened the climate. Subtle romance has been replaced by grunts and groans. Depravity has slaughtered sensitivity. Deafening cacophony has triumphed over deliberate silences, both in voice and music. Suggestion is non-existent.

Even movies that have no explicit ideological flavour exhibit the same blandness. Of late, a good chunk is based on newspaper cuttings with familiar themes: gruesome murders, rapes, and other crimes. Then there is a rush to capture that other new market: biopics. With a few honourable exceptions, most biopics that have been made in India are uniformly atrocious. We also have hilarious adventures like *Toilet Ek Prem Katha* and *Padman,* movies on latrines and sanitary pads, respectively. What next?

Films on handkerchiefs, ties, underwear, and the nuances of urine? But fear not, they'll arrive soon at a theatre near you.

Small wonder that the current crop of films has become mock-worthy memes instead of works of art.

All this is a direct consequence of a variety of factors, the chief of which is the destruction of true education. But to ask a pointed question: what is the kind and quality of literature that these filmmakers read, if at all they read anything of value?

Two anecdotes will clarify this point in a tangential fashion.

A key thread in the plot of the 1984 Telugu blockbuster *Bobbli Brahmanna* was directly borrowed from the celebrated *Sukanyōpākhyāna* (the story of Sukanya) occurring in the Mahabharata.

Likewise, the whole plot of the 1992 Tamil blockbuster *Roja* is based on another immortal Mahabharata episode: the story of Savitri and Satyavan. Interestingly, the plot point for the movie was given by K. Balachander, the film's producer and iconic director. This in itself is a revelation of the solid cultural grounding of veteran filmmakers of his calibre. It is also the starkest contrast between Balachander and Maniratnam. When Maniratnam attempted something similar sans the cultural rootedness of Balachander, he gave us a prolonged dud like *Dalapathi,* a movie allegedly based on the story of Karna. We see Rajinikant, not Karna, in the movie.

In fact, the emergence and rise of new-age directors like Maniratnam, Ram Gopal Varma, Sanjay Leela Bhansali, Ashutosh Gowariker, and Rakesh Omprakash Mehra and company are just the continuation of a downward spiral in Indian cinema.

It can be described using this phrase: *from Independence to Emergency.*

The spread, capture, and subversion, especially of Hindi cinema, by the Marxist artistic squad was the primary casual factor for this spiral. Peddling Marxist propaganda on screen was just one side of this coin. The other side has proven fatal. This was the birth of two generations of writers and filmmakers who consciously ignored and then trashed the ennobling wealth of our classical literature and the finest traditions of Indian theatre. If at all the present generation of filmmakers uses our epic and Puranic characters, they use it to condemn the very culture in which they were born.

Without exaggeration, it can be said that there is almost no 'mainstream' filmmaker in any Indian language who can make a Pauranic movie today. Or even a grand fantasy like the Telugu blockbuster *Jagadekaveerudu Atiloka Sundari* released in 1990. Or an engaging Kannada historical like *Mayura.*

Our filmmakers have deserted our classical aesthetic tradition, and it is only obvious that audiences are quickly deserting our filmmakers. Bollywood, especially, is learning it the hard way.

If the Emergency was the political abyss ushered in by a single dynasty that ran the government like a mafia, the post-Emergency period witnessed the full toxic bloom of the cultural destruction that had been put in motion through the backdoor capture of institutions. Dr S.L. Bhyrappa's novel *Tantu* narrates this ghastly and painful saga with compelling power.

—5—

In 1974, Tom Wolfe, the American journalist and novelist, was rudely jolted awake in his bathtub when he read the following words in *The New York Times* written by Hilton Kramer, dean of the arts at Yale University:

> Realism does not lack its partisans, but it does rather conspicuously lack a persuasive theory . . . to lack a persuasive theory is to lack something crucial.

This ties in with my mention of 'The Theory, The Theory, The Theory!' earlier in this series. Wolfe's awakening culminated in a devastating evisceration of not just Hilton Kramer but the phenomenon that he represented. Titled *The Painted Word,* Tom Wolfe gave a masterclass and a magnificent critique of the art 'scene' in the elite and posh America of that era, something he contemptuously called 'Cultureburg'. Here is a sample:

> Modern Art has become completely literary: *the paintings and other works exist only to illustrate the text*.... Art made its final flight, climbed higher and higher in an ever-decreasing tighter-turning spiral until ... it disappeared up its own fundamental aperture ... and came out the other side as Art Theory!... *Art Theory pure and simple, is words on a page, literature undefiled by vision.* (Emphases added)

What Wolfe lamented and outraged about was the disappearance of the most fundamental element in all art: *beauty.*

And here is the iconic D.V. Gundappa, who expressed the same outrage and lament almost a decade before Wolfe. It was his anxiety and anguish over the loss of beauty in literature.

> [A]rt is the experience of beauty, grandeur and exaltation. But today, the new kinds of art works flooding into India from Europe and America, do they give us this experience? In my case, the answer is no. Perhaps my view might be partially blind owing to my attachment to our artistic tradition. But a person who regards Jakkanachari, Tyagaraja, and Valmiki as Gurus does not get the aforementioned experience in these new works of art. But others who don't have this attachment might experience beauty in them.
>
> In which case, what is beauty?
>
> In today's world, there is no standard to measure it.

> For us, dignity of dressing is beauty; for others nudity is. For us, subtle movement of the human body is beauty; titillation is vulgarity … *new cults in art like the hippies and the Beatles have become popular even in India … to my eyes, their dressing and behaviour appear grotesque in the extreme. Even their painters have followed the same path.*
>
> …
>
> The fate of modern poetry is also similar … the simile is derived from some place and its object of comparison is unclear … it is impossible to understand the feeling or emotion attempted to be conveyed.
>
> Overall, it appears as though anarchy and frenzy are being deliberately spread.
>
> …
>
> In my limited knowledge, a true conception of beauty and exaltation is characterised by choice and proportion. Not all things in this world are endowed with beauty, and not all parts of a thing are equally beautiful…. But there is a fundamental philosophy underscoring choice and proportion. *The vision of beauty and grandeur should not pervert the connoisseur's mind. The painting or play or scene must imbue joy and not inflame crude passions.* The enabler of beauty and profound values is a cultivated inward attitude of bashfulness…. *Bashfulness is the protective armour of all art. Without this, the work of art becomes an exhibition of depravity.* Thus, the work of an artist is one that carries immense responsibility. *Just as how the artist needs freedom, he must also erect restraints upon himself.* (Emphases added)

Clearly, filmmakers of our own time continue to flagrantly violate every single warning that D.V. Gundappa issued more than 60 years ago.

But to state it in polite language, today's movies make us leave the theatre after having merely *witnessed* them, not experienced them. We have facts, not plots. We have real people, not characters. Expertise in technique and craft have become convenient bypasses for circumventing art. In fact, at some point in this race towards the bottom, acting or performance has been slowly murdered. We now have stock expressions for emoting that last for fleeting seconds instead of the time-honoured art of sustaining an emotion at length. The fine art of the monologue has mostly become extinct, and both monologues and dialogues have become one-liners. Instead of allowing the actor to use his or her innate or honed creativity and wide reading to interpret the character, ready-made factory products are being handed down to the actor. As far as Indian cinema is concerned, we have bodybuilders, gymnasts, and athletes as onscreen 'heroes'. The acclaim received by 'character actors' is precisely because *the main leads are not actors.* Female leads exist to perform one or both of these two functions: to sexually arouse the audience and to spew the woke ideology.

In the final reckoning, this lethal handiwork of the Left, which has succeeded beyond its wildest dreams, serves another defining purpose. The example of Lenin's hounding of intellectuals and artists is illustrative. The moment he captured power, he decreed that all art was meant only to propagandize communism. In other words, the Left uses art, literature, drama, and cinema not merely to make an ideological statement but to ultimately topple governments. No section of society is immune from it. The first step to do that is to kill the very foundations and goals of all art—beauty and joy—and to replace them with pessimism and agitation. The downfall of Indian cinema has occurred exactly on these planes.

19

Jamba Lakidi Pamba: An Underrated Classic that Foretold the Woke Epidemic

The pre-climax sequence of the Telugu blockbuster *Jamba Lakidi Pamba* was an eerie prediction of a sinister reality that is exploding out of control in the United States and Europe. In the scene, a Sadhu foretells how society will hurtle into utter degeneration and collapse in five phases:

1. Women will become men and vice versa
2. Children will behave like adults and vice versa
3. Dressing, language, and speech will become bestial, demonic, and unintelligible
4. Everyone lapses into insanity to the extent that insanity becomes the new normal
5. Bodily organs will undergo bizarre transformations: female body parts will appear on male bodies and vice versa

Thirty-one years after *Jamba Lakidi Pamba* was released, almost all these phases have become part of what we mistakenly call 'reality'. These five phases constitute the combined definition of the degeneracy known as woke. It is also its most accurate definition, and its malevolence becomes starker because it appears in a fictional movie.

Back then, the audience laughed uproariously. It was still a naïve and untainted audience, which actually believed that the world depicted in *Jamba Lakidi Pamba* could only exist in the realm of fantasy. Little did this audience imagine that this fantasy could ever come alive and consume its own children and grandchildren, who are today slowly being sucked into the woke vortex. In urban India.

Released in 1992 on a shoestring budget, *Jamba Lakidi Pamba* is a highly underrated classic made by the late E.V.V. Satyanarayana (or EVV as he was popularly known). The movie is solidly anchored in the Jandhyala School of filmmaking. EVV was not only mentored by Jandhyala but was also his most distinguished legatee. Jandhayala Subrahmanya Sastry stands tallest among the handful of Telugu filmmakers who have delivered compelling social and cultural commentaries using classy humour as a powerful medium. A distinctive element in the cinematic oeuvre of both Jandhyala and EVV is their powerful rebuttals to agenda-driven Leftist moviemakers seeking to overturn society through miseducation, perversion, and violence.

The plot-seed for *Jamba Lakidi Pamba* originated when EVV was working as Jandhyala's assistant. It sprouted after he read the Telugu novelist Madireddy Sulochana's play on the same theme. After substantial modifications, EVV developed into a full-fledged screenplay.

The basic theme of *Jamba Lakidi Pamba* is breathtaking in its simplicity: what happens to society when time-honoured gender roles are literally and *physically* reversed?

When *Jamba Lakidi Pamba* was conceptualized and released, feminism had neither acquired the aggression nor the political clout that it has acquired in the last 15 years. This is also why a *Jamba Lakidi Pamba* cannot be made today. In fact, a cheap rip-off of the same movie with the same title was released in 2018, with catastrophic results for the producer.

Which is also why *Jamba Lakidi Pamba* endures as a futuristic and visionary classic. There was no way EVV could have known in advance that something called a woke 'culture' would emerge in the near future. However, like all sane observers of society and popular trends, he had spotted the long-term dangers of toppling enduring social structures, which are the products of millennia of evolution. The social trend that was steadily gaining steam in India in the 1990s was feminism. In hindsight, it is clear that feminism was indeed the original virus that paved the way for today's woke insanity.

Jamba Lakidi Pamba works at multiple levels. It is primarily a social satire housed in the genre of fantasy-comedy. Apart from its opening and closing minutes, the whole movie is both unreal and surreal. This is its greatest strength and is also the reason for its popularity and repeat value. It is also a dire warning. The Indian society depicted in *Jamba Lakidi Pamba* has eroded at a rapid pace in an astonishingly short period, as we shall see.

The fantasy world of *Jamba Lakidi Pamba* is located in Vishakapatanam, but it could be set in any Indian city or town. Its society is what has been theorized as the oppressive patriarchal Hindu society. All men are lazy wastrels, busy playing cards, drinking, smoking, debauching, and generally beating up their wives. All women are helpless victims of this male-dominated, oppressive society. Not only are they victims, they are also oppressors of their own miserable sisters. Life goes on like this until a 'city-educated' (unmarried) firebrand lady decides to completely reverse this society.

She's the female protagonist of the movie. One day, she is led to a forbidding cave inhabited by a swamini (female monk) who had renounced this male-dominated society decades ago. Ever since, she has been engaged in severe penance to find out the best method of seeking vengeance against men. She finally finds it: a magic potion named 'Jamba Lakidi Pamba', a concoction that she has prepared. And she awaits a kindred soul to put her potion to work. The female protagonist takes the potion and mixes it in the tank that supplies water to Vishakapatanam.

The consequence is immediate: overnight, gender roles are reversed in the whole city. Men become women, and women become men.

For the next hour or so, we witness the real-life consequences of this reversal. Men wear *bindi* and *mangalasutra* and cook and draw *rangolis*. Men also get pregnant with bloated bellies and experience labour pains, but women deliver the baby with zero pain. Women play cards, smoke and booze, have rollicking extramarital affairs, and rediscover old flames. Women also visit brothels, where the brothel owner parades the most delectable male whores for selection.

The irony of this upended society is stark. In the old order—i.e., the time-tested gender relationships and social structures—both men and women are aware of their respective roles. In the surreal new order, both men and women are no longer aware of their gender; they have become automatons, dehumanized, and controlled by the external agent known as 'Jamba Lakidi Pamba'.

The whole thing is shown in graphic detail, leaving nothing to the imagination. In fact, *Jamba Lakidi Pamba* is a fine example of *vācyata* (explicitness) that actually works. It works because it is vācyata dipped in splendid humour. And it is humour that's tasteful. But for this tastefulness, vācyata can easily slip into disgust and vulgarity.

And when *this* 'society' finally becomes unhinged, the avenging female protagonist admits to her folly and takes the male protagonist to the aforementioned cave. This is when another layer of storytelling brilliance unfolds. The swamini, who had prepared the original Jamba Lakidi Pamba potion, is dead. There is no antidote to reverse the reversal. The swamini character is actually a superb symbolism for all the mindless and irresponsible feminist cheerleaders and activists of the past and present. Two random names come to mind: the pioneering feminist Virginia Woolf and the manic-depressive Sylvia Plath. The swamini who dies in *Jamba Lakidi Pamba* symbolizes all such unchained feminists who evade responsibility for the horrors they have unleashed by creating a monster that hurts others and not them.

It is at this juncture that we arrive at the pre-climax sequence mentioned at the beginning of this essay. The swami in the cave is her male disciple, who delineates the five-phased destruction of society. He also prepares the antidote for Jamba Lakidi Pamba, and the movie ends on a happy note,i.e., the old order is restored.

But before that, society has tottered to the very brink. It is no longer limited to gender role reversal. Now we witness children behaving like adults and vice versa. Parents attend kindergarten wearing shorts and frocks. Kids have become stick-wielding teachers. In the next phase, male and female voices will be transmuted. And the male protagonist warns that in the succeeding phase, men will start breastfeeding.

While the old order is restored in the movie, it appears that contemporary American society has entered the third or fourth phase shown in *Jamba Lakidi Pamba*. Misguided medical science is now being used for dangerous experiments on live human beings like gender transformation and deadly hormone 'therapies' with unpredictable but disastrous consequences. Male children as young as six are being fed with drugs to make them more 'feminine'. Puberty blockers have become normalized. There is an entire body of research trying to find out ways to make men pregnant. YouTube videos showing adult males breastfeeding are garnering millions of hits. A leading American university published a 'research paper' that tries to 'prove' that lactating mothers need 'consent' from their own infants to breastfeed.

The nightmarish list is endless. Even the creative powers of George Orwell and Aldous Huxley couldn't envision this dystopian hell in *1984* and *Brave New World.*

Alarmingly, this American woke virus has already crept into and is infecting Indian youth. And every voice calling for reason and sanity is being ruthlessly suppressed by the woke mob. This is *Jamba Lakidi Pamba* in savage action in real life. Except that there is no saviour swami or his antidote.

The whole movie is an extraordinary metaphor in and of itself. The term *Jamba Lakidi Pamba* has no meaning. It is a string of rhyming and alliterative sounds. Like an incantation of insanity. Which begets kindred sounds. In the movie, these become *Pamba Lakidi Jamba, Pamba Jamba Lamba Lakidi*, and so on. What is notable is that all these sounds are actually potions, which have specific uses and outcomes—yet another brilliant metaphor. Vishakapatanam is also a metaphor. Its water tank is a metaphor. The deeper we dig, the more artistic and storytelling nuances emerge.

The unstated brilliance of *Jamba Lakidi Pamba* is its awesome use of satirical humour to deliver a grave message, a portent even. We know we're watching arrant nonsense, but for example, like *Alice in Wonderland,* it sucks us into its world, making us simultaneously connoisseurs, observers, and participants. It makes absurdity enjoyable because the absurdity is painted and beautified by the brush of art.

Jamba Lakidi Pamba was and remains a film far ahead of its time. By satirizing a destructive and soulless political ideology like mindless feminism, it has shown its innate nature: silly, absurd, toxic, and devastating. Indirectly, E.V.V. Satyanarayana has provided a fine model for aspiring filmmakers who want to combat the Left-liberal ecosystem on its own turf.

20

The Universal Parallels between Vrtrasura's Story and the Nehruvian Legacy

The story of Vrtrāsura is as timeless and universal as the genius of the civilization that birthed it. First appearing in the *Rg Veda*, it has deservedly captivated the imaginations of generations of artists and devotees alike. The Rishis of the Veda birthed the story, and the *Itihāsakāras* (Maharshi Valmiki and Veda Vyasa) and *Paurāṇikas* (authors of the Puranas) embellished it in spectacular and multilayered forms. In recent times, Devudu Narasimha Sastry's Kannada novel *Mahakshatriya* has brought the story to life in a thrilling and dignified manner.

Vrtrāsura's story works at multiple levels. Its universal symbolism has few parallels. As a literary metaphor, it has stood the test of time. Above all, its kernel contains a profound *darshana* or philosophical revelation.

The word *Vrtra* literally means 'enveloper', 'obstacle', 'cover', 'darkness', 'absence of natural light', etc. The Veda has the synonym *ahi* for Vrtra. Ahi means a fearsome, venomous snake. Ahi is also a synonym for Rāhu, the planet which is represented as a serpent eclipsing the sun and the moon.

In the *Rg Veda*, Indra fights one of his toughest battles with Vrtra, who, in his serpentine form, has blocked the waters of the world. It is a battle in which Indra suffers severe reverses.

Vrtra breaks Indra's jaws, but undaunted, Indra shatters the 99 forts of Vrtra and eventually slays him with his *Vajrāyudha*—the invincible thunderbolt. Indeed, one of the celebrated sobriquets of Indra is *Vrtrahan*—the killer of Vrtra.

On the symbolic plane, here is Indra—the deity of rain—engaged in a fierce war against a demon who has blocked all the waters, i.e., life itself. The synonyms for the Sanskrit word *jīvana* include 'life' and 'water'.

The Story in the Puranic Corpus

In the Puranic lore, the Vrtra story has been significantly transformed without altering its Vedic core. It occurs variously in the *Bhāgavataṃ, Devī Bhagavata*, *Padma Purāṇa*, and *Viṣṇudharmottara Purāṇa*. The *Padma Purana*, for example, has a celebrated version of the Vrtra story in which Indra is terrified of Vrtra's power and resorts to deceit in order to slaughter him.

The Ramayana and the Mahabharata, too, have creatively exploited the Vrtra story. The Mahabharata, especially, has used the story as a backdrop to narrate the life and legacy of the glorious king Nahusha.

But the *Viṣṇudharmottara Purāṇa* has quite a nice twist to the aftermath of the Vrtra story.

Although Vrtra was an asura, he was also a Brahmana. Thus, by killing him, Indra incurred the *Brahmahatyā-dōṣa* (the sin of killing a Brahmana) and had to expiate it. The *Viṣṇudharmottara Purāṇa* tells us that Indra killed Vrtra when the latter was engaged in tapas—penance. The *Padma Purāṇa* tells us that Indra induced the celestial danseuse Rambha to seduce Vrtra and make him consume liquor, which was an unambiguous sign of his downfall. And when Vrtra blacked out due to excessive drinking, Indra unleashed his thunderbolt and killed him.

This is how the *Viṣṇudharmottara Purāṇa* describes what transpired next:

> Stricken with the *Brahmahatyā-dōṣa,* Indra immediately lost his resplendence and was afraid to stay in *Svarga-Loka*. He fled to the *M*ānasa *Sarovara* (literally, Lake of the Mind). There, he assumed his Subtle Form and hid himself inside a lotus stem.
>
> Now leaderless, the rest of the Devatas too, fled *Svarga-Loka.* Spotting an empty *Svarga-Loka,* the great emperor of the earth, Nahusha, invaded it and occupied Indra's throne. He had earned this honour by performing a hundred *Aśvamēdha-Yāgas*. For, the Veda says that a human being who has performed one hundred *Aśvamēdha-Yāgas* automatically becomes an Indra.
>
> But the throne of Indra instilled disdain in Nahusha. He ordered Shachi Devi, the Indrāṇi (Indra's wife and queen) to become his wife. She became mortified when she heard the news of this vulgar demand. Then she hit upon a plan and sent the following message to Nahusha: I will agree to become your wife only if you build an ornate palanquin and receive me personally. The palanquin must be carried by the *Saptarṣis* (The Seven Eminent Sages) on their shoulders and you must show your regal pride befitting your status as Indra.
>
> Accordingly, Nahusha built the palanquin and made the *Saptarṣis* carry it. This was an unprecedented act of effrontery. No Indra had ever done something as vile as this. At the height of his haughtiness, Nahusha kicked the Rishi Agastya with his foot, chiding him for being slow. He commanded the sage, '*sarpa! sarpa!* Faster! Faster!' The outraged sage cursed him: '*bhava sarpo Mahīpate*! May you become a serpent!' The word *Sarpa* also means a serpent.
>
> The next moment, Nahusha was transformed into a serpent but he repented for his brashness. Agastya took pity on him and said that he would regain his human form when he met Yudhishtira.

> The *Svarga-Loka* once more became leaderless. The Devatas who had remained there became inflicted with extreme *Rajas* (unrestrained passion) and *Tamas* (dullness, sloth). They were also imbued with melancholy and lost even the notion of joy. As a result, all good deeds and Dharmic rituals disappeared from the *Svarga-Loka.*
>
> Naturally, this state of disorder directly impacted the mortal world as well. Famine-induced deaths became rampant. People stopped performing propitiatory rituals and stopped offering sacred oblations to the Devatas (*Yaga, Yajna*) as had been the norm. No longer were the melodious chants of *Svāhā*, *svadhā* and *Vaśaṭ* heard.
>
> The whole earth was being wiped out by drought and people stood on the brink of death by starvation. Cattle wealth (*Go-dhana*) was obliterated. A large section of both virtuous and wicked people had turned into demons killing whatever they could find just in order to survive. The mortal world had become a mountain of corpses. Market streets were abandoned.
>
> Agriculture had disappeared. Water bodies had dried up. Parents carried their children and infants on their shoulders, distraught and wailing. People had no strength even to shed tears of sorrow. Indeed, what is joy and sorrow when you are starving? Gradually, the demonic element entered the nature (*svabhāva*) of these starving people and they became demons in human form.
>
> Eventually, those who could, began migrating out of *Āryāvarta* and settled in *Mleccha* lands. They lost all sense of Dharma, virtue and pure conduct. They abandoned even basic hygiene and began eating impure and rotting food. It appeared as if the whole earth would be transformed into a gigantic *Mleccha* hell-hole.

The story ends with the Devatas beseeching Vishnu to restore order and peace in all three worlds. Moved by their plight,

Vishnu restored Indra to his former throne, and all is well that ends well.

Timeless Lessons and Profound Insights

To the 'modern' mind which is incurably mired in 'reality' and literalism, this story might sound laughable and ridiculous. But the truths and lessons that it contains are universal and have eternal relevance.

The *Svarga-Loka* can be roughly taken as a metaphorical expression of Rta or the invisible cosmic order. By deceitfully killing Vrtra, Indra no doubt commits a crime, but that crime eventually serves to maintain the cosmic order. Yet he is only too aware of his own guilt and embarks on tapas as a form of repentance.

On another plane, Indra is also the *Indriyābhimāni Dēvata*—the guardian or deity of sense organs. This is why, when he abdicates his throne, his subordinates—other Devatas—are afflicted by rajas and tamas.

The Nahusha interregnum is also illustrative of the disaster that occurs when even a qualified and virtuous person occupies high office. He has merely acquired the trappings of Indra's throne but not the wisdom, experience, or restraint to hold on to it. Nahusha is justly celebrated as a noble emperor in our Puranic lore, but as this episode shows, lust and pride become his Achilles' heel. The sweet fruit of a hundred Aśvamēdha-*yāgas* turns into lethal venom with one kick of his foot, and he himself is physically turned into a venomous creature.

The fate of the Svarga-Loka after Indra's abdication and Nahusha's ignoble exit also provides superb insights into the nature of anarchy. When the cosmic order is itself thrown into disorder, it consumes everything. This is the underlying tenor of the horrifying descriptions of the human world that we read in the *Viṣṇudharmottara Purāṇa*. This is especially notable in the portions dealing with:

The 'demonic element' entering into starving human beings whose world is now ruled by anarchy. An independent India ruled by Nehru-imposed socialism precisely created such demons out of millions of ordinary Indians. It was a starvation economy that forced decent people to become cut throats.

The migration of people from *Āryāvarta* into *Mleccha* lands. The infamous 'brain drain' that occurred after the 1970s was another byproduct of the self-same starvation economy. But more fundamentally, it was an outcome of a vile anarchy that Nehru's fondness for Soviet-style socialism had engineered and which Indira Gandhi had nurtured. Thus, devout middle-class Hindus who fled to the US as students during that period reconciled themselves to the plight of serving beef burgers to Mlecchas in order to meet their expenses rather than living in their sacred *matrubhoomi*. Thus, sans this engineered anarchy, it is doubtful whether such a large population of NRIs would have existed today.

Defining Mleccha-ness

The alarm that the *Viṣṇudharmottara Purāṇa* sounds about the Mleccha-fication of the whole earth is premised on Rta and Dharma. From one perspective, a major block of the history of the West is simply a history of anarchy. This is especially true of the history of various 'revolutions'. The graphic, eyewitness details of absolute monsters like Robespierre clarify this point like no other. Will Durant tangentially captures this truth in brilliant prose: 'When liberty destroys order, the hunger for order will destroy liberty.' Viewed from the Darshanic perspective, the trajectory of the post-Christian West is one continuous history of rampantly tampering with Rta. An unbridled desire to conquer nature is a defining trait of the Mleccha-ness.

Whether or not we wish to believe in the existence of Indra, Vrtra, or Svarga-Loka, or whether we choose to dismiss the whole thing, is beside the point. What Indra, Vrtra, et al. really symbolize is an unalterable philosophical tenet. One of the outstanding expositions of this theme is available in Devudu Narasimha Sastri's vivid description of the whole process of creating an alternate Svarga-Loka for Trishanku, in his masterpiece *Mahabrahmana.*

Our Puranic and epic literature has created all these fantastic tales and incredible worlds, gods, sages, and kings to delineate these unalterable truths in a thrilling, intimate, evocative, and emotional fashion. Nothing educates the mind and illuminates life like an unbelievable story told unbelievably.

The Devatas, who finally appeal to Vishnu to save them from their leaderless and anarchic ordeal, present a highly logical end to the story. Vishnu is, after all, the Stithi-Karta, the preserver of order and stability.

21

Bharatavarsha Must Consciously Reject Western Ideological Universalism and Accelerate Decolonization

—1—

A recent WhatsApp forward that had spread like wildfire euphorically heralded some sort of glorious revival of Right-Wing ideology across the Western hemisphere. Its conclusion basically is that because Giorgia Meloni, Javier Milei, Geert Wilders, et al., have been elected with thumping majorities, Narendra Modi too will return to power in 2024.

At the very least, this is the latest exemplar of an old logical fallacy: confounding correlation with causation. At worst, it is the return of another old ailment that has plagued the Hindu community for the last 150 years: seeking Western validation for our own successes, which have nothing to do with the West. To say it bluntly, such behaviour is the outward expression of our subconscious colonization, which clings to the alien and fears taking ownership of our own triumphs.

Even in the limited sphere of electoral politics, equating Narendra Modi with Geert Wilders or Giorgia Meloni is akin to forcing a simile between Christ's alleged Second Coming and Krishna Janmashtami.

The West has a well-defined Right wing. India has only a well-defined Left wing fully populated by spectral Indian imitators of the West. Members of this Indian Left wing are equal opportunity timeservers; they are happy to do the bidding of both the soul-harvesters of the Joshua Project as well as dangerous globalists like George Soros and Pierre Omidyar.

India, thus, is a freak case where the ideological opponents of the (Indian) Left are yet to define themselves unambiguously. Defining themselves as 'Right wing' causes more self-inflicted harm than good in the long run. Since its inception, the Indian Left has at least been honest about its psychological colonization and proudly flouts it. But because the Indian Left's opponents have had no clear self-definition, they have had to resort to drawing feel-good parallels between Wilders and Modi, Trump and Modi, and so on. This is not to question the genuine commitment of the Indian non-Left to their pet causes, but to point out a historical and commonsense reality: that the best weapons in your arsenal pose the constant danger of backfiring.

I recall the eminently wise words of the literary scholar Dr L.V. Shanta Kumari, who once told me, 'wings on human beings look ugly and stupid'.

The Right wing of the West, if it acquires absolute power, will, for example, further accelerate the pace of Christian conversions in India. History demonstrates that the missionary apparatus loves nothing more than a civil war within the society of its targets. The story of how the 1994 Rwandan genocide was the climax of sustained missionary conversions is a chilling instance in recent memory.

The Right versus Left battle in the West has a reasonably long history. What has made it so stark and visible to the rest of the world today is the unprecedented level of global connectedness, plus the demonic transformation of the Left into woke. The ongoing backlash in the West against the Left has occurred precisely because woke has singlehandedly destroyed the family unit out there and has been the most loyal bedmate of Islamic terror. By all counts, this is the West at war with itself, divided into Left and Right.

The Hindu society in India should watch it with caution, and while it is tempting to celebrate the electoral losses of the Left in the West, it is wiser to introspect and draw lessons and not participate in it.

— 2 —

The phenomenal success of the Ramajanmabhoomi Movement, the consecutive victories of Narendra Modi, and the evolving Hindu resurgence—all of these are fully homegrown. They are not merely political, social, or cultural changes, but epochs. But because they've unfolded before our own eyes, it is hard to grasp their far-reaching magnitude. When their history is written with honesty after half a century, posterity will better appreciate the true import of the term *epoch*. Their inspiration was Indian. Their methods were homespun. Their appeal was rooted in an ethos that has nothing to do with Western 'wing' political ideologies. And so, viewing them in the light of these 'wing' ideologies is, like I said, an expression of subconscious colonization.

I see two ways forward.

The first is a *conscious rejection* of the Western model of ideological universalism, i.e., viewing every phenomenon through the Western ideological lens. That model has clearly failed in the very society and culture that birthed it. It would have been hilarious if only it was not so serious: both the (non-woke) Left and the Right in America are incessantly breaking their brains over the same question: why is America so broken and how to fix it? Their final prognosis is uniform: a corrupt elite has colonized the US. And their solutions, such as they are, are no solutions. The philosophy of history says that what is known as American civilization has reached its expiry date because its society has become dysfunctional. The same philosophy also tells us that the political class cannot fix society. So, what is needed for America is a tombstone, not a repair kit.

The second. This rejection should be concomitant with all-encompassing decolonization, a term and a process that originated in India even as the British were colonizing it. The field is almost infinitely vast, and stalwarts of the past have handsomely fertilized it. It would be both foolish and arrogant to claim to improve upon their work. The best we can do is carry that legacy forward. This work has also acquired lightning urgency in our own period of byte-sized attention spans, in an era of fleeting emotions and a complete lack of respect for anything that is grand, magnanimous, quiet, sustained, slow, and rhythmic.

—3—

Decolonization is a national duty and a future national asset. Duty, to borrow the Bhagavad Gita's eternal edict, is a profound, lifelong inner calling that has to be pursued for its own sake. An army of ants will flock to the sweet fruit of duty, but its bitter yield is that of a serpent that bites the doer. As a future national asset, if the value of decolonization is fully realized, Bharatavarsha will re-emerge as perhaps the only palliative for the global wreckage, whose pronounced feature is instability.

Decolonization is a diagnosis, a scholarship, a process, and a civilizational continuum. It is both foolish and impossible to do justice to it, even in the space of, say, 20 volumes. What I can do at best in this space is to offer some outlines that will hopefully stimulate a deeper and wider study.

Apart from Sri Dharampal's inner calling, which transmogrified as a lifelong study of how Bharatavarsha looked before the British colonized her, no comprehensive study of decolonization has been done till date with the gravity it merits. His work has been ably continued—both in letter and spirit—by stalwarts of our own time such as Sri J.K. Bajaj, M.D. Srinivas, et al.

While their findings have been widely published, the impact has been rather minimal because the state apparatus that India inherited in 1947 has remained stubbornly colonial. This embedded colonial nature is the direct cause of how easy it is, even today, to stir separatist sentiments along various fault lines. A thorough decolonization makes for a truly united India.

My own limited studies in this area lead me to the following conclusion: even after three-fourths of a century, Indians—Hindus especially—have actually become more colonized than they had ever been under British rule. All attempts at decolonization have met with feeble success, and that success has at best been sporadic and short-lived.

True decolonization reflects itself in lasting and culturally rooted changes in the life and lifestyle of the individual; it will rebuild the family, the community, society, and political and administrative institutions. This was—and still is—the pulsating mantra of everyone working in this sphere. However, the power and grip of the negative legacy of colonization have proven remarkably enduring.

So, it is better to face the bitter truth bravely and with confidence if we honestly need to find long-term solutions.

— 4 —

A first step in decolonization involves all-encompassing study and scholarship. This will help us evolve practical and implementable solutions towards comprehensive decolonization. Thus, decolonization is both an academic discipline and a practical process. The discipline should guide the process, and the process should enrich the discipline. It is also a mistake to think that decolonization is a specific 'goal' to be achieved. It is a continuum.

But at an even more fundamental level, decolonization is the recovery of memory. In our case, it is the recovery of the Hindu civilizational and cultural memory across space and time. When we recover this memory, we automatically recover our narrative memory, as we shall see in more detail.

As an all-encompassing phenomenon, decolonization includes everything from politics to performing the daily puja at home. In the contemporary, hyperconnected era, this becomes even more stark. At least one generation of the Hindu diaspora has completely embraced the woke epidemic, which poses one of the most lethal threats to Hindu Dharma.

In one sense, decolonization is a negative process aimed at achieving a positive outcome. This is akin to rebuilding a destroyed structure. Even if the rebuilding is complete, the original structure has still been lost forever. We can consider a random example to illustrate this: the rebuilding of the Sri Rama Mandir. The new temple is certainly a brilliant civilizational victory. It promises to be grand, but it is not the original temple that was destroyed. This is to emphasize the kind of challenges that decolonization encounters even in the physical space.

To fully grasp the extent, scale, and complexity of this challenge, it is essential to understand the obvious phenomenon that led to all this: colonization. We need to answer very basic questions: How do we understand our own Hindu society today? What are the sources and tools that shape this understanding? Is our present Hindu society the same as what it was, say, even in 1970s? If so, what are the common features? If not, what are the key differences?

History is our indispensable guide for finding answers to all such questions. It is crucial for us to understand how and on what all planes we have been colonized. This mandates us to travel back about 250 years. We need to study the history of this period to comprehend the nature of the forces that permanently changed India.

Simultaneously, we need to get a clear picture of how Indian society functioned back then. But our greatest handicap in this endeavour is the fact that we no longer have access to that society. But it is undeniable that the maximum damage occurred at the level of our psyche, and this damage was deliberately engineered.

The Lost Access to the Hindu Societal Past

The clearest differentiator that marked India before the advent of the British is available in the realm of social engineering. For the preceding 600 years, successive alien Muslim regimes had not mucked around with the traditional and social institutions of Hindus. Muslim invaders, who had come from abroad, had permanently settled in India after establishing empires.

However, from the start, the British knew that their stay in India would be temporary. The copious archives they have left behind show that they were aware that they would have to eventually pack their bags and leave. The British hated everything about this country—its climate, its people, its culture, and its society. The oppression of Hindu society by Muslim kings was extremely crude, violent, and evoked instant outrage. But the British oppression was more deliberate and long-term. It was imbued with a single goal: to extort the maximum amount of wealth with maximum efficiency and speed. Guns and swords would only take them so far. In his classic book *The Case for India,* Will Durant gives us a desolate picture of British oppression:

> When the British came there was, throughout India, a system of communal schools, managed by the village communities. *The agents of the East India Company destroyed these village communities* … [the British] spent most of its [funds] for education on secondary schools and universities, where the language used was English, the history, literature, customs and morals taught were English, and young Hindus, after striving amid poverty to prepare themselves for college, found that they had merely let themselves in for *a ruthless process that aimed to de-nationalize and de-Indianize them, and turn them into imitative Englishmen.*
>
> …
>
> British ownership of India has been a calamity and a crime … the present plunder has now gone on beyond bearing; year by year it is destroying one of the greatest and gentlest peoples of history…. This is the conclusion … taxation, exploitation, starvation, death. (Emphases added)

By the mid-19th century, the British had initiated a generational project of social engineering. Among its chief outcomes were introducing a new education system, an alien legal framework, and a wholesale dismantling of traditional Hindu institutions and replacing them with British models. For example, the university system and the elaborate court hierarchies that we're all familiar with now did not exist before the British disruption of India.

The overall scenario looked like this: by the second half of the 19th century, India was being transformed in an unprecedented fashion, and this transformation had an irreversible quality to it. Nowhere was this transformation more pronounced than in education, beginning with the infamous Macaulay's Minute, which aimed to create a class of Indians who would think like the British and blindly imitate them in all respects. Apart from education, the British also inflicted colossal damage on our traditional institutions of, say, charity, community-based economics, guilds, and so on.

All these changes naturally left a deep and lasting impact on Indians as a people and India as a civilization.

And so, to fully grasp the challenge of decolonization, we also need to understand the psychological impact of the kind of government that the British ran in India. Its fundamental purpose was heartless economic exploitation, and all structures that they erected were solely meant to serve it. Thus, education was transformed into a device for serving this extortionate government, aided by a well-oiled and subservient bureaucracy manned by a class of people slightly better than automatons. The Sanatana conception and practice of education as a sacred calling, ideal, and value lost their philosophical primacy. Laws were concocted overnight to circumvent inconvenient systems that had been in place for more than two millennia.

— 5 —

By the third quarter of the 19th century, a new India had emerged: for the first time in 5,000 years, we had two countries within the same country: England, as represented by its colonial government, and the 'original' India, still untainted by the British infection. This naturally birthed two societies within the same society: the new, English-educated Indian elite and the 'original' Indians, who were anchored to their roots. At no point in our history did this situation exist.

Until the British began vandalizing our social institutions, a king, a chieftain, or a rich zamindar would only tell a poor man, 'You can't build a bigger house than mine.' He never said, 'You can't eat more than me.'

In other words, despite differences in economic status, religious beliefs, etc., there was an internal harmony between the ruling class and the plebians in India. This harmony is the reason we never find a single mass revolution in the entire history of India, unlike in Europe.

So, how was this harmony achieved? Here are two quotes that provide the answer to this question. The first is by Dr S. Srikanta Sastri, an eminent scholar of Indian history.

> In the history of the world, it is only Hinduism that gave not only to India but also to all her neighbours an organic conception of society based upon economic as well as spiritual needs. It is the very antithesis of 'the principle of accumulation based on inequality' which is a vital part of the Western order of society. It recognized frankly the hard fact that perfect equality in all spheres is impossible of attainment. Therefore, it attempted to mitigate the evil consequences of great disparity by aiming at only the essentials. It reconciled the antagonism between rights and obligations, so that the individual by asserting his 'inherent' right might not break up social solidarity, nor could society impose such obligations as to cripple the spirit of individualism. Liberty and law were synthesized to achieve spiritual freedom.

The second quote is by another luminary D.V. Gundappa. He delineates perhaps the clearest contrast between our traditional forms of government and the British system of parliamentary democracy:

> There has always been present in the body politic of England an element distrustful of authority and critical of its ways … we in this country never had, as the British had, a conflict between the king and his barons or bishops, and never a split in the citizen-body as royalist and roundhead, Tory and Whig, Conservative and Liberal. There was no occasion for our ancestors to develop such a bifurcation of the public life…. Our party life of today is an artificial creation.

Both D.V. Gundappa and Dr Srikanta Sastri wrote their treatises in the 1950s. So, when DVG declares that 'our party life of today is an artificial creation', he clearly points at the political impact of colonization even after India had attained political freedom. In other words, this time-honoured harmony that had existed for millennia had been irreversibly shattered by British colonization.

— 6 —

Even as the British were busy tampering with our traditional and social institutions and impregnating the Macaulayite model of education, a parallel development was occurring.

This was the Indian response to these social engineering efforts.

It took two major forms.

The first was the backlash that English education received. It began in Bengal because it was the first laboratory of the British colonization of the Hindu mind. When Hindu society realized what English education was doing, it hit back ferociously.

Mass public campaigns were launched to discourage Indians from attending British schools, colleges, and universities. British educational institutions were branded as *Gholam-Khanas* or factories producing slaves for the British Empire.

The second response forms the crux of this essay. This was the birth of the New Indian Renaissance, a unique epoch in our civilizational history. It is truly the golden age of India under British enslavement. The fact that Hindus were able to spawn such an age in such an oppressive climate is one of the greatest testimonies to the immeasurable worth of the cultural continuity that our people so dearly valued. This period spanned roughly an entire century, from the second half of the 19th to the second half of the 20th century.

In fact, the Indian freedom struggle, which eventually became a mass movement, was only the political facet of a deeper and far more profound struggle—a struggle to recover the battered, bruised, and wounded ethos of the ancient Hindu civilization, which had attracted the whole world continuously for more than 2,000 years as the global magnet of education, culture, and prosperity.

The New Indian Renaissance also witnessed the birth of an entirely new class of extraordinary philosophers, spiritual masters, intellectuals, thinkers, writers, artists, scholars, and statesmen.

This class began to chart a fresh process and a journey of re-evaluating and rediscovering its own roots using the tools introduced by the British (the West, broadly speaking). Gradually, as Indians began travelling to Europe in greater numbers, they got first-hand experience of that society and its conditions. They were able to produce fine and clear comparative analyses of the Indian condition. One major finding was that the so-called 'modern', 'scientific', 'rational', and 'progressive' British society was, after all, none of these on the ground in its own land. The 19th and early 20th century British society was a deeply status-conscious society, and London, for example, was notorious for rampant teenage prostitution. But back in India, the same British had already compiled voluminous treatises about the inherent evils of a 'caste system', which they had invented and declared was the primary reason for Hindu society's backwardness.

Armed with such findings, the luminaries of the New Indian Renaissance began broadcasting these foreign truths to their own countrymen.

The outcome was nothing short of a nationwide explosion of civilizational reawakening and cultural renewal helmed by the brightest minds endowed with the most compassionate hearts that beat and bled for Bharatavarsha.

Today, it might be astounding to learn that these luminaries were household names in their own time. For example, Jadunath Sarkar was primarily a scholar of history, but he had become a household name because he was something far higher and profounder than a mere historian in the limited sense of a professor teaching a class or writing books.

They were also luminaries in the sense that they exuded a light that re-cultured Indian society both in parts and whole. The other notable feature of these stalwarts was the fact that they knew each another, appreciated each other's good work, and actively sought out each other. A substantial corpus of correspondence—both personal and scholastic—among them is still available to the patient researcher. Often, all it took to initiate the first correspondence was a scholarly paper, a new research finding, or even a straightforward request for help on a knotty problem. These would sometimes lead to lasting friendships and camaraderie. One only needs to read the acknowledgements section of, say, P.V. Kane's volumes on the Dharmasastra or

R.C. Majumdar's volumes on history. What bound all these giants together was Bharatiya culture.

Thus, if we need to seek inspiration and guidance for decolonization in our own time, we inevitably need to study the legacy of these seminal decolonizers. They emerged at a time when they had no past masters to guide them in their respective fields. They had to build their own tools and methods through trial and error and by the dint of their sheer determination, hard work, and perseverance. Aurangzeb consumed more than a quarter of Jadunath Sarkar's life. Dharmasastras devoured more than half a century of P.V. Kane's life.

These were truly original minds who combined talent, scholarship, courage, selflessness, and virtuous conduct. They were exalted patriots driven by a sense of purpose, undaunted by failures, inwardly aloof from fame, and distinguished by a glaring absence of pettiness.

Here is a brief list of names I've selected at random: Raja Rammohun Roy, Swami Nārāyaṇa, Debendranath Tagore, Swami Dayananda Saraswati, Sri Ramakrishna Paramahansa, Keshub Chandra Sen, Chattambi Swamikal, Sri Narayana Guru, Swami Vivekananda, Rabindranath Tagore, Mahatma Gandhi, Sri Aurobindo, Jadunath Sarkar, G.S. Sardesai, V.S. Rajwade, R. Narasimhachar, M. Hiriyanna, V.S. Agarwal, D.V. Gundappa, S. Srikanta Sastri, Govinda Pai, R.C. Majumdar, S. Krishnaswami Iyengar, P.V. Kane, P.K. Telang, U.N. Ghoshal, A.S. Altekar, C.S. Srinivasachari, V.V. Mirashi, B.A. Saletore, B.C. Law, R.D. Banerji, Motichandra, D.C. Sircar, Ramachandra Dikshitar, S. Srikantayya, R.N. Saletore, G.S. Dikshit, C. Hayavadana Rao, and Radhakumud Mukherjee.

Apart from the aforementioned virtues of their character, only sheer madness can explain the priceless treasure they have bequeathed to us. To borrow a quote that John Kenneth

Galbraith stated in a different context, 'if there must be madness, something may be said for having it on a heroic scale'.

—7—

The sunny trait common to all the luminaries of the New Indian Renaissance is this: they were polymaths in the most extensive sense of the term. In our context, they had a solid training and grasp of the Bharatiya tradition and had also mastered the Western intellectual and philosophical milieu dating way back to ancient Greece, Rome, and all the way up to, say, Huxley. This command enabled them to confidently hold the fort in any argument or debate with Western scholars.

An enchanting pleasure in life is to repeatedly savour the clinical demolitions of ill-informed Westerners pontificating on Hindu philosophy, culture, society, and history with the omniscient air of a fundamentalist padre preaching from the pulpit. Five random names come to mind.

In terms of both volume and excellence, Mahamahopadhyaya P.V. Kane ranks first. A big chunk of the six thousand-plus pages of his *History of the Dharmasastra* is a scrumptious feast of roasted Western scholarship. Of special note is how Kane repeatedly treats Dr J. Jolly's misinformed scholarship as if it were a football.

Likewise, Dr S. Srikanta Sastri blazes like a lone, confident torch of truthful dissidence against the enduring hoax called the Aryan Invasion Theory. He stood apart and solitary in this courageous endeavour in a climate clouded by this colonial fog. Dr Sastri was also among a handful of Indians who headbutted celebrated Western intellectuals of the calibre of Oswald Spengler.

In terms of sublimity, precision, and unambiguity, few can match the prowess of Professor M. Hiriyanna. He is perhaps the best model for us to learn the art and craft of how we can reinvigorate and preserve the continuity between the best ideals and traditions of Bharatavarsha and respond to ideas informed by the onslaught of Western ideas, trends, and fashions. For example, when he writes an austere declarative sentence that 'Vedanta is the art of right living more than a system of philosophy', we are left dumbstruck at the simple but unerring profundity of this statement. About a century ago, he predicted the ensuing hijack of our Darshana Sastras by Western scholarly imperialism: 'Owing to the impact of hostile forces and the growing secularization of life, there is a great risk of the true Indian ideal being obscured and even lost.'

And then there is Ananda K. Coomaraswamy, whose best and most prolific missiles against errant Western scholarship is found in his corpus of what are incorrectly known as 'art criticism'. For example, his essay 'Indian Images with Many Arms' remains a classic in the genre. Art apart, Ananda Coomaraswamy was perhaps the most pugnacious reviler of the catastrophe called the British education system.

The final name in this enumeration is D.V. Gundappa. He is unlike the four others who precede him on this list. DVG's formal education had stopped well before his matriculation. But 'formal' is what it exactly means: something related to mere form. DVG's real education was substantial, which derives from *substance*. Just as he had sat at the feet of great Sanskrit and Kannada vidvans and pandits in his boyhood, he had also read all the volumes of Gibbon's history of the Roman Empire twice—cover to cover—when he was just 16 years old. He could expound on the nuances of Rta, Satya, and Dharma in the pages of his *Public Affairs* journal with the same breezy elan that he employed to blast Western mediocrities like Rousseau and Spencer.

A profuse contributor to this standard of scholarship was their early education, which was entirely rooted in the traditional Hindu system. Memory, depth, and error-free expertise are the greatest strengths of this system.

DVG, for example, learned the alphabet by writing on sand, a practice as old as the Hindu civilization itself. An impoverished R.C. Majumdar wrote and rewrote his school lessons on dried bamboo leaves.

When these stalwarts reached adulthood and studied in the English model of education, their early grounding made the transition relatively effortless. They also quickly understood an elementary truth: English was not just another language but a highly inferior language compared to Sanskrit or any other Bharatiya bhasha.

Purely on the intellectual plane, traditional training in the Hindu sastra system actually broadens and embellishes an intellect already fine-tuned by the rigours of sastric scholarship. The truth of this statement will become evident through an honest contrast with the post-Renaissance and post-Enlightenment intellectual traditions of Europe. The kernel of this tradition is rooted in intellectual abstractions and unresolvable dichotomies based almost entirely on the vicissitudes of the material world. They are unresolvable precisely because they are worldly and operate on the plane of the intellect. They not only do *not* recognize a plane higher than the intellect but explicitly reject these planes. In which case, how does a fundamental darshanic framework like the *Pañcakōśa vidyā* become accessible to the Western tradition? But even on a relatively mundane level, the mistranslation of *ātma* as soul is a classic marker of this Western error. In this backdrop, how does one even understand the various prefixes and suffixes to *ātma*, such as *jīvātma, paramātma, ātmānanda, ātmōd'dhāra*, etc? We shall return to this point later.

The giants of the New Indian Renaissance had clearly grasped precisely this fundamental contrast. We can re-quote Professor Hiriyanna's golden aphorism that 'Vedanta is the art of right living more than a system of philosophy', to clarify this further. We don't see this definition of Vedanta anywhere in our substantial corpus of *sutras* (aphorisms), *bhāṣyas* (commentaries), and *nibandhas* (digests), whose combined timeline spans a minimum of 3,000 years and is spread across various *matas*, *panthas*, and *mārgas* throughout Bharatavarsha. Yet, here is Hiriyanna giving us this contemporary definition of Vedanta in the idiom of the 20th century in English. This becomes more significant when we recall the fact that no British or European scholar who studied Hindu philosophy was Hiriyanna's contemporary and was able to supply this definition of Vedanta in his own mother tongue. This is a core strength that we've lost—hopefully, not permanently.

In other words, our luminaries exercised authoritative command over the strengths and weaknesses of both systems and could evaluate both with clarity and precision. And they carried out this evaluation in multiple disciplines: philosophy, art, aesthetics, language, law, literature, and epigraphy.

Just two examples will suffice to illustrate this point. The first quote is by DVG, delineating the fundamental difference between Indian and Western society:

> In Chapter six of the Bhagavad Gita, two types of civilization viz., Daivi or divine and Asuri or material, are described. *The civilization of the West is … of the latter type.* If Socrates and Plato, Wordsworth and Carlyle, Goethe and Emerson … represent that civilization, it is not then, very different from our own. *But they are not its exponents. It has grown in spite of them.* Their teachings have mostly been cries in the wilderness. *Bigotry,*

> *intolerance, jealousy, competition, aggression, and selfishness are among the most salient features of the civilization of the West.* Therefore, while assimilating it, we should beware of its evils. It has its virtues also. Unanimity, cooperation for a common cause, public spirit, and resistance to unjust aggression—these are some of the qualities that we have yet to learn from the West. *We have lost sight of our ancient ideals. Our Rama and Bhishma fall flat on our own ears. We have unlearnt that love for everything our own which formed such an important character of our ancestors....* Therefore, [our] duty is to assimilate these virtues from the West if they can be found there, taking care ... not to mistake vices for virtues. (Emphases added)

The second is by U.C. Sarkar:

> *A certain class of Hindus were the peculiar products of Western civilisation and Western education.* They did not understand the underlying spirit or genius of the Hindu culture and religion. Nor did they understand how to accept and assimilate what is best in a foreign culture and civilisation. *They were always attracted more by the exterior rather than by the intrinsic worth. It may be said that those who were really benefited by Western contact were never unwise enough to denounce their own cultural achievements* and contributions. (Emphases added)

Overall, these stalwarts of the New Indian Renaissance and their legacy are still the best archetypes for our present attempts at decolonization.

— 8 —

The easiest job is to gloat and feel proud about the luminaries of our New Indian Renaissance. But the enormity of the difficulty facing us begins when we attempt to walk on the path that they have gravelled for us. This difficulty has acquired an insurmountable quality in post-independence India for two major reasons.

The obvious first is the deracinated power elite that seized the government in 1947 and wrecked our social harmony by uprooting a moral and ethical order that was based on the code of Dharma. Roughly since the 1960s, our courts have become flooded with disputes that for centuries had been resolved by a single angry glare from an elder in a village or community. Even a superficial reading of the Privy Council judgements reveals the caution that the British took in sticking to these age-old customs and usages prescribed by our Dharmasastras. 'Independent' India has thoroughly abandoned even the notion of Dharma in areas that even the colonial British were scared to touch. This perversion was not only allowed but actively encouraged by the aforementioned power elite.

The second reason was both the consequence and a servant-maid of the first. In practical terms, this was the emergence and rapid inbreeding of a new class of mentally colonized slaves, which called itself variously 'intellectuals' and 'opinion-makers'. At no point in our history did this class exist. As we've seen earlier, this class was impregnated in India by the Macaulayite education system. But it amassed frightening levels of power and influence after independence. The largest component of this class included the Communists, Marxists, socialists, progressives, and others who awarded fancy appellations to themselves. They arrogated unearned power to pronounce sweeping public verdicts on topics ranging from thermodynamics to Dharma. Here is a sample of their intellectualism:

> [W]e should not overlook the fact that this objective force cannot be accepted as unconditional, and that particular historical reasons should be taken into consideration. The bourgeoise becomes a revolutionary factor when it raises the standard of revolt against backward, antiquated forms of society.

What does this even mean? Yet, people who churned out such incomprehensible nonsense were deified as intellectuals and profound thinkers by the rootless ruling class for more than half a century. M.N. Roy, the Marxist ideologue who wrote the aforementioned quote, was regarded by Prime Minister Jawharlal Nehru as the 'greatest Indian intellectual alive'. And so, bereft of such high political patronage, it is doubtful whether these 'intellectuals' could have gone very far. Gene Overstreet and Marshall Windmiller provide the key to unlocking the secret behind this brand of intellectualism:

> The ostensible purpose of Communist theoretical literature is to provide a conceptual framework by which political and economic processes can be understood. In actuality its primary purpose is *to surround a particular course of action with an aura of scientific correctness,* and thereby to mobilize support for that specific plan among the Party rank and file, and its followers. *Because the body of theoretical witing is so large and complex, only a priesthood in the Communist movement is really familiar with it.* This priesthood is therefore armed with a potent means of influencing *the rank and file, which is awed by the theory and by the intellects of those who are able to discourse learnedly about it.* (Emphases added)

India was a freak case where the term 'intellectual' became a synonym for 'Marxist', 'progressive', etc., for a straightforward reason: it was a Western import, and its importers were Indian lackeys of Marxism, communism, and variants thereof. The stalwarts of the New Indian Renaissance were not intellectuals in this sense.

This needs a brief explanation in our context.

The term 'intellectual' or 'public intellectual' is fairly recent, dating back roughly to the early 18th century. Its most influential progenitor was a Frenchman named Jean-Jacques Rousseau.

The growth of the phenomenon known as intellectualism was an outcome of mediaeval European society's revolt against the prolonged stranglehold of the Church. The British writer Paul Johnson gives a succinct assessment of this class of people:

> With the decline of clerical power in the eighteenth century, a new kind of mentor emerged to fill the vacuum and capture the ear of society.... He brought to this self-appointed task a far more radical approach than his clerical predecessors. *He felt himself bound by no corpus.... For the first time in human history, and with growing confidence and audacity, men arose to assert that they could diagnose the ills of society and cure them with their own unaided intellects:* more, that they could devise formulae whereby not merely the structure of society but the fundamental habits of human beings could be transformed for the better. *Unlike their sacerdotal predecessors, they were not servants and interpreters of the gods but substitutes.* (Emphases added)

'Unaided intellects' persist as the distinctive hallmark of the so-called intellectuals. And when an unaided intellect acquires the frenzy of a permanent fever, it produces a prophet. This is precisely what we notice in Swami Vivekananda's immortal description of Prophet Muhammad:

> This state of going beyond reason, transcending ordinary human nature, may sometimes come by chance to a man who

> does not understand its science; he ... stumbles upon it.... In a good many cases there is the danger of the brain being deranged ... you will find that all those men, however great they were, who had stumbled upon this superconscious state without understanding it, groped in the dark.... *They opened themselves to hallucinations. Mohammed claimed that the Angel Gabriel came to him in a cave one day and took him on the heavenly horse.... Think of the good Mohammed did to the world, and think of the great evil that has been done through his fanaticism!* Think of the millions massacred through his teachings, mothers bereft of their children, children made orphans, whole countries destroyed, millions upon millions of people killed! *Real inspiration never contradicts reason, but fulfils it.* (Emphases added)

From this perspective, every intellectual from Rousseau onwards is a quasi-prophet. Personal hubris, a total negation of the past, a personalized and only version of a grandiose utopia, and an obstinate refusal to admit any error—these are traits common to all prophets, from Muhammad to Marx.

Western intellectuals, beginning with Rousseau, have had the bad luck and misfortune to live in drastically altered spatiotemporal circumstances. 18th-century Europe was not 7th-century Arabia, where a hallucinatory warlord could wage wars to implement his messianic religious vision by raising fanatical armies. However, the long-term outcome of Rousseau's brand of intellectualism has been no less fatal than what the jihad and plunder-hungry armies of Islam have achieved over the centuries. Prophet Muhammad built armies comprising trained and indoctrinated soldiers. Rousseau and his intellectual progeny have spawned generational academics and committed legislators.

Negating the past is perhaps the most powerful ingredient of any prophetism. The past is either a force for good or a pesky obstacle, depending on an individual's mental makeup. In the

Hindu tradition, the past is merely a point in a continuum, and it is in this context that the term *parampara*—tradition—acquires its most profound meaning. Hence, by definition, the question of negating the past does not arise. On the contrary, prophetic creeds, including the creed of intellectualism, have no historical basis to stand on unless they vilify or negate any history that does not fit the core doctrine of their prophetism. The alleged 'dark ages' that predated Christianity, the concept of *Jahiliya* in Islam, and the 'regressive/feudal era' of Marxism are clearly cut from the same cloth. Dr Koenraad Elst's incisive work *Negationism in India* is an outstanding exposition of this phenomenon. The late V.S. Naipaul describes this negationist phenomenon slightly differently:

> Islam . . . makes imperial demands. A convert's worldview alters. His holy places are in Arab lands; his sacred language is Arabic. *His idea of history alters.* He rejects his own; he becomes, whether he likes it or not, a part of the Arab story. *The convert has to turn away from everything that is his.* . . . The disturbance for societies is immense. . . . People develop fantasies about who and what they are; and *in the Islam of converted countries there is an element of neurosis and nihilism.* (Emphases added)

The Indian variant of this Western intellectual class imported this negationist formula wholesale with its eyes wide open. That is what gave it the confidence to declare, for example, that Dharma is superstition. It is really quite incredible. In the last volume of his monumental *History of the Dharmasastra*—a sacred yajna that consumed 60 years of his life—P.V. Kane makes a humble submission. No matter how many times we read it, we feel like a mere speck, and a lump automatically forms in our throat:

> I could not arrange or plan my life. I had to oscillate between education, literature and law, between Government service and an independent profession like that of law, I have, however, lived a very active, full and varied life for over sixty years. *Thinking over the vast Sanskrit literature and the labour and time that I had to spend on one branch of it,* I am inclined to close this Epilogue with two lines from Browning's poem, 'The last ride together',
>
> 'Look at the end of the work, contrast
> The petty done, the undone vast.' (Emphasis added)

For more than half a century, the aforementioned Indian 'intellectual' class literally dictated what the 'true' history, culture, and civilization of India were. It branded someone of Kane's eminence as a regressive Hindu communalist and got away scot-free. It decided and destroyed countless careers. It could do all this because its prophetism had political shelter. One is reminded of Allan Bloom's pithy diagnosis of this mindset: 'Only Socrates knew, after a lifetime of unceasing labour, that he was ignorant. *Now every high-school student knows that. How did it become so easy?* (Emphasis added).'

In this light, what has been the Hindu experience of intellectual tradition? Is it even an intellectual tradition in the sense that the West understands it?

—9—

The Hindu tradition of philosophical inquiry makes three clear distinctions: *adhibhūta* (the physical plane), *adhidaiva* (the plane of the deity, god, etc.), and *adhyātma* (the spiritual plane). It has well-defined logical rules for debating any topic. A primary rule is that one cannot mix these three planes. For example, if you are analysing the Ramayana on the adhibhūta plane, you cannot bring in the adhidhaiva elements into that analysis. Thus, on the adhibhūta plane, the Ramayana's characters become just normal human beings, and they must be analysed as such. On the adhidhaiva plane, Rama becomes an avatara of Vishnu, Sita, an avatara of Lakshmi, etc. On the adhyātma plane, Rama symbolizes the *Parabrahman*. And so, at the outset, you have to state your premises, i.e., on which plane the Ramayana is being analysed.

Over the last 100 years or so, these fundamental and time-honoured rules of debate have remained valid only in their flagrant violations. Forget a literary work like the Ramayana, there has been a rampant tendency towards force-fitting adhibhūta arguments in realms as abstract as the Vedanta.

This kind of basic confusion is at the root of much of the failure to confidently establish the Hindu position in public discourse.

Which then takes us back to the aforementioned fundamental difference between the Western and Indian intellectual traditions. The Western tradition, which developed as a consequence of a revolt against Church hegemony, completely rejected the Christian God and replaced him with materialism. Such an opposition to God does not exist in the Santana tradition because we have harmonized the material with the spiritual and elevated the spiritual to the philosophical. Thus, each had its own well-defined place. We can understand this point with greater clarity with examples from our philosophical history.

Since very ancient times, Bharatavarsha has always had a tradition of emperors and kings who renounced everything and became Sanyasins and *Brahmajnanis*. This tradition has a history spanning a minimum of 5,000 years, from Janaka of the Vedic era to the 10th century Chandela monarch, Dhanga. Janaka, for example, engaged as equals in deep philosophical debates with the celebrated Brahmajnanis of his era, like Yājñavalkya. Then we have the brilliant example of a haughty Kshatriya monarch like Vishvamitra, who waged war against the forest-dwelling Brahmarshi, Vasistha. Vishvamitra repeatedly ate humble pie, and his vengeful quest to crush Vasistha transformed him into another Brahmarshi. This is the Vishvamitra who later became the guru of Sri Ramachandra.

However, in the entire history of the West (including its pre-Christian past), we don't find a single king like Janaka, Vishvamitra, or Dhanga. Rishis, as we understand them here, are conspicuous by their absence in the West.

Therefore, when we talk about intellectual discourse, decolonization, etc., we need to begin here, at the fundamentals.

— 10 —

At the core, Bharatavarsha is a spiritual civilization rooted in darśana whereas Christian theology is the basis even of spirituality in the West. And the basis of this theology is an irrational faith in an alleged son of God who was born out of a virgin's womb and who was supposed to appear again in the calendar year 2000. Christianity collapsed in Europe the moment enough number of people questioned the faith in this fiction. Thomas Aquinas, widely regarded as the theologian par excellence in history, ties himself in inextricable knots when he tries to 'prove' this fiction in his *Summa Theologiae*.

When we examine the post-Christian intellectual tradition of the West, we clearly notice a continuation of the same Christian trend. Whereas the Christian period was split along the lines of Churches and denominations, the subsequent period was populated by godless sects founded by individuals who believed in *nothing*. Just as how Catholicism and Protestantism are cults, these godless sects are also cults. In the last 150 years, capitalism and communism have emerged as the most influential and destructive post-Christian cults.

Faith in the individual, faith in economics, faith in godless politics, and faith in the state (communism) had supplanted faith in the Christian God. But it was still faith. When we consider any intellectual school in the West, we observe that it operates primarily in these realms. All of these schools are named after theorists: Rousseau, Kant, Hegel, Descartes, Spinoza, Marx, Sartre, Foucault, Derrida, et al. These schools had flourished as long as that theorist was alive. After that, they became merely historical records and museum pieces, not unbroken, living traditions that were actually a force for good. In fact, some of these 'intellectuals' became irrelevant and discredited in their own lifetimes for two reasons verifiable through human experience. The first reason: their fabulous but unreal theories did not match the kind of life they themselves led. In other words, they did not practice what they preached and were eventually exposed as frauds. The second reason: every new generation finds heroes and role models who are closer to them in age and speak the same idiom. To draw a pedestrian analogy, *Animal* Ranbir Kapoor is a bigger star today than Amitabh Bachchan, who has been downgraded to veteran status. In the history of Western intellectualism, few people have fallen so miserably in their own lifetime as Jean-Paul Sartre. This is how his last days looked:

> *In the 1970s Sartre was an increasingly pathetic figure, prematurely aged … often drunk,* worried about money, uncertain about his views…. His last years were brutally described by de Beauvoir in her little book, *Adieux: A Farewell to Sartre*: *his incontinence, his drunkenness, made possible by girls slipping him bottles of whisky,*

> the struggle for power over what was left of his mind. *It must have been a relief to them all when he died* … de Beauvoir … survived him five years, a Queen Mother of the French intellectual left. *But there were no children, no heirs….*
>
> Sartre, like Russell, failed to achieve any kind of coherence and consistency in his views of public policy. No body of doctrine survived him. In the end, again like Russell, he stood for nothing more than a vague desire to belong to the left and the camp of youth. The intellectual decline of Sartre, who … at one time did seem to be identified with a striking, if confused, philosophy of life, was particularly spectacular … Sartre … was given a magnificent funeral by intellectual Paris. Over 50,000 people, most of them young, followed his body into Montparnasse Cemetery. To get a better view, some climbed into the trees. One of them came crashing down onto the coffin itself. To what cause had they come to do honour? What faith, what luminous truth about humanity, were they asserting by their mass presence? (Emphases added)

Sartre perhaps represents the most flamboyant nadir of the journey of societal destruction that 'intellectual schools', beginning with Rousseau, caused. Their overall legacy has been awful for humankind, to say the least.

— 11 —

We see the exact opposite climate in India. Our Rishis and sages did not establish any individual-centric schools. They bequeathed living traditions, which were the consequence of years of contemplation and a philosophical realization of changeless universal principles. These principles are, for example, Rta, Satya, and Dharma. Their practical application includes the whole of the Hindu ethical system or Dharmasastras. Some of the major ingredients of this ethical system are the triad of yajña (sharing), d*āna* (charity), tapas (penance), and more generally, the 10 traits that constitute Dharma as defined by Manu Maharshi:

> dhṛtiḥ kṣamā damo'steyaṃ śaucaṃ indriyanigrahaḥ I
> dhīrvidyā satyaṃ akrodho daśakaṃ dharmalakṣaṇam I I
> Patience, forgiveness, self-restraint, non-stealing, hygiene, control of sense organs, courage, knowledge, truth, and non-anger constitute the ten traits of Dharma.

Dr S. Srikanta Sastri provides a penetrating insight into this Indian philosophical tradition.

> Indian culture gives immense importance to individual freedom. Differences of opinion exist among various schools of Indian philosophy on the subject of the nature of the relationship that exists between an individual, the Supreme Being and the material world. However, *all these schools also universally recognize the fact that the individual, based on nature and temperament, is free to lead a life of his or her choosing. It is because of this that there is no scope for totalitarianism in Indian culture.*
>
> The spiritual outlook that lies at the heart of Indian culture is the reason it is still alive and flourishing in the world. It is also the reason every single facet of Indian culture—food, social mores, business ethics, philosophy, aesthetics, investigations into the nature of truth and beauty—holds a special distinction. *Not only does Indian culture embody universal values, it has also infused its unique value system both at the level of the individual and the society.*
>
> Indian culture is thus like Atman, the Self: timeless and imperishable. (Emphases added)

D.V. Gundappa, too, mirrors the same insight in his masterly contrast elucidating the Indian philosophical tradition with that of Western notions of liberalism.

> [T]here is nothing peculiarly British or European in these ideas [of liberalism]. Their validity is universal. So far as India is concerned, the ideas are implicit in the Hindu concept of Dharma...
>
> Dharma is individual self-sustenance or one's being oneself.... None can perform the Dharma of another. The eye cannot hear; the leg cannot taste.... Liberty is opportunity for ... self-fulfilment. *Sva-tantra* or liberty is a condition indispensable to *Sva-Dharma*. It should be noted that, *while the word liberty, denoting absence of restraint, is negative in its import, the word Sva-Dharma* (one's own duty prescribed by the principle of the general good) *is positive.* The notion of duty is implied and not explicit in liberty, while the notion of *Sva-tantra* (liberty) is implied and not explicit in *Sva-Dharma* (duty). The relative emphasis in the two phrases is characteristic of the two scales of value. *That liberty is incidental and ancillary to Dharma is the Hindu view*.... Self-fulfilment is not in solitude, but in and through society.... Law or *Nyaya* is the working of Dharma....
>
> Dharma is thus charity or philanthropy, citizenship, or public spirit.... The progress of the soul is from self-expression under the law of justice to self-dissolution in life universal—from Dharma to Moksha, from individualism to universalism, from life limited to life limitless. (Emphases added)

Thus, the Hindu tradition holds that society and politics are just means or vehicles for attaining a higher goal. We can paraphrase D.V. Gundappa's brilliant analogy in this regard: a thirsty man needs water. A utensil is required to drink water. And so, the utensil acquires value because of water. Likewise, worldly life acquires value because it enables the attainment of an exalted state of existence. Society and politics acquire value because of worldly life.

The fact that no Western philosophical canon or doctrine was able to produce such insights once again points to the same thing: the fundamental difference in outlook between the West and Bharatavarsha. The Sanatana philosophical core can easily assimilate and Hinduize even a messiah of exclusivity like Jesus Christ. The reverse is impossible.

— 12 —

The West understood Bharatavarsha primarily through the Christian, colonial, materialist, and sociological prisms. Its understanding stemmed from a conqueror's mindset. Colonial scholars of India never became honest participants in the same Hindu society and culture that they studied while living in it. Study, understanding, interpretation, and analysis are words that have specific meanings. Thus, their studies and analyses of our culture, philosophy, and traditions resemble nothing higher or are more meaningful than inert reports of an archaeologist's field study or a museum curator's documentation. They had no feel for our culture, languages, customs, and traditions. The most depraved proofs of this fact are the lucrative auction houses in the West like Sotheby's that openly hawk the *murtis* of our Devis and Devatas. This is a double crime. One, a majority of these murtis are items that the West has plundered. Two, these auctions are ongoing felonies called cultural annihilation and a rape of sanctity: your reverence is our tradable commodity. That all this is still being done without remorse shows the levels at which the phenomenon of cultural contrast operates.

To cite an oft-repeated insight of Shatavadhani Dr R. Ganesh, Europeans discovered Sanskrit at the same time we discovered English. After 250 years, India has a thriving market for Indians writing in English. In contrast, how many works in Sanskrit (or Indian languages) has Europe or America produced during the same period?

But the situation is worse.

Four or five generations of Hindus have internalized the colonial and Christian West's understanding of India and have been using those frameworks, methods, and arguments in their own work, both fiction and non-fiction. This class of Hindus belongs to three broad categories.

The first are the genuine converts—the incurably colonized Hindus who sincerely believe that there was nothing good in India before the British civilized it.

The second class comprises opportunists. They are beneath contempt.

The third class consists of Hindus who sincerely work towards decolonization, especially in what is known as the 'intellectual' realm. A good chunk of this class continues to use the aforementioned Western frameworks in a mistaken and wasteful endeavour to somehow defend our own traditions. Some even chase the mirage of 'beating them at their own game', forgetting the elementary truth that the West had set the rules of that game centuries ago. Contemporary Indologists like Sheldon Pollock win the game repeatedly, precisely for this reason. *There is no neutral turf in the colonial game called Indology.* However, it has assumed lethal and gargantuan proportions today compared to what it was during direct colonial rule. This is because generational armies of Hindus trained and indoctrinated in the Indology departments of America are playing the game on behalf of their White masters, such as Wendy Doniger, Paul

Courtright, Steve Farmer, Sheldon Pollock, et al. It is worth recalling the memorable warning that P.V. Kane gave in 1953 in this regard:

> *Conquerors rarely adopt the words of the language of the conquered. It is the conquered who adopt many words from their conqueror's language as we did when the Moslems or the British ruled over India.* It is best to confess one's ignorance than put forward fantastic views about combinations of words from different dialects for producing Vedic words. (Emphasis added)

There is a second historical point. India's experience with alien invasions and regimes dates back to nearly a millennium. The story of the all-round oppression of Hindus by these regimes is as prolonged and painful as it is well known. Yet, throughout that period, not one alien philosophy or religion has managed to influence our philosophical core even one bit. The Hindu society still hasn't perhaps realized that this is the unmatched strength that it has at its disposal and that it needs to rediscover it.

— 13 —

Finally, decolonization cannot be taught through books or in classrooms. Those are crutches at best. Decolonization is a civilizational endeavour in which the entire Hindu society should consciously participate. This quote, drawn from Sita Ram Goel, gives a sample of the magnitude of the effort involved:

> *[I]n today's India it is not sufficient to be a Hindu by birth.* Hindu society and culture are under attack from several quarters. *One has to be a convinced and conscious Hindu to meet and survive* that attack. One has to find one's roots in Sanatana Dharma. (Emphases added)

Thus, decolonization is a function of both the immediate and the larger cultural and social atmosphere that incubates, nurtures, and preserves it.

The stalwarts of the New Indian Renaissance mentioned earlier had lived in an ambience that had not been fully colonized. A major aspect of their trailblazing work was to prevent the destruction of this ambience and to preserve its best elements.

Professor M. Hiriyanna, for example, had learned sastras, Sanskrit, etc. in a traditional gurukulam. His immediate surroundings were thickly permeated by the Hindu cultural ambience. Such an atmosphere silently and invisibly imbibes us with lessons that we can never forget. These are too subtle to be formally taught. A whole ecosystem works to create these kinds of stalwarts. That ecosystem has pretty much disappeared. Small wonder that we are no longer able to produce luminaries of that calibre.

There is an additional difficulty. Today, we live in an almost exclusively materialistic world. American-style capitalist materialism hasn't spared any piece of the earth. The emphasis in such a system is a constant striving for wealth for its own sake. This also conditions the mind to view everything through this materialist lens, or at any rate, through the lens of hardcore utilitarianism.

Even in the 1970s, we had a familiar phrase: cultivating leisure. Today, we have either endless work or mindless entertainment, but not leisure. Leisure is a precondition for the sort of cultural decolonization needed today. Leisure is the midwife of culture and gives it expression in different realms—art, music, poetry, literature, philosophy, etc. We notice an earnest and philosophical side of leisure in this verse in Sri Krishnadevaraya's classic *Āmuktamālyada*:

varṣārthamaṣṭau prayateta māsān
niśārthamardham divase yateta |

> vārdhakyahetorvayasā navena
> paratrahetoriha janmanā ca ||
> To savour the rainy season, we must suffer for (the rest of the) eight months.
> Thus, for (resting at) night, in the day, thus for old age, in youth, and
> Thus to attain the Other World (Moksha) must we suffer in this world.

In other words, unbroken cultural continuity and social stability are both necessary and sufficient conditions for any meaningful attempt at decolonization. Studying how it practically worked in the past and the lessons we can learn from it, looking back at our own childhood experiences, understanding how our own previous generations lived, a conscious cultivation of the serene and subtler aspects of life, and above all, reading our past masters, especially our literary and artistic heritage, is perhaps the best guide for decolonization.

We can conclude this on an ironic note. This is what J.G. Herder, the 18th-century German indologist wrote:

> Do you not wish with me that instead of these endless religious books of the Vedas, Upavedas, and Upāṅgas, they should give us the more useful and more agreeable works of the Indians, and especially their best poetry of every kind? It is here that the mind and character of a nation is best brought to life before us, and *I gladly admit that I have received a truer and more real notion of the manner of thinking among the ancient Indians from this one Śakuntalā*, than from their Upāṅgas and Upavedas. (Emphasis added)

References

Chapter 1

Mani, Vettam, *Puranic Encyclopedia* (1975).

Pratama, Rifqi Listyawan, and Junianto, 'Banana Leaves as A Natural Food Packaging: A Review', *Global Scientific Journals*, Volume 9, Issue 12 (December 2021).

Priceless Onam Gift: https://www.thehindu.com/features/metroplus/society/priceless-onam-gift/article3812324.ece. Last accessed: 23 August 2012.

Substantial portions of this essay owe a deep debt of gratitude to a brilliant monograph titled *The Plantain*, published in the January 1891 issue of *The Calcutta Review*.

Chapter 2

Bhattacharya, B., 'Royal Prerogative in Ancient India' in *Dr S. Krishnaswami Aiyangar Commemoration Volume* (Madras, 1936).

Dikshitar, Ramachandra V.R., *The Mauryan Polity* (University of Madras, 1932).

Gundappa, D.V., *Vruttapatrike* (Kannada) (Hubli: Sahitya Prakashana, 2020).

News: https://www.etymonline.com/search?q=news. Last accessed: 4 December 2023.

Shamasastry, R. (tr. & ed.), *Arthashastra of Kautilya*, (Mysore: Mysore Printing and Publishing House, 1929).

Chapter 4

'Annual Report of South Indian Epigraphy' (Madras, 1907).

Acharya, P.K., *Indian Architecture: According to Manasara-Silpasatra*, Manasara Series (Delhi: Munshiram Manoharlal Publishers, 1996).

Auboyer, Jeannie, *Daily Life in Ancient India* (Delhi: Asia Publishing House, 1961).

Bhandarkar, D.R., 'The Junnar Cave 18' in *Some Aspects of Ancient Indian Culture* (University of Madras, 1940).

Bhyrappa, S.L., *Saartha* (Kannada) (Bangalore: Sahitya Bhandara, 1998).

Dharampal, *Dharampal Collected Writings* (5 Volumes) (Goa: Other India Bookstore, 2016).

Foundations of Sanatana Dharma: Yajna, Dana, Tapas. https://www.prekshaa.in/foundations-sanatana-dharma-yajna-dana-tapas. Last accessed: 16 July 2023.

Hultzsch, E., 'Archaeological Survey of India', *Epigraphia Indica*, Vol 8 (Delhi, 1905–06).

Kane, P.V., *History of Dharmasastra* (in 5 Volumes) (Poona: BORI, 1930–62).

Konow, Sten, 'Archaeological Survey of India', *Epigraphia Indica*, Vol 12 (Delhi, 1913–14).

Krishna Sastri, H., *South Indian Inscriptions* ,.Vol 3, Part 1 (Madras: Government Press, 1920).

Majumdar, R.C., *Corporate Life in Ancient India* (Poona: The Oriental Book Agency, 1922).

Majumdar, R.C., *The Classical Accounts of India* (Calcutta: Firma K.L.M. Publishers, 1960).

Mill, James, *The History of British India*, ed. H.H. Wilson (London: James Madden, 1858).

Narasimhacharya, R., 'Inscriptions at Shravanabelagola', *Epigraphia Carnatica*, Vol. 2 (Bangalore: Mysore Government Press, 1923).

The Civilisational Wisdom of Sri Dharampal: Excerpts from an Interview. https://www.dharmadispatch.in/dispatches/the-civilisational-wisdom-of-sri-dharampal-excerpts-from-an-interview. Last accessed: 7 April 2023.

Chapter 5

Gode, P.K., 'Recipes for Hair-dyes in the Navanitaka (2nd Century A.D.)' *Studies in Indian Cultural History*, Volume 1 (Hoshiarpur: Vishveshvaranand Vedic Research Institute, 1961).

Gundappa, D.V., 'Cambodia and India', *Public Affairs Journal*, Vol. XIV-9 (Bangalore, September 1970).

Hoernlé, A. F. Rudolf, *The Bower Manuscript* (Facsimile Leaves, Nagari Transcript, Romanized Transliteration and English Translation with Notes) (Calcutta: Office of the Superintendent of Government Printing India, 1893–97).

Puri, *Buddhism in Central Asia* (Delhi: B.N. Motilal Banarsidass Publishers Private Limited, 1987).

Sergeev, Evgeny, *The Great Game, 1856–1907: Russo-British Relations in Central and East Asia* (Baltimore: John Hopkins University Press, 2013).

Shaw, Robert, *Visits to High Tartary, Yarkand and Kashgar* (1871). Reprint with introduction by Peter Hopkirk, Oxford University Press, 1984.

Singh Mohan, Kaviraj Balwant, *Navanītakaṃ* or *The Bower Manuscript* (Lahore: Mehar Chand Lachman Das, 1925).

Teh, Jennifer, 'The Caravan'. https://jenniferteh1.com/2020/06/27/the-caravan/. Last accessed: 14 December 2023.

Chapter 6

Gode, P.K., 'Recipes for Hair-dyes in the Navanitaka (2nd Century A.D.)', *Studies in Indian Cultural History*.

Hoernle, A.F. Rudolf, *The Bower Manuscript*.

Mohan, B.S., *Navanitakam*.

Chapter 7

Coomaraswamy, Ananda K., 'Picture Showmen', *The Indian Historical Quarterly*, Vol. 5 (Delhi: Caxton Publications, 1929).

Raghavan, V., 'Picture Showmen: Mankhas', *The Indian Historical Quarterly*, Vol. 12 (Delhi: Caxton Publications, 1936).

Sivaramamurti, Calambur, *Vijayanagara Paintings* (Delhi: Publications Division, Ministry of Information and Broadcasting, Government of India, 1985).

Steingrass, F.J., 'A Comprehensive Persian-English Dictionary'. https://dsal.uchicago.edu/cgi-bin/app/steingass_query.py?page=795. Last accessed: 24 November 2023.

Chapter 8

Bbanu, Runa Shelina, *A Critical Study of the Progressive Art Movement in Bengal* (Aligarh: Aligarh Muslim University, 2009).

Coomaraswamy, Ananda K., *Essays in National Idealism* (Delhi: Munshiram Manoharlal, 1981).

Ganesh, Shatavadhani Dr R., 'Bharatiya Puranagalu' (Kannada), 'Ragabharati' (Bangalore: Ayodhya Publications, 2023).

Hiriyanna, M., *Art Experience* (Delhi: Indira Gandhi National Centre for the Arts, 1997).

Kramrisch, Stella, 'The Ṛg Vedic Myth of the Craftsmen (The Ṛbhus)', *Artibus Asiae*, Vol. 22, No. 1/2 (Zurich, 1959): pp. 113–20.

Mookerji, Radhakumud, *Ancient Indian Education* (Delhi: Motilal Banarsidass, 2011).

Raghavan, V., 'Picture Showmen: Mankha', *The Indian Historical Quarterly*, Vol. 12 (Delhi: Caxton Publications, 1936).

Raghavan, V., *Adult Education in Ancient India* (Madras: Memoirs of the Madras Library Association, 1944).

Raghavan, V., 'Methods of Popular Religious Instruction in South India', *The Journal of American Folklore*, Vol. 71, No. 281 (Illinois, 1958): 336–44.

Sastri, S. Srikanta, *Bharateeya Samskruti* (Bangalore: Kamadhenu Pustaka Bhavana, 2015).

Srirangachar, Vajapeyam, 'Preface' to the *Matsya Purana* (Mysore: Jayachamarajendra Grantharatnamala, 1946).

Chapter 9

Hughes, *Dictionary of Islam* (Delhi: Munshiram Manoharlal, 1995).

Lewis Rice, B., *Epigraphia Carnatica* (Vol. 8) (Bangalore: Mysore Government Central Press, 1904).

Majumdar, R.C. (ed), *History and Culture of the Indian People* (Vol. 6) (Bombay: Bharatiya Vidya Bhavan, 1967).

Rajahmundry, *Journal of the Andhra Historical Research Society*, Vol. 7, Part 1, 1932.

Saletore, B.A., *Social and Political Life in the Vijayanagara Empire* (2 Vols) (Madras: B.G. Paul & Co, Publishers, 1934).

Sircar, D.C., *Indian Epigraphical Glossary* (Delhi: Motilal Banarasidass, 1966).

Sircar, D.C., *Select Inscriptions Bearing on Indian History and Civilization* (2 Vols) (Delhi: Motilal Banarasidass, 1983).

Thomas, F.W., *Epigraphia Indica* (Vol. 14) (Bombay: British India Press, 1918).

Chapter 11

Balakrishna, Sandeep, *Invaders and Infidels* (Book 1) (Delhi: Bloomsbury, 2020).

Curry, Anne, *The Hundred Years' War 1337–1453, Essential Histories* (Vol.19) (Oxford: Osprey Publishing, 2002).

Ganesh, Shatavadhani Dr R., *Vibhuthi Purusha Vidyaranya* (Kannada) (Hubli: Sahitya Prakashana, 2011).

Ganesh, Shatavadhani Dr. R., *Kshattra The Tradition of Valour in India*, translated by Sandeep Balakrishna and Hari Ravi Kumar (Hubli: Subbu Publications, 2023).

Goel, Sita Ram, *Heroic Hindu Resistance to Muslim Invaders, 636 CE to 1206 CE* (Delhi: Voice of India, 1994).

Gundappa, D.V., *Vidyaranyara Samakaaleenaru* (Bangalore: Sahitya Bhandara, 2020).

Majumdar, R.C. (ed), *History and Culture of the Indian People*, Volume 05, *The Struggle For Empire* (Bombay: Bharatiya Vidya Bhavan, 2001).

Nagaraju, H.M., *Devaraya II and His Times-History of Vijayanagara* (Mysore: University of Mysore, 1991).

Robinson, Seward D., *The Hundred Years War: The English in France, 1337–1453* (London: 2003).

Row, B. Suryanarain, *A History of Vijayanagar: The Never to Be Forgotten Empire* (Madras: Addison & Co, 1905).

Saletore, B.A., *Social and Political Life in the Vijayanagara Empire* (2 Vols) (Madras: B.G. Paul & Co, Publishers, 1934).

Sewell, Robert, *A Forgotten Empire* (Delhi: Asian Educational Services, 2011).

Srikantayya, S., *Founders of Vijayanagara* (Bangalore: Mythic Society, 1938).

Various authors, 'Vijayanagara Sexcentenary Commemoration Volume' Vijayanagara Empire Sexcentenary Assocation and Karnatak Historical Research Society (Dharwar, 1936).

Venkataramanayya, N., 'The Early Muslim Expansion in South India', Madras University Historical Series No. 17 (Madras, 1942).

Weir, Alison, *The Wars of the Roses* (New York: Ballantine Books, 1996).

Chapter 12

Austin, Granville, *Working In A Democratic Constitution* (Oxford, 2003).

Baru, Sanjaya, *The Accidental Prime Minister: The Making and Unmaking of Manmohan Singh* (Delhi: Penguin Books Limited, 2014).

Battle Over Delhi Gymkhana Club: Why Govt Wants to Take Over National Capital's Iconic Landmark: https://www.indiatoday.in/mail-today/story/battle-over-delhi-gymkhana-club-why-govt-wants-to-take-over-national-capital-s-iconic-landmark-1674844-2020-05-06. Last accessed: 12 December 2023.

Bernier, Francois, *Travels in the Mogul Empire* (Oxford University Press, 1916).

Bhushan, Prashant, *Bofors: The Selling of a Nation* (Delhi: South Asia Books, 1990).

Bhyrappa, S.L., *Bhitti* (Kannada) (Bangalore: Saahitya Bhandaara, 1996).

Dalvi, John P., *Himalayan Blunder* (Natraj Publishers, 2021).

Despite the hostile reception, Indira Gandhi's visit to Britain turns out to be a tour de force: https://www.indiatoday.in/magazine/special-report/story/19781215-despite-the-hostile-reception-indira-gandhis-visit-to-britain-was-a-tour-deforce-823183-2014-03-07. Last accessed: 10 December 2023.

Edwardes, Michael, *Nehru: A Political Biography* (London: Allan Lane, 1971).

Frank, Katherine, *Indira: The Life of Indira Nehru Gandhi* (Harper Perennial, 2007).

Gene and Windmiller, *Communism in India* (Bombay: The Perennial Press, 1960).

Goel, Sita Ram, *Nightmare of Nehruism* (Delhi: 'How I Became a Hindu', Voice of India, 1992).

Goel, Sita Ram, *Genesis and Growth of Nehruism* (Delhi: Voice of India, 1993).

Gorl, Sita Ram, *Nehru's Fatal Friendship* (Delhi: Society for Defence of Freedom in Asia, 2017 (reprint)).

How Nehru's friend Jayanti Dharma Teja went from Lutyens' darling to international fugitive: https://theprint.in/past-forward/how-nehrus-friend-jayanti-dharma-teja-went-from-lutyens-darling-to-international-fugitive/867452/. Last accessed: 14 December 2023.

Jahagirdar, I.K., *Arasu āḍaḻitaraṃga* (The Theatre of Devaraj Urs' Administration, Kannada) (Bangalore: Chanakya Prakashana, 1979).

Jayanti Dharma Teja: An unheralded comeback: https://www.indiatoday.in/magazine/special-report/story/19830331-jayanti-dharma-teja-an-unheralded-comeback-770561-2013-07-24. Last accessed: 14 December 2023.

Jayanti Dharma Teja: The Original Nehruvian Crony Capitalist: https://www.dharmadispatch.in/history/jayanti-dharma-teja-the-original-nehruvian-crony-capitalist. Last accessed: 14 December 2023.

Lal, K.S., *The Legacy of Muslim Rule in India* (Delhi: Voice of India, 1992).

Markham, Clements R., *The Hawkins' Voyages* (London: Hakluyt Society, 1878).

Mathai, M.O., *Reminiscences of the Nehru Age* (Delhi: Vikas Publishing House, 1978).

Moreland, W.H., *India at the Death of Akbar* (London: Macmillan, 1920).

Moreland, W.H., *From Akbar to Aurangzeb* (London: Macmillan, 1923).

Palkhivala, Nani A., *We, the Nation: The Lost Decades* (Noida: UBS Publishers Distributors, 1994).

Pelsaert, Francisco, *Jahangir's India* (Cambridge: W. Heffer and Sons Ltd, 1925).

Rajiv Gandhi's Lakshadweep Holiday; Guess who else was there: https://www.newindianexpress.com/galleries/nation/2019/may/10/from-our-archives-rajiv-gandhis-lakshadweep-holiday-guess-who-else-was-there-102271.html. Last accessed: 12 December 2023.

Remote Mindset: https://openthemagazine.com/features/india/remote-mindset/. Last accessed: 6 December 2023.

Sahgal, Nayantara, *On Dynastics*, 'The Seminar', Delhi, 1984.

Sarkar, Jadunath, *History of Aurangzib* (5 volumes) (Calcutta: M.C. Sarkar & Sons, 1912).

Sarkar, Jadunath, *Fall of the Mughal Empire* (4 volumes) (Calcutta: Orient Longman, 1971 (reprint)).

Sezhiyan, Era, 'Shah Commission Report: Lost and Regained', Aazhi Publishers (Chennai, 2011).

Shourie, Arun, *These Lethal, Inexorable Laws: Rajiv, His Men, and His Regime* (Delhi: ASA, 1997).

Shourie, Arun, *Mrs. Gandhi's Second Reign* (Delhi: Vikas Publishing House, 1983).

Shourie, Arun, *Governance and the Sclerosis That Has Set In* (Delhi: Rupa, 2004).

Shourie, Arun, 'Lifting the Veil over Pratibha Patil', *New Indian Express*, 28 June 2007.

Singh, K. Natwar, *One Life Is Not Enough* (Delhi: Rupa Publications, 2012).

Singh, Tavleen, *Durbar* (Delhi: Hachette India, 2013).

Sitapati, Vinay, *Half-Lion: How P V Narasimha Rao Transformed India* (Delhi: Penguin Viking, 2017).

Swami Dhirendra Brahmachari: A Man with No Official Standing but Awesome Power: https://www.indiatoday.in/magazine/cover-story/story/19801130-swami-dhirendra-brahmachari-a-man-with-no-official-standing-but-awesome-power-821648-2014-01-04. Last accessed: 5 December 2023.

Thakur, Janardhan, *All the Prime Minister's Men* (Delhi: Vikas Publishing House, 1977).

The Men in Indira's Life: http://timesofindia.indiatimes.com/articleshow/2039423.cms?. Last accessed: 12 December 2023.

Tripura DM Shailesh Kumar Yadav suspended for trashing marriage party video had gone viral: https://apnlive.com/india-news/tripura-dm-shailesh-yadav-marriage-party-video/. Last accessed: 15 December 2023.

Vasudev, Uma, *Two Faces of Indira Gandhi* (Delhi: Vikas Publishing House, 1977).

Chapter 13

Bernier, Francois, *Travels in the Mogul Empire* (London: Oxford University Press, 1916).

Foster, William (Ed.), *The Embassy of Sir Thomas Roe to the Court of the Great Mogul, 1615-1619* (2 Vols) (United Kingdom: Taylor & Francis, 2017).

Ovington, John, *A Voyage to Surat in the Year 1689* (London: Oxford University Press, 1929).

Priolkar, A.K., *The Goa Inquisition: The Terrible Tribunal for the East* (Panaji: Rajhauns Vitaran, 2010).

Chapter 15

Ganesh, Shatavadhani Dr R., *Vibhuthi Purusha Vidyaranya* (Kannada) (Hubli: Sahitya Prakashana, 2011).

Personal guidance given to the author by Shatavadhani Dr Ganesh.

Shivaramaiah, B.K., 'Dr S. Krishnaswami Aiyangar Commemoration Volume' (Madras: Mysore Palace Publications, 1936).

Sri Jayachamarajendra Grantharatnamale (Kannada), review by Dr N. Anantarangachar (appended to the volumes).

Sri Jayachamarajendra Grantharatnamale (Kannada), review by Dr H.V. Nagaraja Rao (appended to the volumes).

Sri Jayachamarajendra Vedaratanamala (Vols 1–36) (Kannada) (Mysore: Various publishers, 1947–61).

Chapter 17

Dalvi, John P., *Himalayan Blunder* (Natraj Publishers, 2021).

Goel, Sita Ram, *Nightmare of Nehruism* (Delhi: 'How I Became a Hindu', Voice of India, 1992).

Chapter 18

Bhyrappa S.L., *Tantu* (Bangalore: Sahitya Bhandara, 1993).

Bhyrappa S.L., *Bhitti* (Bangalore: Sahitya Bhandara, 1996).

Bradley, A.C., *Oxford Lectures on Poetry* (Glasgow: Good Press, 2020).

Evans, A.B., *Leicestershire Words, Phrases and Proverbs* (London: Trubner & Co, 1881).

Ganesh, Shatavadhani Dr R., *Musings on Indian Aesthetics*, https://www.prekshaa.in/musings-indian-aesthetics. Last accessed: 10 December 2022.

Global Over-The-Top/OTT Market Insights: https://www.skyquestt.com/report/over-the-top-ott-market. Last accessed: 23 August 2023.

Hiriyanna, M., *Art Experience* (Delhi: Indira Gandhi National Centre for the Arts, 1997).

The Opium Den: Somerset Maugham, 'On a Chinese Screen': https://standardebooks.org/ebooks/w-somerset-maugham/on-a-chinese-screen/text/single-page#chapter-14. Last accessed: 16 July 2023.

Wolfe, Tom, *The Painted Word* (New York: Bantam Books, 1975).

Chapter 19

Dalrymple, Theodore, 'The Rage of Virginia Woolf' *City Journal* (Summer 2002).

Dolan, John, 'Sylvia Plath's Son?', *The Exiled*, 24 March 2009.

I'm A Dad - And I Breastfeed My Baby, https://www.youtube.com/watch?v=FgFdwKIeVsQ. Last accessed: 9 April 2024.

Radzyminski, Sharon, and Lynn Clark Callister, 'Mother's Beliefs, Attitudes, and Decision Making Related to Infant Feeding Choices', *National Library of Medicine* 25(1) (2016: 18–28).

Chapter 21

Bhattacharjee, G.P., *Evolution of the Political Philosophy of M.N. Roy* (Calcutta: The Minerva Associates, 1959).

Bloom, Allan, *Closing of the American Mind* (United Kingdom: Simon & Schuster, 2008).

Chakrabarty, Dipesh, *The Calling of History: Sir Jadunath Sarkar and His Empire of Truth* (University of Chicago Press, 2015).

Complete Works of Swami Vivekananda: https://www.ramakrishnavivekananda.info/vivekananda/complete_works.htm. Last Accessed: 23 November 2023.

Durant, Will, *The Case for India* (New York: Simon and Schuster, 1930).

DVG Kruti Shreni (The Complete works of D.V. Gundappa in 11 vols Kannada) (Bangalore: Kannada and Culture Department, Government of Karnataka, 2013).

Elst, Koenraad, *Negationism in India: Concealing the Record of Islam* (Delhi: Voice of India, 1992).

For a brilliant exposition of the concepts of Rta, Satya, Dharma, and allied topics, see *Your Dharma and Mine*, Shatavadhani Dr R. Ganesh (translated by Hari Ravikumar), Subbu Publications, Hubli, 2021.

Foundations of Sanatana Dharma: https://www.prekshaa.in/foundations-sanatana-dharma-yajna-dana-tapas. Last Accessed: 20 October 2023.

Goel, Sita Ram, *Genesis and Growth of Nehruism* (Delhi: Voice of India, 1993).

Goel, Sita Ram, *How I Became a Hindu* (Delhi: Voice of India, 1993).

Hiriyanna, M., *The Best of Hiriyanna* (Bangalore: Wise Words & Prekshaa Pratishthana, 2018).

Johnson, Paul, *Intellectuals: From Marx and Tolstoy to Sartre and Chomsky* (United States: HarperCollins, 2007).

Kane, P.V., Presidential Address, Proceedings of the Indian History Congress, https://www.jstor.org/stable/i40180148. Last Accessed: 20 October 2023.

Kane, Pandurang Vaman, *History of the Dharmasastra* (5 Vols) (Poona: Bhandarkar Oriental Research Institute, 1930–62).

Longman, Timothy, *Christianity and Genocide in Rwanda* (Cambridge University Press, 2009).

Naipaul, V.S., *Beyond Belief* (New York: Vintage Books, 1998).

Neelakandan, Aravindan, and Rajiv Malhotra, *Breaking India: Western Interventions in Dravidian and Dalit Faultlines* (Bhopal: Amaryllis, 2011).

Nehru, Jawaharlal, *Discovery of India* (Delhi: Penguin Random House India Private Limited, 2008).

On Ananda Coomaraswamy, see for example: (1) *Dance of Shiva* (2) *Bugbear of Literacy* (3) *Essays on Indian National Idealism* (4) *Spiritual Authority and Temporal Power* (Various publishers).

On the methods of primary school learning in ancient and mediaeval India, for example, see this article: 'A Jilted Italian Lover's Description of Primary Arithmetic Education in Gerusoppa': https://www.dharmadispatch.in/history/a-jilted-italian-lovers-description-of-primary-arithmetic-education-in-gerusoppa. Last accessed: 18 November 2023.

Overstreet, Gene D., and Marshall Windmiller, *Communism in India* (Bombay: The Perennial Press, 1959).

Ramaswamy, Krishnan, et al., *Invading the Sacred: An Analysis of Hinduism Studies in America* (Delhi: Rupa & Company, 2007).

Sarkar, U.C., *Epochs in Hindu Legal History* (Hoshiarpur: Vishvesharanand Indological Series, 1958).

Sastri, Dr S. Srikanta, *Geopolitcs of India and Greater India* (Bangalore: Madhu Publishers, 1943).

Sastri, S. Srikanta, *Bharateeya Samskruti* (Bangalore: Kamadhenu Pustaka Bhavana, 2015).

Sastri, S. Srikanta, *Srikanthayana* (Collected Works of Dr S. Srikanta Sastri in 2 Vols) (Bangalore: Mythic Society, 2016).

Stead, W.T., 'The Maiden Tribute of Modern Babylon', *Pall Mall Gazette*, 6 July 1885.

Swarup, Ram, *The Word as Revelation* (Delhi: Biblia Impex, 1980).

Tripathi, Radhavallabh, *Vada in Theory and Practice* (Delhi: D.K. Printworld, 2016).

Why the woke support Hamas: Richard Samuelson, https://highlandcountypress.com/why-woke-support-hamas#gsc.tab=0. Last accessed: 20 November 2023.

About the Author

Sandeep Balakrishna is a veteran write, author, editor, public speaker, and independent researcher. He has been writing on Indian history, culture, and literature for about 20 years, authored over 900 articles, essays, critiques, and academic papers, and delivered lectures related to these themes at institutions such as the Indian Council of Philosophical Research, IIM Bangalore, Sri Aurobindo Society, Shree Somananth Sanskrit University, Bangalore University, and Amrita University, to name a few. He writes in both English and Kannada.

Sandeep is the author of the bestselling books *Tipu Sultan: The Tyrant of Mysore, Madurai Sultanate: A Concise History, 70 Years of Secularism: Unpopular Essays on the Unofficial Political Religion of India,* and *Stories from Inscriptions*. He has translated the legendary Kannada novelist Dr S.L. Bhyrappa's critically acclaimed work *Aavarana* into English as *Aavarana*: *The Veil,* which is now in its 20th reprint.

Sandeep is the founder and editor of The Dharma Dispatch, an online journal dedicated to Indian civilization, culture, and history, and serves on the advisory board of Prekshaa.